1781

The Decisive Year
of the Revolutionary War

ROBERT L. TONSETIC

CASEMATE
Philadelphia & Oxford

Published in the United States of America and Great Britain in 2013 by
CASEMATE PUBLISHERS
908 Darby Road, Havertown, PA 19083
and
10 Hythe Bridge Street, Oxford, OX1 2EW

ISBN 978-1-61200-154-8
Digital Edition: ISBN 978-1-61200-078-7

Cataloging-in-publication data is available from the Library of Congress
and the British Library.

10 9 8 7 6 5 4 3 2

Printed and bound in the United States of America.

For a complete list of Casemate titles please contact:

CASEMATE PUBLISHERS (US)
Telephone (610) 853-9131, Fax (610) 853-9146
E-mail: casemate@casematepublishing.com

CASEMATE PUBLISHERS (UK)
Telephone (01865) 241249, Fax (01865) 794449
E-mail: casemate-uk@casematepublishing.co.uk

CONTENTS

Prologue   vii

PART I: A WINTER'S TALE

Chapter 1:   The Darkest New Year   3
Chapter 2:   Disorder, Fear, and Mutiny   11
Chapter 3:   Hills of the South Country   27
Chapter 4:   Hell in Virginia   37
Chapter 5:   Sunrise at the Cowpens   47
Chapter 6:   The Race to the Dan   63
Chapter 7:   We Fight, Get Beat, and Fight Again   75

PART II: NO SPRING NOR SUMMER REST

Chapter 8:   Everything Has Changed   99
Chapter 9:   The Lion Sleeps at Yorktown   125
Chapter 10: We Have Pursued Them to the Eutaws   145

PART III: THE GUNS OF AUTUMN

Chapter 11: The Siege of Yorktown   161
Chapter 12: Capitulation   197
Chapter 13: Aftermath   211

Epilogue   217
Notes   231
Bibliography   241
Index   249

For
Miranda and Mitchell

I have the honor to inform Congress, that a reduction of the British Army under the Command of Lord Cornwallis, is most happily effected.

—General George Washington to the President of the Continental Congress, October 19, 1781

PROLOGUE

This book traces the events of one of those rare years in American history, when the fate of the nation hung in the balance, and only the fortitude, determination, and sacrifices of its leaders and citizenry could save it. After six years of war, the new nation faced seemingly insurmountable challenges and difficulties. Like the years 1776, 1865, and 1945, the year 1781 changed the course of American and, indeed, world history.

By 1780, the Revolutionary War in the northern theater had reached a stalemate. The British army continued to occupy New York City with some 7,000 troops, while most of the American army was deployed in a wide arc from northern New Jersey across the Hudson highlands and on into New England. However, after six years of war, the American army was fast approaching the breaking point. The troops were in a worse situation than ever before, including the harsh winter of 1777–78 at Valley Forge. By January of 1781, the number of Continental troops had shrunk from a high of nearly 23,000 men in 1778 to a meager force of less than 10,000. The Americans faced other problems as well.

The American army was critically short on all classes of military supplies and equipment, including muskets, artillery, and ammunition of all types, as well as uniforms, blankets, tents, and medical supplies. Additionally, General George Washington found it increasingly difficult to feed his troops. Lacking funds to make purchases, Washington had to resort to requisitioning food and other supplies from surrounding farms and towns, angering the war weary and increasingly apathetic civilian population. Making matters worse, the troops had not been paid in months, and many were nearing what they believed to be the end of their three-year enlistments. When the three-year soldiers were told that their enlistments were actually for the duration of the war, threats of mutiny reverberated through the camps.

There was little Washington could do to resolve the shortages of supplies, lack of pay, and disputes over enlistment contracts. He kept Congress fully informed of the army's requirements, but the U.S. Treasury was empty, and the value of Continental paper money had plummeted to the point that it was considered worthless. Moreover, Congress had no power over the states to levy taxes to fund the war or draft men for the army. Each state was largely responsible for enlisting, clothing, equipping, and paying its own troops, and Washington could only appeal to Congress and state governments to fulfill their obligations to the army. As a result, recruitment of new soldiers for the Continental Army became next to impossible, and the enlistments and drafts from the state militias proved inadequate to replace the army's personnel losses.

America's alliance with the French was also under severe strain. Beginning in 1777, France had supplied the Americans with large quantities of armaments, munitions, clothing, and money, but by 1780 the flow of supplies and funds had slowed to a trickle. Disappointed by the lack of progress in the war, the French Foreign Minister Vergennes proposed a summit of European powers to mediate a peace conference between the belligerents. A ray of hope arrived in July of 1780, when a small French fleet arrived off Newport, Rhode Island, and landed some 6,000 French troops under the command of General Comte de Rochambeau. However, the French General was reluctant to begin combined operations with the Americans before the remaining 2,000 troops of his army arrived from France. Those troops were left behind due to a lack of ships to transport them to America. The French government had ordered its strongest naval fleet and most of its transports to sail to the Caribbean to protect French interests in the West Indies. France was increasingly reluctant to challenge British naval superiority off the American coast.

On their part, frustrated by lack of progress in the northern theater, the British adopted a new southern strategy to secure the remainder of the rebellious colonies for the Crown. The British believed that they had strong Loyalist support in their southernmost colonies. In December 1779, Lieutenant General Henry Clinton sailed to South Carolina with a joint army and naval task force to reestablish British control in the Carolinas and Georgia. By April 1780, the city of Charleston was completely invested and siege operations began. On May 12th, 1780, American General Benjamin Lincoln surrendered the port city to the British. Some 5,700 American soldiers and 1,000 sailors were taken prisoner, the largest number of prisoners taken by the British in a single campaign.

After the capture of Charleston, General Clinton returned to New York leaving Lord Cornwallis in command of 8,000 troops in the Carolinas and Georgia. Cornwallis was urged by the British government to follow up the victory by reestablishing control over the interior of the Carolinas, where Patriots and Loyalists were already engaged in a bloody civil war. The British offered clemency to all rebels who would swear allegiance to the Crown, but most refused. The Patriots took refuge in the coastal swamps and foothills and mountains of the interior. Patriot leaders Francis Marion, Andrew Pickens, Thomas Sumter, and others organized bands of partisans to carry on the fight against the British invaders and their Loyalist allies. Operating from their bases camps in the tangled cypress swamps, forests, and estuaries, the small partisan bands struck suddenly and ruthlessly at British patrols, outposts, and their own Loyalist neighbors. Supply and communication lines from Charleston were under constant threat.

Meanwhile, a limited number of Continental troops marched south to form the nucleus of a new Southern Army, around which militia could rally to defend their states. Congress appointed General Horatio Gates, the hero of Saratoga, to command the Southern Department. Gates soon gathered a force of 4,000 Continentals and militia, and marched against the British post at Camden, South Carolina. Cornwallis hurried north from Charleston with reinforcements, and routed Gates' force at Camden on the 16th of August 1780. Following Gates' devastating defeat, Washington sent General Nathaniel Greene south to the Carolinas in October of 1780, hoping to stem the tide of British victories in the Carolinas. Meanwhile, flushed with his easy victory at Camden, General Cornwallis marched north and invaded North Carolina.

As events unfolded in the Carolinas during the fall of 1780, General

Washington uncovered Benedict Arnold's treasonous plot to deliver the American defenses at West Point in late September, just in time to foil it. Two months later, General Washington moved his headquarters to New Windsor, New York to keep his eye on the strategically important Hudson corridor. He remained concerned about the threat posed by the 7,000 British regulars occupying New York City. If the British marched north and took control of the Hudson highlands, the American army's lines of communications and supply between the Middle Atlantic and New England states would be severed.

As the year 1780 drew to a close, the American cause seemed to be at its lowest ebb since the war began. Defeat in the southern states appeared imminent, and in the north, General Washington struggled to hold his small, poorly provisioned, and equipped Continental Army together. After six years of war, the patriotic enthusiasm and fervor that marked the early years of the war was all but gone. It was the nadir of the American Revolution.

PART 1

A Winter's Tale

"It's with inexpressible pain that I now inform your Excellency of the general mutiny and defection which suddenly took place in the Pennsylvania Line, between the hours of nine and ten o'clock last evening."

—General Anthony Wayne
January 2, 1781

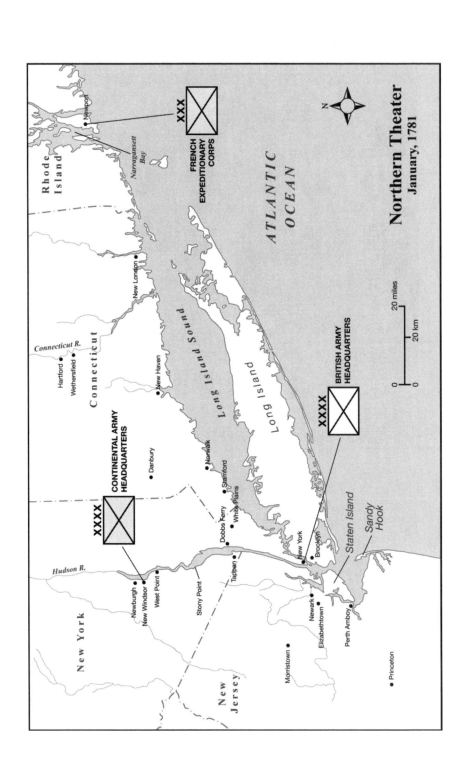

Northern Theater
January, 1781

1

THE DARKEST NEW YEAR

After crossing numerous frozen streams and struggling through treach-erous snowdrifts with bone chilling winds howling around them, the small party of horsemen reached Army headquarters in New Windsor late in the afternoon on January 1, 1781. Lieutenant Colonel David Humphreys' grueling three-day, near hundred-mile journey from Brunswick, New Jersey to New Windsor, New York, was at an end. The twenty-nine-year-old dismounted his horse and handed the reins to one of the grooms tending several horses outside the modest two-story Dutch farmhouse that served as Washington's headquarters. Several sentries were posted around the house trying to ward off the cold by stomping the ground to keep their feet warm, clutching their muskets close to their bodies at order-arms under their cloaks. Bounding up the snow-covered steps and onto the wrap-around porch, Humphreys stomped the snow off his boots, and after returning the salute of the sentry posted at the door, he entered the house prepared to render his report on his unsuccessful mission to his commander-in-chief. The New Year, 1781, was off to an inauspicious start.

ARMY HEADQUARTERS—NEW WINDSOR, NEW YORK
January 1, 1781

January 1, New Year's Day, was a major holiday in eighteenth century America, even during wartime. A popular way of celebrating the passing of the old year and the arrival of the next was to hold open houses and to go visiting friends and neighbors.[1] Thus, there was only a minimum of

3

staff work conducted at Army headquarters on New Year's Day 1781. Most of the day was spent receiving guests. In keeping with Army customs, subordinate commanders, whose units were in winter quarters nearby, called upon the General and his Lady at their residence. Additionally, in keeping with local Dutch custom, George and Martha Washington also received civilian guests from the local community. Appointments and invitations were unnecessary. Despite his deepening concerns about the future of Army and its prospects for victory, the Army's commander received his guests with the utmost courtesy and respect. His reserved, genteel manner belied the increasing level of stress that he felt.

The day prior, the General had returned to his winter headquarters exhausted after an inspection trip of the fortifications and garrisons at West Point, some ten miles downriver from New Windsor.[2] It was Washington's second recent visit to the area, reflecting his growing concern for the security of the fortifications at the Point. West Point was the linchpin of the American defenses in the strategic Hudson corridor. If the British gained control of the corridor, they would sever the lines of communication between the New England States and the rest of the newly declared nation. Benedict Arnold's plot to turn the fortifications over to the British in September 1780 was a near miss. Adding to Washington's concern was the fact that the New England regiments defending the forts at the Point had been weakened after the discharge of large numbers of levies. Additionally, Washington lacked full confidence in Major General Heath, the Highlands Department Commander, who was responsible for the security of the Hudson corridor. Approaching his forty-ninth birthday, the commander-in-chief looked, and no doubt felt, much older than his years.

After all the guests departed, Washington retired to his small office in an upstairs room, and summoned Lieutenant Colonel Humphreys to receive his report. Humphreys was one of Washington's most trusted aides and confidants. The twenty-nine-year-old Yale graduate had been chosen by Washington to lead a clandestine expedition into British occupied New York. His mission was to capture either the sixty-year-old General Wilhelm von Knyphausen, the commander of Hessian troops, or the British commander in chief, General Sir Henry Clinton. Both the Americans and the British attempted to capture prominent general officers during the war. On more than one occasion, the British laid plans to capture Washington.

Benedict Arnold's scheme to turn over the fortifications at West Point to the British could also have led to Washington's capture. The general had been on his way to West Point when he learned of Arnold's plot.

Washington selected David Humphreys to lead the covert mission based on his experience on two previous raids. During the spring of 1777, Humphreys accompanied Colonel Meigs on a successful raid on Sag Harbor, New York. A year later he led his own 30-man raiding force to the Long Island shore and destroyed three British vessels without losing a man. Washington knew that if anyone could pull off the scheme to capture Knypahusen or Clinton, it would be Humphreys.

During the evening of Christmas Day 1780, Lieutenant Colonel Humphreys' hand-selected detachment of 27 men set out by barge and whaleboats from Dobbs Ferry on the Hudson River. Humphreys hoped to cover the 25 miles to New York City around midnight, but nature did not favor the plan. As the boats approached New York, high northwest winds swept them past their intended landing sites. One boat was driven down toward Sandy Hook, New Jersey, and another put in on a remote section of Staten Island. Over the next few days, Humphreys managed to locate all of his boats and land near Brunswick, New Jersey. From there, the raiders were able to reenter the American lines.[3] The unsuccessful raid was the first disappointment of the New Year for the Americans, and a continuation of a long series of and setbacks experienced during the preceding year. Nonetheless, Washington knew that Humphreys had done his best, and he was relieved when his trusted aide returned safely with all of his men.

After receiving Humphreys' report, Washington's household settled in for the night, and only the groaning, creaking, and cracking of the river's ice broke the nocturnal stillness. As Washington and Martha prepared to retire for the night another major calamity involving the American army was underway. As the General slumbered, couriers raced across the snow-covered New Jersey hills toward his headquarters bearing news that troops of the Pennsylvania Line had mutinied and were planning to march from their encampment at Mount Kimble, New Jersey to Philadelphia to present their grievances to Congress. The mutiny had the potential to trigger others throughout the ranks leading to the dissolution of the entire American army, and dooming the revolution.

DOWNING STREET, LONDON—JANUARY 1, 1781

It was a frosty, gloomy day in London. The Thames was not frozen over, but ice was beginning to form along the banks. Chimneys throughout the city belched thick clouds of black soot into the city's foggy air. A malodorous mixture of cinder smoke, decaying garbage and open sewage kept most Londoners indoors on New Year's Day.

Great Britain's Prime Minister, Lord North, spent the holiday with his wife and children. There was time that day to reflect on his accomplishments as Britain's steward. Having led his nation for ten years, the corpulent 49-year-old Frederick North, 2nd Earl of Guilford, was the longest serving Prime Minister since Robert Walpole (1721–42). He had led Great Britain through the ups and downs of the American War of Independence, since the first shots were fired at Lexington and Concord in 1775. Despite a string of victories that led to the capture of New York and Philadelphia, some of Britain's best generals were unable to secure a decisive victory that would bring an end to the costly war. After the French allied themselves with the American rebels in 1778, Spain quickly joined the war in 1779 as an ally of France, followed by the Dutch Republic a year later. In addition, there was a lingering fear that Russia would enter the war in support of the Dutch. Within a three-year period, Great Britain had found herself in a global war on four continents, with no major allies.

After the humiliating British loss at Saratoga in 1777, and France's entry into the war in 1778, North had offered to resign, but King George III refused to accept his resignation. Opposition to the once popular war continued to increase during most of 1780, but the headline news of major British victories at Charleston in May and at Camden in August of 1780, resulted in a gradual shift of public opinion in favor of the war. Those victories seemed to prove the efficacy of Britain's new southern strategy, and renewed hope that the war could be brought to a successful conclusion. As a result, Lord North's government retained its majority in Parliament after the first elections since the war began were held during the fall of 1780.

Despite the electoral victory, the Prime Minister remained deeply concerned about the war. Great Britain's resources were stretched thin. The British army was under increasing strain due to its worldwide commitments stretching from India to North America. New regiments were needed to replace old ones that were seriously understrength due to losses on the battlefield, and from disease and desertion. Moreover, the recruitment pool was drying up, and the quality of new recruits continued to decline. The British navy was also stretched close to the breaking point. In addition to protecting the homeland from invasion, the navy was faced with the enormous task of supplying the army in North America and transporting troop reinforcements to that theater. The shipping of supplies and reinforcements was beginning to seriously restrict the execution of strategic plans in all theaters of war.[4] There was also growing concern within the government about the financial costs of the effort. The national debt had almost doubled since the beginning of the war.[5] Moreover, it was likely that future loans would have to be made at increasingly higher interest rates.

Lord North knew that pacifying the countryside in South Carolina, particularly the backcountry, was not going well. The American victory over the Loyalists at Kings Mountain in October of 1780 raised significant doubts about the capability of the Loyalist militias to prevail over their rebel neighbors. The year 1781 was a critical one for the British. If their southern strategy was to succeed, the rebels in South Carolina, North Carolina, Georgia, and the "real prize," Virginia, had to be crushed. Lord North believed that victory over the American rebels was still possible, but only if Britain remained resolute in the coming months. If the southern strategy succeeded, Britain would, as a minimum, retain its four southern colonies. North was confident that he had the monarch's full support in continuing the war.[6]

THE CHATEAU DE VERSAILLES, FRANCE—JANUARY 1, 1781
After attending mass, the sixty-three-year-old Charles Gravier, comte de Vergennes, Foreign Minister of France, retired to his luxurious Versailles apartments. The stately career diplomat gazed out the windows of his salon at the expansive ornamental gardens. A light dusting of snow sparkled on the trees and shrubs under the January sunlight. The Minister strode to his writing desk and opened a packet of unread dispatches.

Vergennes was appointed as France's Foreign Minister after King Louis XVI's accession to the throne in 1774. The appointment came after a thirty-five-year career in the French diplomatic service; all of it spent abroad. Vergennes advanced a foreign policy that was based on his conviction that Great Britain's power was on the rise and had to be kept in check. He viewed the American War of Independence against the British as an opportunity to avenge French losses during the Seven Years' War, and greatly diminish the British domination of North America. Vergennes' foreign policy views were endorsed by the 27-year-old King Louis XVI, who wanted the Americans to succeed in their war for independence. Due in large part to Vergennes' efforts, a "Treaty of Alliance" between France and the United States was signed in 1778.

Officially, the treaty was non-negotiable; however, both parties knew that alliances survive only as long as they are judged to be useful. After more than two years, Vergennes was having second thoughts about the alliance. The disturbing American losses at Charleston and Camden during 1780, along with Arnold's betrayal, had weakened support for the war within the French ministries. General Comte de Rochambeau's army of 6,000 troops landed at Newport, Rhode Island during the summer of 1780, but the French and American forces had yet to begin joint operations. Despite extensive correspondence, and three personal meetings, Washington and Rochambeau could not agree on a strategy for the future conduct of the war. Washington stubbornly held out for an attack on the British garrison at New York, but Rochambeau refused to commit his army, since the British fleet controlled the waters surrounding the city. France was determined to protect her interests in the Caribbean, and Admiral de Grasse's powerful French fleet was committed to the West Indies. Vergennes was also concerned that the seemingly interminable war was driving the treasury toward insolvency, and that a peace faction was gaining strength within the French ministries. America's appetite for more and more cash, armaments, and supplies was insatiable. Although Vergennes respected the American Minister Plenipotentiary (Ambassador) Benjamin Franklin's intelligence and diplomatic skills, he was rapidly tiring of his endless requests for more and more military and economic assistance. On the other hand, Vergennes had little respect for American Minister Plenipotentiary John Adams. The French Foreign Minister viewed Adams, who lacked Franklin's finesse, as an amateur in the realm of diplomacy. Vergennes was irate that the blunt provincial, John Adams, was meddling in European affairs, particularly with the Dutch.[7] By the beginning of the year 1781, the French Foreign Minister knew that France's foreign policy with respect to the United States was in serious trouble, and he was looking for a way to end the war at the negotiating table.[8]

2

DISORDER, FEAR, AND MUTINY

New Year's Day was a traditional day of celebration in the Army, and the normal daily formations, drills, and work details were not scheduled. At the Pennsylvania Line's winter encampment, the day began quietly. Most of the troops stayed in their huts, while a few ventured into the snow-covered woods to gather firewood to prepare the breakfast meal. In the officers' quarters, preparations were underway for elegant regimental dinners complete with entertainment. For some, it would be the last time that they would dine together. In several huts, groups of sergeants met to finalize their own plans for the day. In hushed voices, the non-commissioned officers reaffirmed their determination to take action to obtain redress of their longstanding grievances. Bottles of rum passed from hand to hand as the sergeants worked out the final details of their plan.

The Pennsylvania Line was formed in 1775, and was originally comprised of thirteen regiments and several independent companies. Along with the Massachusetts and Virginia Continentals, the Pennsylvania regiments provided the backbone of the American army. During the first five years of the war, the Pennsylvania regiments fought heroically in most of the major battles in New York, New Jersey, and Pennsylvania, including Brooklyn, Stony Point, Trenton, Princeton, Monmouth, Germantown, and Brandywine. Casualties suffered in those battles were significant, and the number of replacements was never adequate to fill each regiment's ranks. It made no sense to continue the war with "hollow" regimental formations on the battlefield. Something had to be done

Under a reorganization plan for the Continental Army that became effective on January 1, 1781, the Pennsylvania Line was consolidated into six infantry regiments, an artillery regiment, a legionary corps, and an artificer regiment. The reduction in the total number of Line regiments was necessary due to battlefield losses, non-battle casualties, and desertions. Recruitment of replacements was increasingly difficult after the harsh winters of 1777–78 and 1779–80. The reorganization did not affect the terms of enlistments of the men serving in the ranks. The companies of the deactivated regiments were transferred to one of the remaining regiments. However, the number of officer billets was reduced causing some dissatisfaction and confusion in the officer corps. The discontent was not just in the officer ranks, however. The enlisted troops had their own list of grievances.[1]

No issues caused more distress and discontent among the troops than the terms of their enlistments and their pay. Many soldiers who enlisted in the first years of the war believed that they had joined for a period not to exceed three years; however, Congress determined that the enlistments were for three years or the duration of the war. Since many of the soldiers were young and illiterate, unscrupulous recruiting officers often duped them into believing that they were enlisting for three years at the most. Some were told that the "duration of the war" clause meant that they could be discharged if the war ended prior to the end of their three-year commitment. When their officers could not produce the enlistment papers that they had signed, the men became even more suspicious.[2]

Adding to the men's discontent was the fact that they had not been paid for nearly twelve months. During that period, the value of the Continental currency had become significantly devalued. Another issue adding to the unrest involved the payment of enlistment bounties. The battle-hardened veterans, who endured the hardships of three years service, never received the full bounties promised them. On the other hand, the men who enlisted after July 1, 1780 received bounties of about twenty-seven dollars in silver immediately upon their enlistment, and were promised a bonus of two hundred acres of land after the war. Many veteran soldiers believed that they should be discharged at the expiration of three years service and then be permitted to re-enlist and receive the latest bounties authorized by Congress. There were other complaints as well.[3]

There was a severe shortage of clothing and rations at the Pennsylvania Line's Mount Kimble encampment. Congress placed primary reliance on states to supply their own regiments, but the arrangement proved unsatisfactory. Congress then levied specific quotas on each state for supplies, but by January 1781, despite urgent appeals by Congress and the army, none of the states had met their quotas. Procurement problems and faulty organization and supervision at the state level were to blame.

Washington was acutely aware of the supply problems and wrote no less than five letters to state authorities in the last three months of 1780, complaining of the lack of subsistence and clothing in the army. Procurement of clothing for the troops posed a problem for the states. Eighteenth-century America was not a manufacturing country, and linen was in short supply. Clothing could be woven in individual homes, but wool and woolen cloth were scarce. By 1780, the veteran soldiers who had participated in three years of hard campaigning had long worn out their initial issue of clothing, and were clad in tattered remnants of garments and rags, often sharing a blanket with another soldier to stay warm.

By the beginning of January 1781, the discontent in the ranks throughout the army was extremely serious, particularly in the Pennsylvania regiments. Major General Anthony Wayne of the Pennsylvania Line was well aware of the discontent and dwindling patience of his troops. In December 1780, he wrote from Mount Kimble to Colonel Johnson at Philadelphia expressing his concern about the situation in his command.

> My Dear Col., —I sincerely wish the Ides of Jany was come & past—I am not superstitious, but can't help cherishing disagreeable Ideas about that period . . .You may believe me my D'r Sir that the exertions of the House were never'more necessary than at this Crisis to adopt some effectual mode & Immediate plan to Alleviate the distress of the Troops & to conciliate their minds & sweeten their tempers which are much soured by neglect & every extreme of wretchedness for want of almost every comfort & necessary of life . . .[4]

The authorities in Philadelphia ignored Wayne's dire prediction and admonition, and there was no immediate action taken by Congress or the state authorities to remedy the problems and issues raised by General Wayne and the army's commander-in-chief, General Washington. By January 1st, 1781, time had run out.

WINTER ENCAMPMENT OF THE PENNSYLVANIA CONTINENTAL LINE—MOUNT KEMBLE, NEW JERSEY
January 1–4, 1781

As New Year's Day was a traditional day of celebration in the army, the normal daily formations, drills, and work details were not scheduled, and according to Captain Joseph McClellan of the Pennsylvania Line, "The day was spent in quietness."[5] Lieutenant Enos Reeves, Regimental Quartermaster of the 10th Pennsylvania Regiment, wrote in his letter book that the officers of his regiment ". . . planned an elegant regimental dinner and entertainment at which all the field and other officers were present . . ."[6] Reeve's regiment was one of the Pennsylvania regiments that were to be consolidated with another regiment under the reorganization plan, and this was the last opportunity for the officers to dine together.

While the officers celebrated the occasion, the non-commissioned officers and private soldiers were doing a bit of celebrating of their own. In honor of the holiday, each soldier was issued a half pint of liquor, and some of the men supplemented this ration with local purchases. Plans formulated by a group of sergeants to take action on their longstanding grievances were about to be put into action. Having lost confidence in their officers' efforts to redress their grievances with the Congress, the sergeants were determined to take matters into their own hands. Their plan was to march to Philadelphia and present their grievances directly to the Continental Congress and state authorities. The sergeants established their own temporary chain of command under the leadership of a "Board of Sergeants." Their intent was to maintain good order and discipline in the ranks, maintain unit integrity, so far as possible, and march as an organized force to Philadelphia.

Accounts differ on the exact time that the plan was enacted, but it is likely that initial actions began between 8:00 and 10:00 pm in the 11th Regiment's cantonment area.[7] Captain Joseph McClellan wrote that, "...a number of men in the 11th Regiment began to huzza and continued some time, but it was generally thought it only proceeded from the men drinking, as they had drawn half a pint of liquor this day."[8] The regiment's officers managed to quiet the men and convince them to return to their huts. A short time later another disturbance was reported on the right section of the encampment, followed by another on the left. Lieutenant Reeves of the 10th Regiment proceeded to the parade ground where he "found numbers in small groups whispering and busily running up and down the line."[9] Gunfire soon erupted from the right and left sides of the encampment, and a skyrocket was fired as a signal for the men to fall out of their huts with their arms and knapsacks, and assemble on their respective parade grounds. The officers of the various regiments attempted to restore order and get their men to return to their huts, but they were unable to control the situation. As the officers moved among the unruly armed men trying to regain control, the inevitable soon happened.

Lieutenant Francis White of the 10th Regiment was shot through the thigh when he confronted one group of soldiers, and Captain Samuel Tolbert, a company commander in the 2d Regiment, was shot through the body by a member of his company. His assailant, Absalom Evans, who later deserted to the British, recalled that his Captain had run him though the thigh with his sword causing him to shoot his commander in the stomach. Both men survived their wounds, but Captain Tolbert was unfit for further field service and spent the remainder of his service in Pennsylvania before retiring in 1783.[10] According to General Wayne, a number of other officers were injured as well, by "strokes from muskets, bayonets, and stones, and there were a number of mutineers who bore wounds from the officers' swords and espontoons."[11]

As a result of the bloodshed, the men became even more unruly, shouting and discharging their muskets throughout the encampment. It soon became clear to the officers that the situation was beyond their control, and there was no chance of restoring order.

Any further attempt to do so would likely cost them their lives. The mutineers then turned their attention to seizing the artillery, which they planned to take with them on their march to Philadelphia. At the arsenal where the artillery was stored, one of the mutineers was killed by one of his compatriots who mistook him for an uncooperative sentry. After the cannon were seized, the mutineers fired a number of rounds over the heads of two regiments (the 5th and 9th) that had not as yet committed to the revolt. Some members of those regiments were assembled on their parade grounds, while others remained in their huts. The mutineers continued their efforts to intimidate the more timid troops into joining their ranks.

General Wayne was at his headquarters at the Kemble house a short distance east of the camp when the revolt began. He was celebrating his 36th birthday with two of his Colonels, Richard Butler of the 9th Regiment and Walter Stewart of the 2nd. Born in Chester County, Pennsylvania in 1745, Anthony Wayne was the son of a prominent farmer of that county. He attended the Academy of Philadelphia, but never completed his studies, opting instead to become a surveyor. In May of 1766 he married the daughter of a prominent merchant from Philadelphia and turned his attention to farming, also establishing a tannery. As a prominent citizen of his county, he was elected to and served in the Pennsylvania Legislature from 1774 to 1775. When war broke out in 1775, Wayne raised a regiment and was made its Colonel in 1776.

As commander, Wayne had a reputation as a disciplinarian and a stickler for proper military appearance. He insisted that his men shave and dress their hair on a daily basis, and pay close attention to maintenance of their uniforms and arms. Realizing that he lacked a formal military education, Wayne spent hours reading and studying the art of war, from the "Commentaries of Caesar on the Gallic War" to an account of Marshal Saxe's campaigns.

Wayne commanded the 4th Pennsylvania Regiment during the American's ill-fated invasion of Canada in 1775. His regiment fought a successful rearguard action at the Battle of Trois-Rivieres in 1776, and he later led the defensive forces at Fort Ticonderoga, earning a promotion to brigadier general in February of 1777. As commander of the Pennsylvania Line, he led the Pennsylvanians during the battles of Brandywine, Paoli, and Germantown, and during the winter encampment at Valley Forge. Then in June of 1778, he led the American attack at Monmouth. Wayne's most noteworthy victory came in July of 1779, when he led a daring night attack on the British fort at Stony Point, New York. Commanding a Corps of Light Infantry, Wayne personally led the main assault. After suffering a head wound, he remained on the field, and his men seized the fortifications in thirty minutes, killing or capturing almost all the defenders without incurring significant losses. The victory received national attention, and

Congress awarded a gold medal to Wayne for his victory.

Although Washington held Wayne in high esteem, he was well aware of the Pennsylvanian's shortcomings. He knew that Wayne was prone to impetuosity, impatience, and boastfulness, but he placed high value on his loyalty and fearless leadership qualities. General Wayne was also highly respected by his men, who trusted his leadership in battle when their lives were at stake, but nonetheless they felt that they'd been mistreated enough by Congress and their state. On January 1st they took matters into their own hands. It would take all of Wayne's leadership skills to avoid further bloodshed and bring the uprising to a peaceful resolution.

*   *   *

Alarmed by the artillery and musket fire coming from the camp, General Wayne, accompanied by Colonel Butler of the 9th Regiment and Colonel Stewart of the 2d Regiment, galloped at breakneck speed up the Fort Hill road to the scene of the mutiny.

Spotting a group of the mutineers on the side of the road, the general and his party approached them. Wayne and Butler both spoke at length to the men, but to no avail. According to one source the men replied, "They had been wronged and were determined to see themselves righted."[12] Wayne promised that he would do everything in his power to resolve their grievances, but the rank and file, who had considerable respect for their general, believed that it was beyond his power to do anything to assist. Then someone lurking in the darkness fired shots over the heads of Wayne and the colonels. At that moment Wayne reportedly opened his coat and exclaimed, "If you mean to kill me, shoot me at once—here at my breast!"[13] A spokesman for the mutineers exclaimed that their group harbored no ill will against Wayne and had no intent to harm him, but they remained determined to march to Philadelphia.

Meanwhile, confusion still reigned in the encampment as some of the regiments were resisting the efforts of the mutineers to win them over. The 2nd Regiment was allegedly forced to join at "bayonet point," and the 4th Regiment was actively resisting. Officers from the 4th led a charge to recapture the artillery pieces from the mutineers, but were soon forced to retreat amid the confusion. Captain Adam Bettin of the same regiment was coming down an alleyway between the rows of huts when he saw an armed man running toward him. While the Captain was in the process of starting to wield his espontoon, the man shot him through the body. Bettin died two hours later, becoming the only officer fatality during the mutiny.[14] After this sobering event, there was no turning back for the leaders of the mutiny.

The mutineers then began a systematic sweep of all the regimental camps, turning out the soldiers who were less than enthusiastic about the mutiny and inducing them to join their ranks. Others began marshalling wagons, horses, provisions, tentage, and ammunition in preparation for their march on the capital. By 2 am, the sergeants had more than a thousand men in marching formations, complete with a front and rear guard, and were ready to take to the road. With fifes and drums playing a marching tune, the column began to file out of camp.

General Wayne met the mutineers as they began their march, and tried once again to turn them back, fearing that they might decide to join the British. The sergeants assured the general that they had no intention of defecting to the British, and would severely punish any of their men who tried to desert. The leaders further announced that they intended to reach a location where they could meet on equal terms with Congressional and state officials to demand what was owed them. Wayne requested that he and his brigade commanders be permitted to join the march the following day, and the sergeants voiced no objections.

The column then marched off in the darkness down the road that led toward Philadelphia by way of Princeton. About half the men of the Pennsylvania Line initially declined to join the march and remained in camp, but many soon changed their minds and marched to catch up with the column.

As his mutinous troops marched off, Wayne returned to his headquarters and wrote a brief but alarming letter to General Washington.

January 2d, 1781
Half after 4 o'clock, A. M.
DEAR GENERAL—It is with inexpressible pain I now inform your Excellency of the general mutiny and defection, which suddenly took place in the Pennsylvania line, between the hours of 9 and 10 o'clock last evening . . ."[15]

The letter went on to describe a series of events that occurred at the winter quarters of the Pennsylvania Line on the evening of New Year's Day and the early morning hours of January 2nd. The soldiers of the Pennsylvania Line at Mount Kimble had mutinied, a calamity with the potential to tear the entire American army apart.

*   *   *

The mutineer's column reached the town of Vealtown (Bernardsville) after some four hours of marching. The sergeants ordered a halt to allow the men to prepare their breakfast meal, and allow stragglers and groups of women and children to rejoin the column.

Before leaving his headquarters, Wayne wrote a second letter to Washington. This letter provided more detail than the first, and he entrusted his aide, Major Benjamin Fishbourne, to personally deliver it to Washington's headquarters in New Windsor.

After a fatiguing ride through the snowy countryside, Major Fishbourne reached Washington about noon on January 3rd. After reading Wayne's letter, the commander-in-chief asked the major for a detailed verbal account of the events concerning the mutiny. Washington's worst nightmare suddenly became reality. The loss of the Pennsylvania Line was as an enormous loss to the army, one it could ill afford. Washington also realized that now that the mutiny fire was lit, it might spread throughout the Continental Army.

After considering his options, Washington drafted his reply to Wayne's letter. Washington wrote that he approved Wayne's initial handling of the mutiny and recommended that Wayne, Stewart, and Butler "keep with the troops," and try to bring them "to a negotiation" before they reached Philadelphia. Washington was apprehensive that if the troops entered the city, the Congress would flee fearing for their lives, and the troops being deprived of the opportunity to present their grievances would vent their anger and frustrations on the residents.[16] He also recommended to Wayne that force not be used against the mutineers, since it would "either drive them to the Enemy, or dissipate them in such a manner that they will never be recovered."[17]

*   *   *

General Wayne and his brigade commanders rode hard throughout the day to overtake the marching troops, and arrived in the vicinity of Middlebrook the evening of January 3rd. The troops had halted at Middlebrook for the night, occupying a group of huts that were used during the previous winter. By that time the mutineers' ranks had swollen to about 1,500 men. A herd of about 100 cattle that had arrived at the Mount Kimble encampment had also been driven to Middlebrook to supplement the provisions of the marchers.

After arriving in the Middlebrook area, Wayne and his party occupied a patriot's house, and requested a meeting with the sergeants. A delegation of sergeants soon arrived, and presented their complaints; also discussing with Wayne possible means of redress. Before returning to their troops, it was agreed that Wayne and his colonels would address the troops the following day with specific proposals to solve the grievances. The sergeants also insisted on providing a guard of one sergeant and twelve soldiers to insure General Wayne 's safety.

The troops continued their march early the next morning, choosing not to wait for Wayne's arrival. General Wayne and the colonels caught up with the marchers during a halt and made an effort to address them, but the men were not swayed by his remarks, insisting that their intent was to march all the way to Philadelphia.

By the time the column reached Princeton, cooler heads began to prevail, and the march ended in good order. The Board of Sergeants, as they called themselves, recognized the need to enter into serious negotiations to end the mutiny on terms that would satisfy their men, and not provide the British any opportunity to exploit the situation. Gradually, the sergeants began to consolidate their control over their unruly men, as they prepared to start serious negotiations with Wayne.

Upon their arrival in Princeton, the Board of Sergeants took quarters in Nassau Hall, while the main body of troops established a camp on a farm just south of the town. Wayne and his party were lodged in an inn near Nassau Hall. The sergeants insisted on placing Wayne and his colonels under guard, insisting that it was for their protection, but Wayne knew that the real purpose of the guard was to prevent him exerting any direct influence on the troops. All negotiations would be conducted between the Board of Sergeants and the General.

* * *

Lieutenant General Sir Henry Clinton, the British commander-in-chief, was made aware of the mutiny two days after it began.[18] Tories and spies in the vicinity of Mt. Kimble ensured that the British were kept informed of the situation, and the British Secret Service began developing plans to exploit the situation to their own best advantage. Clinton instructed Oliver DeLancey, Chief of his Secret Service, to establish contact with the mutineers, and offer them amnesty and sanctuary. He also ordered his staff to begin planning and organizing an expedition into New Jersey to exploit the situation. Acting on Clinton's instructions, DeLancey prepared a written offer to the mutineers. The British proposal stipulated that the mutineers would be, "taken under the protection of the British Government, with full pardon for taking up arms against their King, and restoration of all rights as loyal citizens."[19] In addition, the mutineers were promised full pay due them as promised by the Congress with no obligation to serve in the British armed forces. Several British agents set off for Princeton by different routes on the evening of January 4th, with copies of the British proposal hidden in their personal effects.

While the agents headed for Princeton, two battalions of Light Infantry, the British Grenadiers, and four battalions of Hessians marched to staging areas on Staten Island where they would prepare for immediate deployment to New Jersey.

* * *

While the British prepared to seize the opportunity presented by the mutiny, formal negotiations between the Board of Sergeants and General Wayne began in earnest. On Thursday, January 4th, Wayne received a written list of demands from the Sergeants. The demands dealt with pay, bounty payments, clothing allowances, and discharge dates. Discharge dates were based on the year in which the soldiers enlisted, and were not to exceed three years. The letter also specified that the demands must be met within six days from January 4th, and left no room for negotiation on any of the particulars. The sergeants also specified that they were relying on Wayne to "represent and repeat" their grievances to Congress and the state authorities.[20]

Wayne replied that he was supportive of the demands as long as they were consistent with the "resolution of Congress, and the late acts of the Honorable Assembly of Pennsylvania for making up the depreciation (in pay arrears), and be discharged from the service of the United States."[21] In simpler terms, Wayne was sending the sergeants a message that while he might support their demands, the ultimate decision was in the hands of Congress and the leaders of the Pennsylvania Assembly.

After reading Wayne's reply, the Board of Sergeants apparently thought that he was hedging on the issue of discharge of those men who enlisted in 1776 or 1777, leaving that decision entirely to the Congress. As a result, a second letter was sent under the signature of Sergeant William Bouzar, one of the leaders of the mutiny. The letter insisted that their demands applied to those men who enlisted in 1776–77, as well as those who had enlisted in later years.[22] Wayne knew he had no authority to commit to a general discharge of those men who had enlisted for three years, or the duration of the war, and he therefore proposed a meeting between the mutineers and a representative of the Pennsylvania Council. The meeting was to take place at Trenton, New Jersey.

The President of the Supreme Executive Council of Pennsylvania, Joseph Reed, decided to manage the crisis himself. Joseph Reed was born in New Jersey, but grew up in Philadelphia. He studied at the Philadelphia Academy and received a bachelor's degree from Princeton University. He subsequently studied law in London before returning home to practice law in Philadelphia and Trenton. Before his 1777 election as a Pennsylvania delegate to the Congress, Reed served in the Continental Army as General Washington's military secretary and aide-de-camp, and later as the Army's adjutant general with the rank of colonel. During 1778, Reed left the Army and was elected President of the Supreme Executive Council of Pennsylvania, a position similar to today's office of Governor.

Even before he opened negotiations with the rebellious troops, Reed took several conciliatory steps to demonstrate his sincerity in resolving the mutineers' grievances. He dispatched auditors to resolve the pay issues, and ordered the movement of provisions, clothing and money to New Jersey, where they could be immediately disbursed once the negotiations were successfully concluded. Reed then made his way to Trenton, arriving on January 6th.

While Reed was on his way to New Jersey, a pair of British agents sent to make contact with the mutineers reached Princeton on the 5th of January. Upon arrival, John Mason, a notorious Tory, accompanied by his guide, James Ogden, delivered General Clinton's written offer to John Williams, President of the Board of Sergeants. Williams immediately ordered that the two men be taken into custody, and to demonstrate his loyalty to the American cause, he informed General Wayne of the British offer. Williams wisely recognized the danger of giving any hint or suspicion that the mutineers were in simultaneous negotiations with the British.

A meeting between Joseph Reed and the Board of Sergeants was arranged for Sunday the 7th of January. When President Reed and his party arrived in Princeton, they were met by a ceremonial formation of troops, with sergeants occupying the officer positions. The mutineers then rendered full military honors to the President of Pennsylvania. Somewhat surprised by the gesture, Reed returned the sergeants' salutes before proceeding on to the meeting.

In preparation for the negotiations with the President of Pennsylvania and General Wayne, the sergeants had reduced their original proposals for resolution of their grievances to a single proposal. It stated:

> That all and every such men as was enlisted in the years 1776 and 1777 and received the bounty of twenty dollars, shall be without any delay discharged and all arrears of pay and clothing to be paid unto them immediately when discharged; with respect to the depreciation of pay the State to give them sufficient certificates and security for such sums as they shall become due.[23]

Reed balked at the general release of such a large group of men, arguing that not all the men who enlisted in the specified years entered the service with the same terms of enlistment. Additionally, some of the 1776 and 1777 veterans had already reenlisted, or extended their terms of enlistment. The sergeants in turn argued that many men had been forced, under threat of punishment, to reenlist, while others had been deceived by their officers as to the exact terms of their enlistments. It was also alleged by the sergeants that some of their officers had failed to pay promised bounties, and that state stores and clothing were withheld, or not equitably distributed.

Despite the lack of proof of these allegations by the sergeants, Reed concluded that there were "some undue methods" used to enlist many of the men into the service, but opined that, if a man voluntarily accepted a bounty exercising his own free will, he should not be discharged.

While Reed continued negotiations with the sergeants, Washington worked to contain the mutiny and keep it from spreading to other military units. On January 5th, he wrote a letter addressed to the governors of four New England states apprising them of the situation, and imploring them to take immediate action to, ". . . furnish at least three months' pay to the troops . . ." to sustain them until "ways and means are devised to clothe and feed them better . . ."[24] Brigadier General Henry Knox, the Army's Chief of Artillery, was given the mission of hand carrying Washington's letter to the governors of Connecticut, Massachusetts, Rhode Island, and New Hampshire.

On January 8th, the mutineers finally agreed to accept Reed's proposals, and the following day they marched to Trenton where the final details of the settlement were to be worked out. One condition of the settlement was that the two British agents sent to Princeton with offers from General Clinton to join the British were to be turned over immediately for trial by a military court-martial. The Board of Sergeants complied with this demand, and the pair was expeditiously tried and hanged the morning after the verdict was announced.

There followed almost three weeks of foot-dragging and haggling with the Committee of Congress appointed to execute the provisions of the settlement. Reed had wisely returned to Philadelphia, leaving the commissioners to settle up with the men of the Pennsylvania Line. In part this delay was due to the lack of immediate access to regimental records. Once the records arrived the tedious process of validating the terms of each soldier's enlistment began.

On January 29th, General Wayne reported to Washington that about 1,250 infantrymen, and 67 artillerymen had been discharged, after it was determined that their enlistments had expired. This left only about 1,150 men in the ranks of the Pennsylvania Line. Additionally, the non-commissioned officers were sent on sixty-day furloughs. Having lost more than half of their numbers, the remaining six regiments of the Line marched off to their newly assigned posts in Pennsylvania, where they were to commence recruiting efforts to fill their depleted ranks.

*   *   *

While the mutiny of the Pennsylvania Line wound down, another mutiny erupted involving New Jersey troops. The enlisted men of the New Jersey brigade in winter quarters at Pompton were well aware that the Pennsylvania line had mutinied, and they followed the events of that rebellion closely. The New Jersey troops had many of the same complaints including lack of pay, and depreciation of that pay, as well as similar disputes over the terms of their enlistments. When they heard the terms of the settlement offered to the Pennsylvanians, the New Jersey brigade followed suit.

On January 20th, the New Jersey mutineers marched from Pompton to Chatam where they met with commissioners from the New Jersey legislature. The commissioners quickly offered a pardon for those involved in the uprising, and then updated the men on what actions were ongoing to settle their grievances. Somewhat mollified by that information, the mutineers returned to their Pompton encampment to await further developments.

Word of the New Jersey mutiny reached Washington's headquarters at New Windsor on the evening of January 21st. The General quickly ordered General Heath at West Point to assemble a force of "five or six hundred men" for a march to New Jersey to quell the mutiny.[25] The following day, General Washington traveled to West Point to direct and expedite the planning of the expedition. General Robert Howe was selected to command the force that was comprised of New England troops. Washington gave Howe specific instructions that only unconditional submission of the mutineers was acceptable. He also instructed Howe not enter into any negotiations so long as the troops were in an armed state of resistance. Washington also told Howe that, if he was successful in compelling the mutineers' surrender, he was to immediately execute a few of the most prominent leaders of the insurrectionists.

Concerned about a possible British move to exploit the mutinies, General Washington, accompanied by French General Lafayette, rode to Ringwood mansion, just south of the New York-New Jersey border, where he established a temporary headquarters. The location was only eight miles from the New Jersey brigade's Pompton encampment.

After a night march across snow-covered fields, General Howe's force reached the vicinity of the Pompton encampment before daylight and quickly surrounded the mutineers' huts with infantry and artillery. The New Jersey mutineers were then ordered to parade without arms to a designated location at the camp, and their officers were asked to identify those who they believed to be the most incendiary leaders. Howe then required the New Jersey officers to select three from that group for immediate court martial. The unfortunate trio was tried on the spot, found guilty, and were sentenced to be shot. A firing squad consisting of twelve of the next most notorious of the mutineers was then ordered to carry out the executions. Two of the men were shot, but the third received a last minute pardon as an act of clemency. That man survived to fight at Yorktown.[26]

* * *

The mutinies of January 1781 were over, and although the Army remained intact, it was seriously weakened. The Pennsylvania Line lost more than half its manpower, and the state had no funds to entice new recruits and reenlistments. There was also doubt whether the furloughed noncommissioned officers would ever return to their regiments. The New Jersey brigade lost fewer men, but could only muster about 148 effectives to march south with Lafayette to confront Benedict Arnold's January invasion of Virginia. In fact, the mutinies could not have come at a worse time for the army. The British under Lord Cornwallis were on the march in the Carolinas, and the turncoat Benedict Arnold was "unleashing hell" in the Old Dominion. In the coming months, General Washington and his army would face some of their toughest challenges of the war. However over the next several months, Washington would meantime have to rely on those generals he had already selected for command positions in the southern theater.

3

HILLS OF THE SOUTH COUNTRY

January 1, 1781
During the month of January, the weather in the Carolinas was wet
and cold. The muddy roads were nearly impassible, and the rivers and
streams flooded over their banks, making communications and supply
difficult. It was Cornwallis's "winter of discontent" in the Carolinas.
As he paced the pine floors of the modest two-story white frame house
that served as his headquarters in Winnsboro, the British general
recalled the events of the past year and the situation facing his army.
After a severe illness in October, the Commander of British forces in
the south was fully recovered and was anxious to launch a winter
offensive that would crush the American army in the Carolinas. It
would prove more difficult than he could imagine.

Cornwallis was far from satisfied with the progress of his campaign in the
Carolinas. Following the surrender of Charleston in May of 1780, General
Clinton, the British commander-in-chief in North America, returned to
New York, leaving Cornwallis in command of the southern army. The
relationship between Clinton and Cornwallis had frayed during the siege
of Charleston, and Cornwallis welcomed the opportunity for independent
command. While he lacked complete autonomy, he did have wide latitude
in complying with General Clinton's guidance. Broadly stated, Clinton's
instructions to Cornwallis were to pacify South Carolina, reclaim North
Carolina, and then move north into Virginia where, with reinforcements
drawn from New York, he would bring that state under full British control.

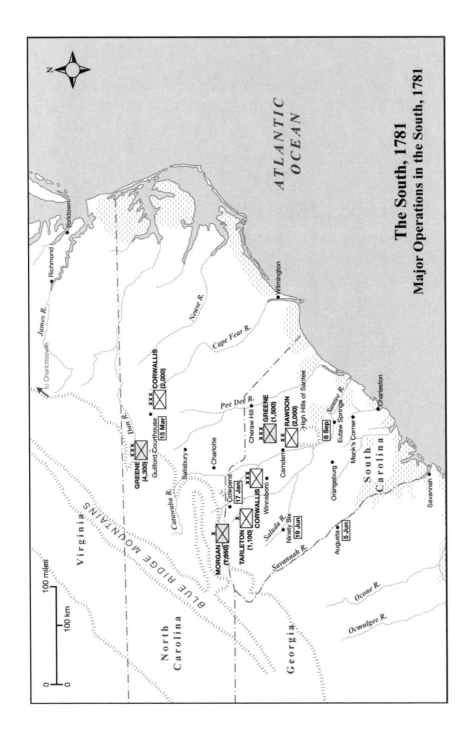

The South, 1781
Major Operations in the South, 1781

It was easier said than done, and Clinton's surrender terms to the Americans at Charleston had added a new dimension to the war in the south.

The Continental troops and the most obstinate local rebels who fought at Charleston were classified as prisoners of war, and were confined in the horrid British prison ships and on islands off the coast. However, some 800 militiamen were paroled. This did not sit well with South Carolina's Loyalists, who expected that all the rebels would be punished. Throughout the summer violence erupted between the Loyalists and their rebel neighbors. Cornwallis attempted a crackdown on the most notorious of the rebel leaders, capturing and imprisoning some, but the fratricidal violence between the Americans spread quickly through the countryside, and was soon beyond British control. Harsh British efforts to crush the local rebels only swelled their ranks with new recruits.

Cornwallis knew that he needed the support and cooperation of the Loyalist forces to conduct a successful campaign against the American Army. He had far too few British regulars to control an area of more than fifteen thousand square miles. As he pushed into the interior of South Carolina, Cornwallis established outposts and supply depots at Ninety-Six, Camden, and Cheraw to support his operations. Local rebel militias and partisan bands harassed the small garrisons of the bases, and attacked couriers and supply trains dispatched from Charleston, as the British battled for control over the interior. The security of the bases and the army's lines of communication and resupply relied heavily on Loyalist forces.

As the British attempted to consolidate their control in South Carolina, a force of 1,400 Maryland and Delaware Continentals under the command of General Baron Johan DeKalb marched into North Carolina. On July 25th, 1780, General Horatio Gates, the victor of Saratoga, arrived to assume command of the southern American army, replacing DeKalb. Reinforced by North Carolina militia, Gates then began a 120-mile march toward the South Carolina border. Cornwallis learned of the threat on August 9, 1780 and marched north from Charleston the following day. The two armies met at Camden, South Carolina on August 16th, and the British decisively defeated the Americans. The battle ended in a rout, as the Americans retreated in disorder. Gates made no effort to regain control over his men. Instead he galloped to the rear ahead of his fleeing soldiers, not halting until he reached Charlotte some sixty miles away.

With the American army in disarray, and with promises of support from nearby Loyalists, Cornwallis launched an invasion of North Carolina. The General believed that he could gain the support of the citizenry of that state, once they saw his army "in motion."[1]

Cornwallis's army reached Charlotte during the last week of September. He intended to continue to Hillsboro (near Raleigh), where he planned to establish a base and lay in supplies from the countryside to sustain his army throughout the winter. However, the arduous march to Charlotte took its toll on his men, many of whom were ill with fevers before departing Camden. His army was in no shape to march another 175 miles to Hillsboro without rest, recuperation, and resupply.

Cornwallis was also concerned about the Carolina highlands to his west. The intelligence reports that he received, along with his own instincts, led him to believe that Loyalist strength was much weaker in the highlands. Mountain folk and frontiersmen, who were not inclined toward allegiance to the British Crown, inhabited the Blue Ridge and the wilderness beyond. Most had immigrated to America to escape the poverty of British-ruled Ireland. Known in America as Scotch-Irish, these folk were fiercely independent and valued their personal freedom to live their lives as they saw fit. Others included French Huguenots and Germans who had been persecuted in their homelands by their own monarchs. Few were loyal subjects of the British sovereign, George III.

Increasingly concerned about his western flank, Cornwallis entrusted the security of that region to an innovative, but at times impetuous, British major, Patrick Ferguson. Cornwallis appointed Ferguson as Inspector of Militia and gave him command of all Loyalist militia on his western flank. Major Ferguson, a Scot by birth, was a brilliant organizer and tactician, but his impetuosity led to his downfall and death. His incendiary message to Americans on the frontier was that, "if they did not desist from their opposition to the British army . . . he would march his army over the mountains, hang their leaders, and lay their country waste with fire and sword." The message ignited a firestorm among the frontiersmen.[2] Hundreds poured over the mountains to reinforce the American militia units east of the mountains, and their combined forces defeated Ferguson's militia force at Kings Mountain in October of 1780. The battle lasted slightly over an hour, and more than two hundred Tory militia were killed, including Ferguson, and the remainder were taken captive.

The American victory at Kings Mountain was a devastating blow to Loyalist morale in the Carolinas, and it spurred many neutral citizens to actively oppose the British and their allies throughout the south. Moreover, it left the British army's western flank exposed, and the supply route to Charleston increasingly vulnerable to partisan attack. As a consequence, Cornwallis decided to withdraw his army 60 miles to the south to Winnsboro, South Carolina. The march over the muddy red clay country roads was a nightmare. The most seriously ill soldiers, including Lord Cornwallis, filled the wagons that followed the marching column.

Cornwallis selected Winnsboro as his destination for several reasons. As a town it was insignificant with only a few citizens and houses, but it was located in the upper Piedmont region equidistant between the towns of Cheraw and Ninety Six. Moreover, the town was only thirty miles from Columbia and Camden. The roads that connected those towns ran through Winnsboro. There was also a network of backcountry roads leading north from Winnsboro toward North Carolina. Thus, Cornwallis had positioned his army to maneuver quickly in several directions, while shortening his supply lines to Charleston. Still with the onset of winter, the British general remained concerned about the security of the Piedmont region. Of particular concern were his outposts at Ninety Six, Brierly's Ferry, and Camden. Those posts were key to the security of the British supply and communication lines.

The American victory at Kings Mountain spurred an upsurge in partisan attacks against the vulnerable outposts, and the main British army at Winnsboro was threatened on both flanks. Partisan leader Colonel Francis Marion operated between the Santee and Pee Dee Rivers, and from that locale he was able to threaten supplies and communications for the British post at Camden and the main army at Winnsboro. On the British left flank, Brigadier General Thomas Sumter's forces operated west of the Broad River threatening Ninety Six. Both Marion and Sumter were determined to make life as miserable as possible for the British.

Cornwallis's main concern, however, was the reinforced American army that moved to Charlotte after he withdrew his army to Winnsboro. General Nathaniel Greene had been appointed to command the Continentals, replacing Horatio Gates. Adding to his worries, Cornwallis learned that a force led by Brigadier General Daniel Morgan, supported by Colonel William Washington's cavalry, had departed Charlotte on December 20th and crossed the Broad River moving in the direction of the British base at Ninety Six, the installation he deemed most vital to his command. Lord Cornwallis therefore concluded that he had to launch a winter offensive to destroy Greene's army.

The first month of 1781 was wetter than normal in the Carolinas, and the roads were turned into morasses of mud impeding the movement of troops and wagons. Moreover, rivers and creeks were swollen and over-flowing their banks in many locations, making fording operations next to impossible. A major offensive against the main American army to the north was risky and fraught with problems. The area between Winnsboro and Charlotte had been heavily foraged by both the British and the Americans, and British supply lines were vulnerable to hit-and-run attacks by Marion's and Sumter's partisans who were on the loose on the British flanks and rear. However, the most dangerous threat to Cornwallis's advance to the north was General Morgan's force that could seriously endanger his western flank and rear. Morgan would have to be dealt with before Cornwallis moved against the major portion of Greene's army.

Dispensing with traditional New Year's Day celebrations, Cornwallis drafted orders to Lieutenant Colonel Banastre Tarleton to pursue and destroy General Morgan's force.[3] The dispatch rider delivered the orders to Tarleton the following day, and he set out immediately in pursuit of Morgan and his men. Meanwhile, Lord Cornwallis continued to fine-tune his plans for a winter campaign to destroy, once and for all, the American southern army.

Cornwallis's plan called for the main British army to penetrate into North Carolina leaving behind sufficient forces in South Carolina to deal with partisan attacks. Offensive operations were to commence around the middle of January, contingent upon the arrival of reinforcements. General Leslie commanding a force of some 1,500 men had sailed to Charleston from Chesapeake Bay, arriving on the 13th of December. Upon his arrival, Leslie received orders to march up-country to reinforce Cornwallis as soon as possible. When Leslie arrived, Cornwallis planned to move north against Nathaniel Greene. His planned line of march took advantage of the Piedmont's upland roads, rather than the lowland routes that presented significant obstacles to movement such as wide rivers, swamps, and fewer fords. He hoped through a series of rapid marches to maneuver his army to a position between Greene's army and Virginia; thereby forcing the Americans into a decisive battle by eliminating any possible withdrawal route, and preventing Greene from receiving reinforcements from the north.

GENERAL GREENE'S HEADQUARTERS— NEAR CHERAW, SOUTH CAROLINA

Thirty-eight-year-old Major General Nathaniel Greene walked with his characteristic limp among the tents and crude log huts toward the fortifications protecting his army's winter camp. As expected, his chief engineer, Thaddeus Kosciuszko, selected an excellent site for the camp, and the work on the fortifications was progressing to his satisfaction. Through the pines and hickory trees, he could see that the Pee Dee River was muddy and swollen from the early winter rains. Rivers he knew would present difficulties for his army, as well as for the British in coming months. The major rivers that flowed through the region including the Pee Dee, the Yadkin, the Broad, and the Wateree, along with numerous tributaries and streams that would pose enormous difficulties in maneuvering and supplying his army during the winter. Upon his arrival in the Carolinas, Greene had studied the terrain and waterways of the region and dispatched men to survey the rivers, measuring depths and currents, and locating fords. Rivers were only one of the numerous challenges he knew that his army would have to face during a winter campaign.

The camp near Cheraw was called "the Camp of Repose," but Greene knew there would be no winter respite for his army. There was no time to rebuild, re-equip, and retrain the defeated army he had inherited. The Rhode Island foundry owner turned soldier knew that Lord Cornwallis would not afford him that opportunity.

Nathaniel Greene, Washington's most trusted general, had arrived in Charlotte, North Carolina on December 2, 1780, after a seven-week journey from New York. He assumed command of the Southern Department of the Continental Army on the following day. The change of command between Greene and his predecessor, General Horatio Gates, went smoothly despite the awkward circumstances surrounding Gates' relief from command. Greene had the authority to conduct an inquiry into the circumstances surrounding Gate's performance during the battle of Camden, including his personal actions during the retreat, but he opted not to order the inquiry. He had more pressing issues on his mind.

His commander-in-chief, Washington, had given General Greene an enormous task. His mission was to rebuild the southern army, defeat Cornwallis, and wrest control of the Carolinas and Georgia from the British and Loyalist forces. With severe shortages of men, arms, clothing, food, and other supplies and money to purchase them, Greene's chances of success were seemingly minimal, but the general undertook the mission with his usual vigor and enthusiasm.

The son of a Quaker farmer, Greene was born in the township of Warwick, Rhode Island in 1742. In 1770, he moved to Coventry to manage the family-owned foundry, and later the same year he was elected to the Rhode Island General Assembly. In 1774, he helped organize a local militia, but his fellow militiamen thought that his limp disqualified him from a leadership position. Nevertheless, Greene devoted himself to the study of military strategy and tactics, acquiring numerous volumes dealing with the art of war. After serving on a committee in the General Assembly that revised the state's militia laws, Greene was appointed as a Brigadier General in the Rhode Island militia. He led his Rhode Islanders during the siege of Boston, impressing the army's new commander, General Washington.

In August of 1776, the Continental Congress promoted him to major general in the Continental Army. Greene came under severe criticism during the New York campaign for advising Washington to hold Fort Washington in upper Manhattan, resulting in the disastrous loss of men and supplies. Nevertheless, Washington continued to entrust Greene with important commands. He successfully commanded the right wing at the Battle of Trenton in December 1776, and also commanded Continental troops at the Battle of Princeton in January 1777, and the Battle of Brandywine in September of the same year. A month later he commanded the army's left wing at the battle of Germantown. In March 1778, Greene was appointed as the army's Quartermaster General, a post he grudgingly accepted. However, despite his distaste for the job, he worked diligently to fix many of the army's supply problems, and greatly increased the efficiency of the Quartermaster Department. Although his post was an administrative one, General Washington still included Greene in his councils of war, and even appointed him to command the army's right with at the Battle of Monmouth Courthouse in June 1778. He next distinguished himself at the Battle of Rhode Island in August of the same year. Greene resigned his post as Quartermaster General in July of 1780, hoping for another field command. Without question, Nathaniel Greene had earned the full confidence of his commander-in-chief, and was a brilliant choice as the Southern Department's new commanding general.

Greene understood from the start that warfare in the southern theater was far different from what he had experienced in the New England, New York, and Pennsylvania campaigns. Given the limited number of Continental regulars under his command, Greene knew that he must not allow himself to be lured into a major battle with Cornwallis's battle hardened British regulars unless all conditions were in his favor. Greene also knew that he would have to depend on the Patriot militias to compensate for the small number of Continentals in his army, and that he would have to rely on partisan and irregular bands to harass the British and their Loyalist allies by attacking their outposts and disrupting their lines of communication. Finally, Greene realized that to defeat the British he would have to out-march and out-maneuver them, forcing Cornwallis to spread his forces over thousands of square miles of territory, gradually and methodically wearing the British down in a war of attrition.

On December 20, 1780, Greene marched the bulk of his army from Charlotte, North Carolina southeast across the South Carolina border to the vicinity of Cheraw. Another detachment of some six hundred men under Daniel Morgan departed Charlotte on the 21st of December. Morgan's men marched southwest into South Carolina and established a camp on the left bank of the Pacolet River at Grindal Shoals.

Greene knew that splitting his army into two parts in the face of Cornwallis's stronger army violated widely accepted military doctrine. By dividing his army and separating the two components by more than a hundred miles, with the British army in the middle, Greene risked the destruction of both wings. With his numerically superior force, Cornwallis could move to destroy either part of Greene's army before turning his attention to the other. Greene justified his actions with simple logic. If Cornwallis moved against his position at Cheraw, the British western flank and supply lines to Charleston would be exposed to General Morgan's force. On the other hand, if Cornwallis moved to attack Morgan, it would provide Greene with an opportunity to move in the direction of Charleston, attacking and destroying British outposts such as Camden along the way.[4] Greene also knew that the movement of two separate American forces into South Carolina would hearten the local militiamen and encourage them to attack the British throughout the state.

Greene believed in his strategy, but he also worried about the poor condition of his army. Supplies were scarce in the backcountry of North and South Carolina, and the anticipated flow of reinforcements and supplies from Virginia had not yet reached him. His second-in-command, General Friedrich Von Steuben, was still in Virginia attempting to recruit men and gather supplies for the southern army. Since Cornwallis was already on the move, sending Tarleton's force after Morgan, Greene had no time to waste.

4

HELL IN VIRGINIA

January 1–19, 1781
At dawn on New Year's Day, a dispatch rider bearing important news arrived in Richmond and ascended Shockoe Hill, headed for the governor's townhouse. He found Governor Jefferson in his garden and delivered the message. On the evening of December 30th, an American ship anchored off Old Point Comfort had spotted a fleet of twenty-seven British ships that had slipped past the Capes of Virginia and were headed in the direction of Norfolk. The long feared British invasion of Virginia had begun.

ON BOARD HMS *CHARLESTOWN*—JAMES RIVER, VIRGINIA
Newly appointed Brigadier General Benedict Arnold, of the British Army, sat at his desk and composed a note to the rebels onshore. He was anxious to mop up the half-hearted resistance by the rebel militia in the tidewater region and continue his advance on his primary objective, the rebel capitol of Richmond. His appetites for plunder and prize money slowed his progress up the James River.

After his traitorous defection to the British, Benedict Arnold was commissioned a Brigadier in the King's army. He then purchased a house and took up residence in Manhattan, a few doors from General Henry Clinton's headquarters. Anxious to prove his newfound loyalty to the King, and secure a means to support the lavish lifestyle of his young and beautiful wife, the former Peggy Shippen, Arnold repeatedly petitioned Clinton for the opportunity to command a major expedition against his former comrades-in-arms. His persistence paid off, and the commander-in-chief of British forces in North America finally granted his request. Recognizing Arnold's attributes as a fearless and aggressive officer eager for fame and fortune, General Clinton selected him as commander of a 1,600-man force that would sail south to Virginia to seize Portsmouth and establish a permanent British naval base. British General Alexander Leslie had seized Portsmouth and begun work on fortifications in late October of 1780, but departed three weeks later when he was ordered to leave Virginia and sail to Charleston, South Carolina to reinforce Cornwallis.

With a British foothold in Virginia's tidewater, Clinton hoped that Loyalists in the Old Dominion would rally to the "cause" and crush the rebel militias. He further hoped that a British force, augmented with Loyalist militia units, could forestall the movement of reinforcements to Nathaniel Greene's southern army in the Carolinas.

Clinton knew that Arnold was aggressive, independent minded, and eager to prove himself to the British. He therefore made it abundantly clear to him that his primary mission was to establish and secure a base at Portsmouth, and from there recruit loyalists for the cause. Clinton did not intend for Arnold to begin immediate follow-on operations into the interior of the state, but he did imply that limited forays into the areas surrounding the base could be conducted, provided that there was not any "danger to the safety of the post . . ."[1] To keep Arnold from acting too independently once he reached Virginia, Clinton told him that he must have the concurrence of his two major subordinate commanders, British Lieutenant Colonels John Simcoe and Thomas Dundas, before launching any major operations. After departing New York, Arnold would soon make clear that he viewed himself as an independent commander, interpreting Clinton's orders as he saw fit.

Arnold's joint navy and army force set sail from Sandy Hook, New Jersey on December 20th, 1780. Aboard the ships were the 80th Regiment of Foot, also known as the Edinburgh Volunteers under Lieutenant Colonel Dundas, the Queen's Rangers, a Loyalist force consisting of light infantry, light dragoons, and artillery under Lieutenant Colonel Simcoe, along with other detachments of loyalists including the Loyal American Regiment under the command of Lieutenant Colonel Beverley Robinson Jr. Rounding out the force was a complement of elite Hessians under the command of Johann von Ewald. All told, Arnold's army contingent totaled some 1,600 men.

A violent gale scattered the convoy on the 26th and 27th of December, but most of the vessels managed to reassemble off Cape Henry on December 29th. Missing were three transports with some four hundred troops on board, and one armed escort vessel. Opting not to wait for the missing transports, the convoy entered Hampton Roads on December 30th, and continued sailing to the mouth of the James River, anchoring off Newport News that same evening. Undeterred by the missing transports carrying one-quarter of his ground force, Arnold quickly ordered the majority of his remaining infantry to transfer from the large transports onto smaller, mostly open boats that were capable of navigating the James River all the way to Richmond. Larger armed escort vessels carrying the cavalry and artillery were to follow the flotilla of small craft. Although the days were warmer than usual for the winter season, the nights were frigid with winds whipping up white caps in the river. Arnold's men huddled together on the small boats and tried to stay warm.

Arnold first ordered the attack on and capture of a number of unarmed boats carrying hogsheads of tobacco that were anchored at Newport News. Throughout the campaign, Arnold's appetite for prizes and plunder was never satiated. Following the seizure of these first prizes, he ordered a landing force of some three hundred men ashore at Newport News. This was a reconnaissance-in-force mission to locate additional prizes and to determine the presence of any rebel militia in the area. The landing force marched eastward across to peninsula to the village of Hampton where the residents were queried about the presence of nearby militia and other information on the region. Meanwhile, Arnold ordered a flotilla of five boats to row across to the western shore of the James to reconnoiter up the Nansemond River on a similar intelligence-gathering mission. Both missions revealed that there were, in fact, rebel militia on both shores of the James. The most formidable force was located on the north bank a few miles northeast of Newport News.

When Arnold learned of the presence of the latter force, he ordered Johann von Ewald and his Hessians to attack at once. Von Ewald led his men ashore in four open boats. As the Hessians rowed toward the shoreline, they were spotted by the militiamen and taken under fire. Undaunted by the hostile fire, Ewald's force landed on the shoreline, and the Hessian general led his men up a steep embankment. The poorly trained militia soon gave way to the Hessians, who set up a defensive perimeter and sent a smaller force to pursue the rebels.

Interrogating several prisoners, Ewald learned that a much larger force than he anticipated had opposed him. He was furious that Arnold had risked his men by ordering them ashore in the face of such a large enemy contingent. Although the action was little more than a skirmish, it did alert the Virginians to the fact that a large British force had arrived in southern Virginia, and that it was moving up the James River. Arnold had set his sights on Richmond. Portsmouth would have to wait.

On January 2nd, Arnold's flotilla sailed further up the James, halting at a ferry landing on the north bank about five miles from Williamsburg. Seizing two American vessels, Arnold ordered his men to prepare to disembark and engage a militia force of unknown size. Hoping that a show of force would be sufficient to entice the rebels to surrender, Arnold sent a messenger ashore under a flag of truce to deliver a written ultimatum under his signature.[2] The brigadier in command of the Virginia militia force, Thomas Nelson, read and immediately refused the terms of surrender. Nelson also asked the messenger if his commander was indeed Benedict Arnold. When the officer confirmed that his commander was the despised Arnold, Nelson replied that he would never surrender to a "traitor." When the officer returned to Arnold's ship, he repeated verbatim Nelson's reply. Arnold opted not to risk a landing in the face of a body of armed militia of unknown strength. Instead, he ordered the flotilla to sail on up the James toward Richmond. Meanwhile, the word spread quickly throughout the region that a large British force under command of the infamous traitor, Benedict Arnold, was sailing up the James headed toward Virginia's capital.

*　*　*

In Richmond, the Governor of Virginia, Thomas Jefferson, ordered the call up of half of the State's militia of some 4,600 men on January 2, 1781.[3] Jefferson, who had no military background or experience whatsoever, thought that his militia force, which was three times larger than Arnold's force, was capable of defeating the British. He did not take into account the time required to muster and assemble the various militia units throughout the region, or the militia's state of training and readiness.

In that hour of crisis, Jefferson called upon the only senior officer readily available to defend Virginia's capitol against the invasion. Major General Friedrich von Steuben of the Continental Army had been in Virginia since the previous November. When Nathaniel Greene was appointed as commander of the southern Continental Army, he had left von Steuben in Richmond to raise badly needed troops and supplies for the army in the Carolinas. Thus General von Steuben, as the highest-ranking Continental officer in the state, became the "de facto" commander of the militia during this hour of emergency. In reality, the widely scattered militia units were under the direct command of their local militia leaders, most of whom did not even know von Steuben or his whereabouts, and had no communication with him.

During his two-month stay in Virginia, von Steuben knew full well the ill-preparedness of the Virginia militia. Other than sheer numbers and familiarity with the terrain, the poorly equipped and trained Virginian militiamen were no match for the British regulars and the crack loyalist units that comprised Arnold's force. On his travels throughout the region, von Steuben had also developed recommendations on how and where the state should develop its defenses against a possible invasion. One location he deemed critical to the defense of Richmond was at Hood's Point on the south bank of the James River about twenty miles downstream. A small battery of two ten pound cannons and one howitzer had been moved to the area, but work on a fort to protect the battery from ground attack was never completed. A meager force of about ninety militiamen was assigned to protect the battery. There was too little time remaining to correct those deficiencies.

During the evening of January 3rd, Arnold's flotilla approached the bend in the James beyond which lay Hood's Point. Wisely, the General ordered his boats to anchor short of the bend so that he could reconnoiter what lay beyond. All but one of the boats received his orders, and that one was taken under fire by the rebel battery as soon as it rounded the bend. Uncertain of what size force protected the cannons, or the nature of the fortifications, Arnold ordered his gunboats to open fire on the rebel battery. He then ordered the landing of two groups of men to launch ground attacks on the position. One group of Hessians and Queen's Rangers moved on the eastern side of Hood's Point, while a second force of British troops worked their way inland to attack the battery from the rear.

Realizing that their escape route was about to be cut off, the militiamen quickly spiked their artillery pieces and made their escape through the darkening woods and tobacco fields before the British closed in on their position. With the Hood's Point battery neutralized, there were no further significant obstacles blocking Arnold's advance on Richmond. After inspecting the unfinished works of the small fort, Arnold decided not to sail directly to Richmond. Instead, he ordered his flotilla to sail to the Byrd family's plantation on the northern shore of the river just a few miles upstream. Upon arrival, he ordered his men ashore, and the plantation was soon transformed into a large British encampment. Arnold had family ties with the owner, the widow Mary Byrd, as his young wife, Peggy Shippen, was a cousin of Mary Willing Byrd. The widow Byrd and Arnold cordially worked out the terms of the British occupation of her estate. In the following days, Arnold's troops pillaged the neighboring plantations including Beckley, the home of Benjamin Harrison, a signer of the Declaration of Independence and Speaker of the Virginia House of Delegates.

Richmond was only a day's overland march from the Byrd Plantation, and the road leading to the capital was only lightly defended by local militia. Nonetheless, Arnold for the first time during the expedition displayed some hesitancy in making his next move. Summoning his officers, he outlined several courses of action to consider, and then asked for his subordinates' recommendations. First, the force could remain at the Byrd plantation and await reinforcements. Second, he could dispatch reconnaissance patrols to determine the rebel strength in the area between the plantation and Richmond, or he could order an immediate attack on Richmond. Uncharacteristically, the hero of Saratoga–turned traitor was hesitant to order an immediate attack, and had to be convinced by his second in command, Colonel Simcoe, that it was the best option. Arnold's hesitation was doubtless based at least in part on a concern for his own personal safety. He was well aware that his capture would result in a quick trip to the gallows.

Nevertheless, Simcoe's compelling argument and reasoning convinced Arnold, and it was agreed that the British force would depart that same evening, despite a driving rainstorm. With Ewald's Hessian Jaegers as an advance guard, Arnold's column of some 900 men and accompanying artillery set off in the darkness following the muddy road toward Richmond. Behind the Jaegers in the order of march were Simcoe's Rangers, followed by a group of sharpshooters, and an assortment of other Loyalist troops and artillery. A small detachment of mounted Rangers constituted the rear guard of the column. The force advanced unopposed to within twelve miles of Richmond before Arnold ordered a halt. After a rest, the British resumed their march in the early morning hours of January 5th.

Virginia's governor, 37-year-old Thomas Jefferson, was informed early in the morning of January 4th, that the British had captured Hood's Point, and that Arnold's fleet was anchored nearby. After sending his wife and three daughters to safety at Tuckahoe, more than a dozen miles further up the James River, Jefferson ordered the evacuation of important state documents before attempting to rouse the city's militia to arms. He had no communication with General von Steuben, who was not on hand in Richmond to organize and direct the defense of the capital.

Jefferson remained in Richmond throughout the 4th, waiting further reports on movements of the British force. He spent the night of 4–5 January at his home, while Arnold marched toward the city, unsure of what further action he should undertake.

As the governor spent a restless night, the British were closing in on the capital, sweeping aside and capturing a few militia patrols along the way. In the darkness, some militiamen mistakenly identified Simcoe's green-jacketed Rangers as some of their own men, who wore the same color uniform. As a misty dawn broke, Arnold's long column of British, Loyalist, and Hessian soldiers and accompanying artillery and wagons reached the outskirts of Richmond. Almost all of the white citizens, including Jefferson, fled the city leaving behind their African-American slaves. Entering the city, Arnold's men spotted a group of several hundred Virginia militiamen gathered on a hilltop on the city's southeast side overlooking the James. Arnold ordered Ewald to storm the steep hill with his Hessians guiding on the Henrico County Church (St John's Episcopal) that stood atop the hill. The ill-trained and poorly equipped militia managed to get off one volley before fleeing, with the ruthless Hessians in hot pursuit.

As Ewald's men chased their prey into the woods, the remainder of

Arnold's troops mounted an assault on Church Hill. Climbing the steep slope, the British and loyalist troops surprised the few militiamen who occupied the height. The startled rebels fled at the sight of the British without firing a single shot. Arnold's troops then launched an attack on Shockoe Hill, where they anticipated a major fight, but even though the Virginia militia outnumbered the attackers, the rebels gave way to Arnold's highly disciplined regulars. Richmond was at Arnold's mercy, and his troops poured into the town in search of any remaining rebels and booty.

The most sought after rebel that Arnold hoped to capture was Governor Thomas Jefferson, author of the Declaration of Independence. Next to George Washington, Jefferson was the man the British would most have liked to see in chains headed for the gallows. However, by the time Arnold and his men reached the Governor's residence, Jefferson was already on the move, staying one step ahead of his pursuers.

As Arnold's men approached the city that morning, the Governor galloped across the river in search of General von Steuben. Querying the local citizens, he was informed that the general was most likely at his residence a dozen miles up the James. Jefferson continued his search, but was unable to locate his military commander. He continued his search for von Steuben for two days. Meanwhile the British laid waste to Richmond.

Arnold, frustrated that Jefferson had eluded him, offered the remaining citizens a deal. If they offered up hostages, he would pay half the price of the goods he intended to seize. As part of the deal, Arnold's men would be guaranteed safe passage back to their base at the Byrd Plantation, with no interference from militia units along the way. When the Virginians refused to take the word of a traitor, the looting and pillaging began in earnest.

Arnold's men emptied the town's warehouses and stores and set them ablaze. Many private residences were also burned. Even churches were robbed of their gold chalices and crosses. Warehouses that were filled with barrels of wine and rum were looted, and the troops helped themselves to the spirits. Arnold also dispatched troops to nearby Westover where a foundry that manufactured most of the state's armaments was located. The British blew up the gunpowder stored in the foundry's magazine, and in some of the surrounding warehouses. They also destroyed the machinery in the mills before putting the buildings to the torch. Their work complete, the detachment returned to Richmond to join their drunken comrades in the pillaging and looting. Even the Hessian commander, Ewald, was aghast at the needless destruction of private property.[4]

Arnold next ordered his troops to load the looted supplies and valuables on a number of boats commandeered from local merchants and residents for transport back to his base on the James. Disappointed that he had failed to capture Jefferson, Arnold decided to return to the Byrd plantation that same day.[5] His second in command, Lieutenant Colonel Simco, argued that the troops were too exhausted to undertake such a march that day. Ignoring Simcoe's advice, Arnold ordered the march to begin immmediately. He believed that the Virginia militia was now gathering in force, and intended to make his withdrawal a costly one.

The call-up of the Virginia militia was proceeding far more slowly than Arnold imagined, particularly in the distant counties. Many of the militiamen who did arrive were lacking in arms and equipment. Nonetheless, mother nature made the British withdrawal a miserable experience for the troops. Heavy winter rains had turned the backcountry roads into quagmires, and artillery and wagons sank to their axels. Numerous men who were too exhausted to continue dropped out of the march, while others became stragglers. The local militia took some stragglers prisoner, but other than a few random shots, no serious efforts were made to ambush the column as it made its way back to the Byrd plantation.

* * *

Arnold's raid on Richmond was a success, and a setback for the Americans in the near-term, but its long-term consequences were less favorable to the British. As word spread throughout the state of the destruction and devastation wrought by the traitor Arnold's troops, Virginians rallied to the cause in ever increasing numbers, and the ranks of the state's militia swelled with new recruits.

For his part, Jefferson was relieved that he had escaped capture and that his family was safe, at least for the moment. On the other hand, he was devastated that his capital lay in ruins. His failure to adequately prepare for such an event was apparent, but he tried to shift responsibility for the lack of preparedness to the State Assembly. On the British side, Arnold viewed his raid as a success, despite the fact that he had not captured the elusive Governor. He had demonstrated to the British that he was a loyal servant of the Crown, while at the same time adding significantly to his personal fortune. He would next turn his attention to his primary mission in Virginia: the establishment of a permanent base at Portsmouth.

5

SUNRISE AT THE COWPENS

January 4–17
Twenty-five-year-old John Whelchel resided in the Union District of
South Carolina when he was drafted into state service in 1776. His
militia company marched to the frontiers of Georgia to protect the
white settlements against the Cherokee and Creek Indians, and he later
fought the British at Stono, South Carolina. He was also a survivor of
the battle of Kings Mountain, after which he joined a mounted com-
pany of light dragoons. In January of 1781, his company, led by Cap-
tain John Thompson, joined Colonel William Washington's cavalry
command near the Cowpens. Whelchel had seen his share of combat
without suffering any serious injury or wounds, but his luck was about
to run out.[1]

By January 4th, Lieutenant Colonel Banastre Tarleton's column had crossed
the Broad River, and moved west some twenty miles in the direction of
the British post at Ninety Six. Finding no sign of Daniel Morgan's force,
he established camp and sent for his baggage train. Tarleton was convinced
that Morgan's corps, including Colonel William Washington's cavalry, was
nowhere near Fort Williams and the post at Ninety Six. He therefore
recommended a joint maneuver that would entrap Morgan and force him
into battle

Tarleton's plan called for his own column to move northeast in the
direction of King's Mountain, pushing Morgan's "flying army" before it,
while Cornwallis advanced north on an axis east of the Broad River. Once

Tarleton overtook Morgan, the Americans would be forced to stand and fight, or cross the Broad River and face Cornwallis' even larger force.[2] Tarleton requested that his command be reinforced with the 17th Dragoons, 7th Fusiliers and the Jagers to execute his part of the plan.

Cornwallis approved Tarleton's plan on January 5th, and agreed to reinforce him with 200 men from the 7th Fusiliers, 50 dragoons of the 17th Regiment, and an additional 3-pound cannon. With those reinforcements, Tarleton's force numbered approximately 1,100 men. The confident twenty-six-year-old light cavalryman was ready to give chase to Morgan's force and destroy it.

Banastre Tarleton was born in Liverpool, England in 1754. The son of a wealthy merchant and one-time mayor of Liverpool, Tarleton studied at Oxford University and intended to pursue a career as a lawyer. However, after receiving an inheritance after his father's death, the young Tarleton quickly squandered most of the money on women and gambling. In 1775, at age twenty-one, Tarleton was able to purchase a commission as a Coronet in the 1st Dragoon Guards. In December of that year, he embarked as an unattached cavalry officer with troops under the command of Lord Cornwallis bound for service in America. After participating in Cornwallis's unsuccessful attempt to capture Charleston in 1776, Tarleton applied for service with the Sixteenth Light Dragoons.

After participating in the successful campaign to capture New York, Tarleton led a daring dragoon raid that captured General Charles Lee— one of the Continental Army's most experienced commanders—in New Jersey. This exploit earned him a promotion to major. After further service in the New Jersey and Pennsylvania, Tarleton was promoted to lieutenant colonel in 1777, and given command of the British Legion that was composed primarily of American loyalists. Two years later, Tarleton's command sailed south with Generals Clinton and Cornwallis to capture Charleston. During the siege, he was ordered by Clinton to cut off the rebel communication and supply lines between the backcountry and Charleston, a mission that he successfully accomplished.

After the surrender of Charleston, Cornwallis ordered Tarleton's Legion to pursue a force of 350 Virginia Continentals led by Colonel Abraham Buford. Tarleton caught up with the Americans and defeated them at the battle of the Waxhaws on May 29th, 1780. Tarleton's men dealt harshly with the rebels, refusing to offer them quarter as they attempted to surrender. Word spread quickly that Tarleton was responsible for a massacre at the Waxhaws, and his reputation as a cruel and vindictive commander followed him throughout his service in America. At the Battle of Camden in August of 1780, Tarleton further enhanced his reputation as a cavalry commander by leading his Legion in a rout of the American forces at the conclusion of the battle. By the beginning of the year 1781, he was hated by more Americans that any other British officer serving in the Carolinas.

As soon as his reinforcements arrived, Tarleton marched north to locate Morgan's force. Heavy rains and swollen creeks slowed the progress of his column. Ahead and on the flanks of the column, Tarleton's scouts and spies reconnoitered the countryside on the lookout for rebels, while his foragers searched for food. Loyalist spies soon reported to Tarleton that rebel militia units were marching to reinforce Morgan.

While Tarleton's men scoured the countryside in search of the Patriot force, General Cornwallis departed Winnsboro on January 7th but halted a day later at the McAllister Plantation where he waited for reinforcements to arrive. Major General Alexander Leslie was marching from Charleston to support Cornwallis, but was delayed by heavy rains that flooded the rivers and creeks throughout the Piedmont region. After a delay of five days, Cornwallis's army resumed its march on January 13th, while Leslie's force still struggled to catch up.

As he neared the Pacolet River on January 15th, Tarleton was informed by his scouts that Morgan had broken camp at Grindal Shoals and was moving in the direction of Burr's Mill, ten miles to the north on Thicketty Creek. Tarleton also learned that Morgan had left men to guard the fords on the Pacolet. Rather than forcing a crossing, Tarleton followed the river upstream for several miles. Morgan's patrols shadowed the British from the opposite bank. When the British made camp that evening, Morgan's scouts did the same. While Morgan's scouts slept, Tarleton ordered his light infantrymen to slip out of camp to secure an unguarded ford at Easterwood Shoals, only six miles from Morgan's camp at Burr's Mill. After the British light infantry secured the ford, the remainder of Tarleton's troops marched to the ford and crossed the fog-shrouded river in the early morning hours of January 16th.[3]

As Tarleton spurred his horse and splashed across the ford at the head of his legionnaires, he was confident that he had Morgan within his grasp. It was just a matter of where Morgan would make his stand. Soon after Tarleton's light infantry crossed the ford at Easterwood Shoals, Morgan's scouts realized they had been duped. Messengers raced through the darkness toward Burr's Mill to alert Morgan that Tarleton was on the move and closing fast. Upon learning that the British were across the Pacolet, Morgan had the alert sounded throughout the camp. In the darkness, officers shouted commands for their men to turn out with their packs and rifles, and assemble in marching formation, while teamsters hastily loaded their wagons. Morgan knew that he only had about an hour's lead-time on Tarleton's fast moving cavalry.

Morgan's column of Continentals, militia, and supply wagons set off in the darkness with detachments of William Washington's cavalry providing the advance, flank, and rear guards. As an additional precaution, Morgan left a detachment of North Carolina militia behind at Burr's Mill to slow the British pursuit. Morgan knew that if Tarleton's cavalry overtook him while he was on the move the results would be disastrous, so he pushed his men hard along the rough roads that traversed the swampy terrain.

Morgan had to clear the swamps and reach defensible terrain before he could make a stand against the British. The Virginian weighed his options. He could continue to push his men hard for twenty miles and cross Broad River, and then establish a defensive position in the hilly terrain beyond. The ground north of the river was ideally suited for the defense, and the Americans could make a river crossing exceedingly difficult for the British. However, Morgan knew there were other factors besides the terrain that he must consider. His column would not reach the river before dusk, and a river crossing in the darkness was risky business, particularly when the stream was swollen and the current was swift. Moreover, Tarleton's cavalry might overtake his column while the river crossing was in progress. He also had serious doubts whether the South Carolina militia would cross the river and march into North Carolina, leaving their own homes and families unprotected.

After conferring with his scouts and militia officers, Morgan learned that the nearest defensible ground south of the Broad River was at the Cowpens. The area was well known to residents throughout the region. It had been used for decades as a site for grazing and fattening cattle before they were driven to markets at Charleston and other population centers to the east. It was also a backcountry road junction. Since the war began, the Cowpens had been used as an assembly area for Patriot and at times Loyalist militia units, when they were called up for service. During October 1780, Patriot militia from throughout the region gathered at the Cowpens before moving against Major Ferguson and his Loyalists at Kings Mountain.

Throughout the march, Morgan continued to confer with his guides and officers. During the early afternoon, he learned that South Carolina militia leader Colonel Andrew Pickens had crossed the Broad River with a mounted militia force and was marching to join him. Armed with that information and the possibility that other militia reinforcements were on the way, Morgan rode ahead to inspect the ground at the Cowpens, reaching the area on the afternoon of January 16th. As he reconnoitered the ground with the keen eyes of a seasoned commander, he weighed the advantages and disadvantages of making a stand there.

The Cowpens was a rolling plain of savanna grasslands with barely noticeable ridgelines and swales. The area was relatively open, allowing for the employment of his cavalry and mounted infantry, but the same held true for the enemy. The swales and low ridgelines offered some concealment for his troops against enemy fire, and the stands of hardwoods and pine offered concealment for his sharpshooters. The general also observed that the ground was much the same all the way to the Broad River some five miles distant. With a river at his back, retreat across open terrain was not an option. Tarleton's cavalry riding hard over the open ground would soon turn any retreat into a disaster. Morgan was also concerned about the willingness of his militia units to stand and fight the British regulars. After the battle Morgan wrote, "Had I crossed the River, one half of the militia would have abandoned me."[4] He knew full well that when men are forced to fight, "they will sell their lives dearly . . ."[5]

As Morgan reconnoitered the terrain, his troops continued marching toward the Cowpens. The main column of Continentals and Virginia and Carolina militia arrived in the late afternoon followed by Colonel Washington's cavalry. Throughout the remainder of the afternoon and evening, militia units and individual militiamen continued to arrive at the Cowpens. The arrival of Colonel Andrew Pickens further bolstered Morgan's confidence. Pickens brought with him 150 men, and after conferring with Morgan, he rode out of camp to gather other units in the vicinity. With militia streaming into camp, Morgan briefed his officers on his battle plan.

Morgan's plan has been called a "tactical" masterpiece, and the details of that plan are still studied today at Army staff and war colleges. The plan was based on the principles of maneuver, surprise, and simplicity. In addition, it made effective use of the terrain, and maximum use of the unique skills and capabilities of Morgan's heterogeneous force. The plan also took into account Tarleton's aggressiveness, and his reliance on tactics better suited to the European battlefield than the American frontier.

Morgan's plan called for a defense in depth with three lines of resistance. The Maryland and Delaware Continentals and Virginia militia formed the main line of resistance. The Continentals and Virginians were deployed in linear formations on the left and right sides of the Mill Gap Road along a low ridgeline. Morgan's reserve force, Washington's cavalry, was assigned an area behind the main line of resistance. The South Carolina militia battalions under Colonel Pickens occupied another ridgeline about 300 yards in front of the Continentals. Both the main position and the forward position were on relatively open ground. The third line, or skirmish line, was about 150 yards in front of the militia position in long neglected fields that were overgrown with weeds and saplings. The Americans also had pickets and cavalry vedettes posted three miles in front of their skirmish line to provide early warning of a British approach.

Morgan made certain that all of his officers and men understood his battle plan, and exactly what was expected of each unit. The skirmishers were instructed to engage the lead British unit, forcing it to deploy before they withdrew from their advanced positions. Unit commanders handpicked the skirmishers, who were all volunteers with exceptional marksmanship skills. The skirmishers were told that their prime targets were the British officers.

Behind the skirmish line, Pickens' militia line was instructed to delay the British assault as long as possible before withdrawing. Morgan's orders were that the militiamen were to fire at least three volleys before withdrawing back through the Continentals to reserve positions near Washington's cavalry. The Continentals and Virginians were expected to stand fast and repel the main British assault, while Washington's cavalry stood ready to counterattack any breakthrough of the main line of resistance, and to counter any flanking movement by Tarleton's cavalry. The cavalry was also on call to pursue any British withdrawal from the field.

The success of Morgan's plan was heavily dependent on the performance of the militia units that comprised about three quarters of his total force. He understood their capabilities, and he knew how to motivate the militiamen. After darkness descended, he visited each militia camp and talked to as many men as possible. The militiamen held Morgan in high regard. He was one of them, a frontiersman, who had fought the French and Indians years before most of them were born. Starting as a wagon master on the ill-fated Braddock expedition, Morgan experienced, firsthand, British distain for the rough-cut American militia. The militiamen were also aware of Morgan's reputation as a fearless leader of men like themselves during campaigns in Canada and the northeast. He even dressed and spoke like them, and they knew he would never ask more than they were capable of doing, or squander their lives recklessly. One militiaman wrote in his memoirs that Morgan ". . . went among the volunteers, helped them fix their swords, joked with them about their sweethearts and told them to keep in good spirits, and the day would be ours." The young militiaman further wrote that he "was more perfectly convinced of General Morgan's qualifications to command militia than I had ever been before." And that even after he laid down, Morgan was "going about among the soldiers, encouraging them, and telling them that the "Old Wagoner" would crack the whip over Ben (Tarleton) in the morning, as sure as he lived."[6]

*   *   *

After crossing the Pacolet, Tarleton's force proceeded toward Burr's Mill, arriving late in the afternoon of January 16th. Upon learning that the Americans had abandoned their camp and were on the move, Tarleton ordered his dragoons to dispatch patrols to follow them until dark. He also ordered his "spies" to query local citizens about Morgan's whereabouts and his intentions. After interrogating a captured militia officer, and receiving other intelligence reports indicating that Morgan was about to be reinforced, Tarleton decided that he would "hang on Morgan's rear" to "impede the junction of reinforcements . . . and likewise to prevent his passing Broad River . . ."[7] Other reports received around midnight confirmed that

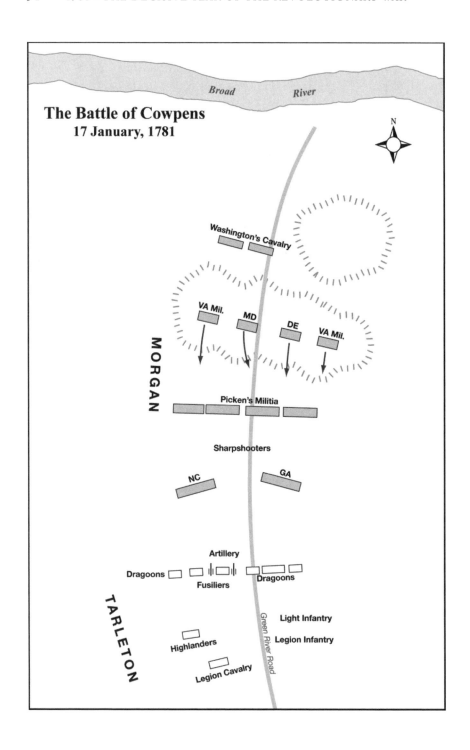

The Battle of Cowpens
17 January, 1781

American reinforcements were on the way to Morgan, and that news spurred Tarleton into action.

At 3:00 am on the morning of January 17th, Tarleton ordered his pickets called in, and roused his men for a night march following the route the Americans had taken toward the Cowpens. Tarleton's column marched off in the darkness with an advance guard of three companies of light infantry supported by the Legion infantry. Next in the order of march were the 7th Fusiliers, the two 3-pound cannon, followed by the 1st Battalion of the 71st Highlanders. Tarleton's cavalry and mounted infantry formed the rear guard of the marching column. The baggage and wagons were left behind with orders to follow the main column at daylight. Tarleton wanted to travel fast and light to close on Morgan's position as early as possible, but creek and stream crossings, and the requirement to maintain constant front and flank security slowed the progress of the night march.

Before dawn, Tarleton ordered an advance guard of cavalry to the front of the column. The horsemen soon made contact with Morgan's pickets and vedettes, forcing them to withdraw. The British cavalry pursued and overtook some of the Americans, prompting Tarleton to reinforce his advanced guard with two troops of dragoons. The officer in command of the advance guard soon reported that Morgan's pickets and patrols were pulling back toward the main American position. The Loyalist guides described Morgan's position as being on open ground, free of swamps, with the Broad River parallel to their rear. Tarleton estimated that he was facing about one thousand militia in the American's first line, five hundred Continentals in the second line, with one hundred twenty cavalry and three hundred "backwoodsmen" in reserve.[8]

Never one to shy from a fight, the British commander ordered his light infantry and Legion (Loyalist) infantry to drop their packs and deploy in an attack formation with the light infantry battalion on the right, the Legion infantry to the left, and one of his two cannon between the two units. Once deployed, the infantry were ordered to advance to within 300 yards of the American skirmish line under the covering fire from the cannon. Once the forward infantry reached their initial objective, the 7th Fusiliers moved forward to the left of the green-jacketed Legion infantry, and the second three-pound cannon was positioned between them. Dragoons galloped forward to provide right and left flank security for the infantry line. Tarleton kept his reserve force, the 1st Battalion 71st Infantry (Fraser's Highlanders), and 200 mounted Legionnaires 150 yards to the rear of the infantry line behind and echeloned to the left of the 7th Fusiliers.

Overconfident of success, Tarleton ordered his troops forward while some units were still marching toward their designated positions for the advance. Officers shouted orders and sergeants harangued their men as they marched through the rough foliage trying to keep in formation. The British were confident of a quick victory, and caution was not the watch-word of the day.

* * *

Pickets alerted Morgan that the British were on the march, and he had moved his men into their assigned positions in the frigid pre-dawn dark-ness. The day broke clear and cold. Morgan's skirmishers, expert riflemen from Georgia and North Carolina, lay in the frost-covered grass and crouched behind tree stumps scanning over their rifle sights at the misty fields and open woods to their front, while others slapped their hands together to stay warm.

At about 7:00 a.m., the marksmen spotted Tarleton's green-jacketed mounted dragoons, followed by crimson and white clad infantrymen emerging from a wood line about four hundred yards to their front. As the infantry steadily approached, the dragoons galloped forward to flush the skirmishers from their positions.

The riflemen drew beads on the horsemen, waiting for them to come within range. John Savage, a South Carolina militiaman, may have fired the first shot of the battle. A British officer rode ahead of his men toward the skirmishers, shouting at them in a loud voice to disperse. According to an eyewitness, "John Savage instantly raised his rifle and fired and the British officer fell from his horse mortally wounded."[9] Savage's fellow skir-mishers followed suit, emptying more than a dozen saddles before sprinting back toward Pickens' militia line. Tarleton then recalled his dragoons and ordered his artillery to open fire on the militia line. As the cannon roared, the British marched forward in near perfect alignment, trying to keep step with the rolling drums and shrill fifes.

When rebel sharpshooters opened with sporadic long-range fire, dropping several officers, the British responded with a cheer and broke into a run toward their enemy. The Americans responded in kind with an Indian yell, and raised their rifles to the firing position. When the British line was within 50 yards, Pickens' militia fired a deadly volley into the approaching mass. Stymied and unnerved by the volley, several Fusiliers took it on their own to return the fire. Reacting to the breach of discipline, the British officers used the flats of their swords to get the men moving again. The militia reloaded and fired two more volleys into the British line, halting its advance for a second time. A lieutenant who commanded a Light Infantry company, reported, "Two-thirds of the British infantry officers had already fallen, and nearly the same portion of privates."[10]

As Fusiliers and Highlanders toppled forward in the grass, sergeants shouted at their men to dress their ranks and charge forward with fixed bayonets. Having fired their assigned number of volleys, Pickens ordered his militia to begin withdrawing toward Colonel Howard's line of Continentals and Virginians, some 300 yards to their rear. When they saw the ranks of Continentals and Virginians standing calmly in formation awaiting the British, the American militiamen remained calm and began an orderly withdrawal. As the retreating militiamen approached their ranks, the Continentals opened gaps in their lines to afford them passage to the rear.

When Tarleton observed the militia moving toward the rear, he ordered Captain Ogilive, who was screening the right side of the British line with fifty dragoons, to charge the militiamen on that flank. Before some of Pickens' men could pass through Howard's line of Continentals, the dragoons were among them, hacking with their sabers. With their route of withdrawal cut off by the British horsemen, some militiamen ran toward the woods where their horses were hidden.

Observing the charge of Ogilive's dragoons, Morgan quickly decided to commit Colonel Washington's cavalry. James Collins was one of the militiamen who ran toward the hidden horses. He later wrote,

> Tarleton's cavalry pursued us; now I thought my hide was in the loft. Just as we got to our horses, they overtook us and began to make a few hacks at some . . . but in a few moments, Colonel Washington's cavalry was among them like a whirlwind . . . The

shock was so sudden and violent, they could not stand it, and immediately betook themselves to flight . . . and they appeared to be as hard to stop as a drove of wild Choctaw steers . . ."[11]

The Continentals held their fire until most of militia passed through their ranks. Meanwhile, the British infantry, having reformed their ranks, began to advance up the gentle slope toward Colonel Howard's Continentals and Virginians. As soon as the last of the militia cleared their front, the Continentals opened a galling fire on the advancing British, slowing but not halting their advance. Observing that Howard's Continentals were standing firm and not retreating, Tarleton decided to commit his infantry and cavalry reserve to break the stalemate. He ordered the commander of the 1st Battalion, 71st Highlanders to advance past the left flank of the Fusiliers, ensuring that his right did not "entangle" with the Fusiliers' left. Tarleton next ordered his Legion commander to assail the American right flank with his cavalry, reinforced with 50 dragoons from the flank guard.

The Highlanders double-timed the 300-yard distance from their reserve position to the front, while the British cavalrymen rode toward the American right at a fast canter. Once in position, the Highlanders overlapped the right of the American line, exposing it to flank attack. Colonel Howard, commanding the Continentals and Virginians, recognized the danger immediately, and took action to thwart the attack. He ordered his right flank company of the Virginia militia to face about and wheel to their left forming a right angle to the Continental line. This maneuver placed the Virginians in a better position to engage the oncoming Highlanders. The maneuver was a bit complicated for the Virginians to execute while under fire, and it was executed in a somewhat confused manner. Amid the smoke, noise, and confusion of battle, the Maryland and Delaware Continentals thought that a general retreat had been ordered. The Continental officers, therefore, had their men face about and start marching toward the rear in good order. Observing the scene, General Morgan rode forward to Howard's location and asked him if his men were beaten and abandoning their positions. Howard replied, "Do they look like they're beaten?" Morgan then rode to the rear to locate a position where the Continentals could halt, face about, and fire into the oncoming ranks of the British.

The British troops, believing that they had broken their opponents' line, neglected their formation and rushed forward in a disorderly pursuit of the Americans. Maintaining their formation, Howard's men crossed a swale and moved up a slight grade before Howard ordered them to halt and face about. He then ordered his Continentals to fire a deadly volley into the oncoming British at a distance of about 40 yards. Reeling from the disciplined, devastating fire, the leaderless British survivors began to fall back in panic. Howard's men charged after the retreating mob with fixed bayonets.

Washington's cavalry, after mopping up Ogilve's dragoons, had returned to their original reserve position behind the Continentals. Observing the fleeing British troops, Washington requested Morgan's permission to charge the onrushing British right flank to envelop the Highlanders and cut off their line of retreat, while Howard's Continentals mopped up the Fusiliers.

Galloping forward, Washington's cavalry quickly enveloped the British right, while Pickens' reformed militia swept around the British left cutting off any possibility of escape. It was a near perfect double envelopment.

In an attempt to forestall disaster, Tarleton sent orders for his cavalry "to form about 400 yards to the right of the enemy, in order to keep them in check while he endeavored to rally the infantry . . ."[12] Tarleton's cavalry refused to comply with their commander's order, despite the fact that they outnumbered Washington's men. Tarleton's efforts to organize his remaining infantry to protect the artillery failed as well. The British commander knew that the tide of battle had turned against him.

Morgan's Continentals and militia shouting "Tarleton's quarter" rushed into the panic-stricken British infantry, shooting and bayoneting their foes. Many of the British tossed their muskets aside and fell to the ground begging for their lives. Morgan and Howard galloped into the melee to prevent a full-scale massacre of their now helpless adversaries.

With the Fusiliers and Highlanders falling apart across the battlefield, Tarleton once again ordered his cavalry to charge the onrushing Americans. Only about forty of the two hundred dragoons were still on the field; the remainder had galloped toward the rear. Tarleton fearlessly led the forty horsemen in a charge to save the remnants of the Highlanders, who were forming for a last stand. Colonel Washington, scanning the field, spotted Tarleton's men charging across the battlefield, and led his own men in a counter-charge. In the violent clash of cavalry, Tarleton's horse went down, leaving the British commander afoot amidst a mass of saber-slashing and pistol-firing horsemen. Accepting the offer of a mount from one of his men, Tarleton swung into the saddle and decided to make good his escape with his surviving troopers. Intent on capturing the infamous British commander, Washington galloped after him in hot pursuit.

Washington's horse outdistanced most of his own troopers' mounts, and he was soon within striking distance of Tarleton and his aides. Suddenly, the British cavalry leader and his escorts wheeled their mounts about to face their pursuers. The fight then became personal. Washington and a few troopers matched against Tarleton and his small escort. One of Tarleton's officers—it may have been Thomas Darley, a former South Carolinian Patriot turned Loyalist—attempted to strike first at Washington. The officer rode forward and swung his saber at the colonel. Washington parried the blow with his sword, but his blade broke off at the hilt. The Loyalist then rose up in his stirrups to deliver a killing blow to Washington's head. However, an on-rushing horseman, possibly Washington's manservant, shot the Loyalist in the shoulder, disabling him. Another of Tarleton's aides then attempted to kill Washington with his saber, but another American horseman drove him off. Henry Wells, one of Washington's men, was struck across the left shoulder by one of Tarleton's officers. He recalled that the he was struck, "with such violence, the collar of my coat, my vest, and my shirt, were each cut." Fortunately, Wells' clothing absorbed most of the damage, and his flesh was only scratched and bruised.[13] Tarleton then rode into the fray to finish off Washington. He struck with his sword, but the American deflected the blow with the hilt of his damaged sword. When he saw the rest of Washington's men approaching, Tarleton wheeled his horse around and galloped after his fleeing dragoons.

The battle at the Cowpens lasted little more than an hour, ending in a humiliating British defeat with Tarleton barely escaping capture. British corpses, muskets, packs and other accoutrements were strewn across the battlefield. Casualty estimates for the battle vary; however, it is generally accepted that British losses were near 200 men killed, another 180 wounded, and some 600 men taken prisoner.[14] In addition, the Americans captured the two British three-pound cannon and 800 muskets, along with a stockpile of ammunition, a traveling forge, a number of horses, and thirty-five baggage wagons.

On the American side, Morgan reported the loss of twelve men killed and 61 wounded, making it a lopsided victory for the Americans.[15] One of the most seriously wounded Americans was John Whelchel, the South Carolina dragoon. Whelchel received several saber wounds from Tarleton's dragoons in the mounted fighting, including a "cut through the skull to the membrane of the brain." No one expected Whelchel to live, and he lay on the ground for several hours before receiving treatment. To the surprise of many of his comrades, though, Whelchel recovered and finished the war as a surgeon's assistant. Afterward he pursued a career as a doctor in South Carolina.[16]

After the battle, Morgan ordered his militia to march the British prisoners north to Virginia for imprisonment. Most of the prisoners including the wounded were stripped of their warm clothing and shoes by the Americans, making it a miserable shivering march to the far-off prison camp at Winchester.

The news of the American victory spread quickly, raising Patriot morale throughout the country. More importantly, the battle demonstrated the inability of the British and Loyalists to exert their control over the backcountry of the Carolinas and Georgia. When supported by a small army of Continentals, the militias were willing and able to defend their states against the British troops and their allies. The tide was beginning to turn against the British in the backcountry, but Cornwallis's army was far from beaten and remained a formidable force, superior in numbers to the Americans. General Nathaniel Greene knew that his only chance of defeating Cornwallis was to reunite his divided army and lure the British deeper into the inhospitable backcountry. To accomplish those aims, he would have to outmarch and outmaneuver the British. Greene also knew that he needed to march is army north toward Virginia, the source of his supplies and reinforcements.

6

THE RACE TO THE DAN

January 18–March 15
After an exhausting 150-mile ride over muddy backcountry roads,
Major Edward Giles rode into General Greene's camp on the Pee Dee
on the 23rd of January. The mud splattered major was one of General
Morgan's trusted aides de camp, and he came bearing thrilling news
of the spectacular American victory at the Cowpens. The camp went
wild with joy and celebration. Rum flowed freely, and muskets were
fired into the air in celebration. Tarleton's defeat sparked new life into
the dispirited American southern army, and set in motion a war of
maneuver that would spread across the breadth of three states.

Throughout the night of January 17–18, Cornwallis received several
unsettling reports that Tarleton had suffered a major defeat at the Cowpens.
The reports were confirmed the next morning when Tarleton himself rode
into Cornwallis' camp on Turkey Creek with the remnants of his Legion.
Cornwallis listened intently as his subordinate described in detail the battle,
emphasizing his own attempts to forestall the disaster that befell his
command, and the poor performance of his mounted arm. It was a galling
admission since Tarleton's cavalry had outnumbered Colonel Washington's
horsemen. Cornwallis could not conceal his anger, but chose not to
relieve his best cavalry leader. Rather, in his report to General Clinton,
Cornwallis praised Tarleton's personal bravery, particularly his futile efforts
to save his artillery, and his successful effort to recover his captured baggage
train.[1]

Having lost almost one quarter of his total army, Cornwallis had a decision to make. He could move against Greene's force near Cheraw, or he could move against Morgan to avenge Tarleton's defeat and destroy Morgan's wing of the southern army. After the arrival of Leslie's force from Charleston and the remnants of Tarleton's command, Cornwallis knew he had a three to one advantage over Greene; however, if Morgan was able to reunite with Greene, the American army would approximate the strength of Cornwallis's force. It wasn't a difficult decision for Cornwallis. He would pursue and destroy Morgan before he could reunite with Greene. He also desired to liberate the 600 British prisoners captured at the Cowpens. Having made his decision, the British commander had to make an educated guess as to Morgan's next move. The vulnerability of the British post at Ninety Six still worried Cornwallis. He thought that Morgan would choose to attack the base before moving to rejoin Greene, and he therefore marched off with his 2,500-man army in the direction of Ninety Six for two critical days.

Despite his brilliant victory at the Cowpens, Daniel Morgan was well aware of his perilous situation. He did not stand a chance in a straight-up fight with Cornwallis's reinforced army. He therefore marched his force northeast hoping to reunite with Greene at some undetermined location. His prudent decision bought him a two-day lead on Cornwallis, a gap that the British general was never able to close.

After finding no sign of Morgan's force on his march, Cornwallis realized his error and changed direction, heading north toward the North Carolina border. After five days of hard marching, the British reached Ramsour's Mill on the South Fork of the Catawba River on January 25th. Morgan's corps was still twenty miles ahead of him approaching the fords of the main Catawba River. Cornwallis realized that his only chance of snaring Morgan was to speed his own rate of march. He could only accomplish that by destroying all of his superfluous baggage and many of the wagons that were slowing his progress. The heavy rains had turned the backcountry roads into quagmires, and crossing the rain-swollen rivers and streams with wagonloads of baggage and supplies subtracted miles from each day's march. After ordering an extra ration of rum for his men, he ordered that a huge bonfire be built using wagons, tents, extra clothing, and beds. Officers' personal baggage, dishes, and silver were also discarded, and casts of wine and rum were emptied on the ground. Cornwallis's implicit message to his troops was clear; there would be no more rest, or rum, until the rebel army was destroyed.[2]

Morgan crossed the Catawba River at Sherrill's ford on January 23rd, the same day that General Greene learned of his victory at the Cowpens and his intent to march north into North Carolina. After crossing the Catawba, Morgan halted to await further orders from Greene. Both men knew that the two American wings had to reunite to stand any chance of success against Cornwallis's reinforced army. When Greene learned that Morgan had halted on the Catawba waiting for instructions, he ordered General Issac Huger to march the main American army north from its camp near Cheraw, South Carolina toward Salisbury, North Carolina. Salisbury was thirty-five miles east of Morgan's camp on the Catawba. It took Huger two days to break camp and organize for the march northward. Meanwhile, General Greene set off with a small escort to find Morgan. Greene was alarmed by a message he had received in which the forty-five-year-old Virginian wrote that his back ailments and rheumatism were growing worse by the day, casting doubt on his ability to continue as a field commander. Greene and his escort rode more than a hundred miles through the rain-soaked Loyalist-contested countryside before linking up with Morgan on the 30th of January.

The following day the two commanders discussed where they would reunite the two wings of the army, and once joined, where they would march. Greene wanted to lure Cornwallis into a pursuit northward toward Virginia. Morgan was skeptical and proposed an alternate plan to march the army toward the mountains of western North Carolina. Greene rejected that plan, opting for Virginia, where he would be closer to supply centers in that state. He was also concerned that the North Carolina militia had not turned out in large numbers to resist the British invasion, and thought that he could rely on Virginia to provide him more troops. Having overruled his subordinate, Greene ordered Morgan to begin marching north that same day toward Island Ford on the Yadkin River, some forty miles away. Once across the Yadkin, Morgan was to link up with the column under the command of General Huger.

As the two American commanders argued over strategy, Cornwallis was preparing to cross the rain-swollen Catawba, no easy task for the

British in the dead of winter. Morgan had left militia units behind to guard the fords and oppose any crossing, and the swift current in the river was hazardous for both men and horses.

General William Davidson of the North Carolina militia was in command of 300 militia assigned to guard the fords and oppose any crossing by the British. But it was too small a force to cover all the fords in sufficient strength. Led by Tory guides, Cornwallis' army feigned a crossing at Beattie's Ford before moving downstream to Cowan's Ford during the early morning hours of February 1st. In the pre-dawn darkness, the British advance guard slipped quietly into the freezing four-feet-deep water. Holding their muskets over their heads, they struggled to reach the distant shoreline some 500 yards away. Peering into the windy darkness, Davidson's pickets were awakened just as the redcoats splashed through the water near the shore. The pickets opened fire on the dark silhouettes struggling across the slippery river bottom. Few if any of the British were hit in the darkness, and they were soon climbing the riverbank headed toward the picket posts. General Davidson heard the firing, and raced to the ford with reinforcements, but the British had already driven off the pickets and established a bridgehead. In the ensuing skirmish Davidson was shot from his horse and killed, along with several other Americans. However, by the time Cornwallis reassembled his army on the far side of the Catawba, Morgan's men were already less than ten miles from Island Ford on the Yadkin River.[3]

Hoping that the heavy rain would delay Morgan's crossing of the Yadkin, Cornwallis pushed on with his slimmed down force. He knew that it was his last chance to destroy Morgan before he crossed the Yadkin and reunited with the other wing of the American army. By mounting some of his infantry on horses that were no longer pulling wagons, Cornwallis's column was able to make good time as it marched down the muddy backcountry roads leading to Island Ford. Fortunately, General Greene had the foresight and experience, as former Quartermaster of the Army, to order boats sent to the ford to transport Morgan's men across the rain-swollen river. It was a close-run affair. As Morgan's rear guard boarded the boats and shoved off, the British advance guard galloped forward trading shots with the Americans. Cornwallis had no boats, and Greene insured that there were none available for the British to commandeer on his side of the turbulent river. As the river was fast approaching flood stage, it was impassible without boats. Cornwallis ordered his artillery to fire on the Americans camp across the river, but the fire was ineffective. The Americans had won the first leg of the race.

After waiting five days for the floodwaters to subside, Cornwallis marched his men nearly forty miles upstream and crossed the Yadkin at Shallow Ford on the 9th of February. Despite the miserable condition of his army after 200 miles of hard marching from his winter camp at Winnsboro to the Yadkin, Cornwallis would allow his men no rest. He was determined to catch up with Greene's army and destroy it, regardless of the hardships and privations suffered by his troops. Shivering in their wet clothing and trying to ignore their gnawing hunger pains, the bone-weary British troops formed in marching column and moved out.

On that same day, Morgan's corps rendezvoused with General Huger's command at Guilford Courthouse about thirty miles south of the Virginia border. After seven weeks of hard winter campaigning, General Greene's army was once again united, but the Americans were still under threat from Cornwallis' fast approaching army. Uncharacteristically, Greene called for a council of war with his major subordinate commanders, Generals Morgan and Huger, and Colonel Otho Williams, who commanded the Maryland Continentals.

Greene told his subordinates that there were only two courses of action that the army could follow. It could turn and fight, or it could continue to withdraw north into Virginia and cross the Dan River where it would be close to the American supply depots. Having reviewed the strength reports of the reunited army, Greene knew that he had only about fifteen hundred Continentals and some six hundred poorly armed and equipped militiamen compared to Cornwallis' army of between twenty-five hundred and three thousand troops.[4] Without reinforcements, Greene knew that a decisive battle would probably lead to defeat and destruction of the southern American army. Greene and his commanders decided by consensus not to accept battle at that juncture. Withdrawing to Virginia was the only alternative, and Greene and his subordinates knew the consequences of such a move. By moving into Virginia, the Americans were abandoning war-torn North Carolina and ceding the state to the British and their Loyalist allies. Moreover, it would undoubtedly lead some in Congress to question

Greene's willingness to fight, and Washington's decision to appoint him as commander of the southern army. Greene therefore ensured that he had the support of his subordinates on record. Morgan, Huger, and Williams all agreed with Greene's assessment that a general engagement ought to be avoided at all costs. Greene forwarded a copy of the proceedings of his council of war in a letter to Washington that same day.[5]

At Guilford Courthouse, Greene was startled when he saw General Morgan's emaciated condition. It was clear that the "old Wagoner" was simply worn out from the hard winter campaigning. Morgan was almost crippled with rheumatism and he grew worse by the day. Consequently, Greene approved his request to be relieved from active service to recuperate at his home in northern Virginia. Greene had lost his best tactician, and ablest commander.

The following day "the race for the Dan" began. The American army departed Guilford Courthouse marching north toward Virginia's Dan River. Greene's troops moved in two columns. Colonel Otho Williams, leading 700 light troops, was directed to move to the east of the main force in the direction of the upper fords of the Dan. Greene further instructed Williams to keep his highly mobile force between Cornwallis, who was less than twenty miles behind, and the main column. Cornwallis was moving on an axis roughly parallel and slightly to the west of the Americans. While Williams lured the British into thinking that the Americans planned to cross the Dan using the upper fords, Greene would turn his column in the direction of the lower fords. Once again Greene had arranged for boats to be waiting at the Dan River to ferry his men across.

The success of the American plan rested on the fitness and stamina of Greene's men, and they were exhausted even before they started. The men were awakened each day at 3:00 am and marched for four miles before halting to cook their breakfast that was then eaten on the march. There were no rest breaks, and the march continued until darkness fell. The intent was to give each man six hours sleep, but that did not take into account the time each soldier spent on picket and guard duty. The Americans moved swiftly, but Cornwallis pushed his men even harder, once again using his surplus horses to best advantage. Five days into the race for the Dan, Cornwallis was within about four miles of overtaking Colonel Williams' column, and less than twenty miles behind Greene. Cornwallis realized that, while he could not overtake Greene before he reached the Dan, he had a good chance of bagging Colonel Williams' force at the Dan's upper fords. His spies reported that there were too few boats upstream to ferry Williams's troops across the river.

On February 13th, Colonel Williams wisely changed his direction of march and moved toward the lower fords where Greene was already preparing to cross. The following day, Williams received a message from Greene that his men were safely across, and to come on. Energized by the good news, Williams' men made a fourteen-mile speed march arriving at the crossing point two hours after sunset. Under the cover of darkness, Williams' men were ferried across the river. Cornwallis was close on his heels, marching his men through the night, but the British troops did not arrive at the crossing site until dawn. The last boat carrying a detachment of American dragoons had just reached safety on the far shore. The Americans had won the race for the Dan.

Cornwallis realized that he could push his men no farther due to their exhausted condition, and there were no boats readily available to pursue Greene deeper into Virginia. He also knew that Greene was likely to be reinforced by Virginia militia and Continentals recently recruited by General von Steuben. Cornwallis therefore opted to return to North Carolina, declaring that he had driven the Continental army from the Carolinas and had reestablished Crown rule in the provinces. He then marched his army sixty miles to Hillsborough, North Carolina, where he formally declared victory with an official proclamation.

General Greene was not, however, prepared to concede defeat and the loss of the Carolinas. On the contrary, after resting his army and receiving badly needed supplies and reinforcements, he recrossed the Dan on February 23rd, and marched back toward North Carolina. He had previously sent Colonel Henry "Light Horse Harry" Lee and his cavalry ahead to harass the British as they marched to Hillsborough. He also ordered Colonel Williams' light infantry to recross the Dan ahead of the main American force and march back boldly back into the Tar Heel state.

By February 28th, Greene had established his headquarters at High Rock Ford on the Haw River in North Carolina. In addition to a shortage of supplies, he was concerned about the low numbers of patriot militiamen that were taking up the fight, and Cornwallis's apparent success in recruiting loyalists and some former rebels for service to the Crown. In his February 28th letter to Washington, he presented "unequivocal and full evidence of the disaffection of a great part of this state."[6] He went on to report that the British had raised seven independent companies in a single day. Something had to be done to discourage the citizens of the state from casting their lot with the British.

When Greene learned that a force of some four hundred Loyalist militiamen had mustered and were marching to Hillsborough to receive British arms and equipment, he dispatched Lieutenant Colonel Lee's cavalry to intercept them. The Loyalists initially mistook Lee's green-jacketed horsemen for Tarleton's men who were protecting the militia column, but they soon found out otherwise. To their surprise, Lee's men charged into their midst, killing ninety and wounding most of the rest. Tarleton and his men fled the scene, leaving the Tories to the mercy of the Americans. The fact that Lee did not lose a man in the bloody clash supported the British claim that most of the loyalist militiamen were unarmed. Though Greene was loath to admit it, the battle was reminiscent of Tarleton's treatment of the Americans at the Waxhaws. Nonetheless, he remained determined to stop the British from recruiting more Loyalist militia using any means possible.

Hoping to lure Greene into decisive battle, Cornwallis led his army out of Hillsborough on the 26th of February, and marched by way of Guilford Courthouse to Tralinger's Ford on the Haw River. He then crossed the Haw placing his army within twenty miles of Greene's headquarters at High Rock Ford. Cornwallis believed that even if Greene refused battle, the British show of strength would reenergize the recruitment of Loyalists. The recruitment of Loyalists for service in the militia became increasingly difficult after what the British called Harry Lee's "Pyles' Massacre." On the American side, the ranks of the Patriot militia began to swell after the incident. The state called up more militia, and the "Over Mountain Men" crossed the Blue Ridge in ever-increasing numbers to join Greene. Adding to these, a regiment of Virginia Continentals arrived, increasing the strength of Greene's army to more than 4,000 fighting men.[7] By mid-March, Greene's army outnumbered the British and their Loyalist allies. Greene no longer had to avoid a major battle with the British.

PORTSMOUTH, VIRGINIA

While Cornwallis pursued the Americans through the Piedmont of North Carolina and southern Virginia, Benedict Arnold continued to occupy Portsmouth, but he made little progress in improving the fortifications. He was preoccupied with searching the surrounding countryside for more plunder, and arguing with his naval counterpart about how to divide the prize money from the captured goods and vessels. It wasn't until early March that Arnold turned his attention to following General Clinton's explicit orders to build an impregnable base at Portsmouth. He was spurred to action when he learned that a French fleet was headed for Virginia, and General Lafayette was preparing to sail down the Chesapeake with a brigade of Continentals to lay siege to the base. British soldiers worked day and night to reinforce the breastworks so that the forts could withstand the cannons of the French fleet. Arnold spent hours in the saddle personally supervising and inspecting the forts around the port.

General Washington had gone to great lengths to convince the French to commit their fleet to Virginia. The Commander-in-Chief made an arduous 200-mile winter journey from his New Windsor headquarters to Newport, Rhode Island to convince French General Rochambeau and Admiral Detouches to commit the French fleet to dislodge the British from Portsmouth. General Washington remained at Newport until the fleet set sail on the 8th of March.

Meanwhile, Lafayette was still at Head of Elk, Maryland trying to assemble a fleet of vessels to ferry his brigade down the Chesapeake. The only craft available were unarmed "Bay craft" and his flagship mounting twelve guns.[8] Once Lafayette set sail with his transports and armed vessel, the expedition only made it as far as Annapolis. A number of small British frigates and privateers that were prowling the Chesapeake scattered the transports. Determined to reach his destination, Lafayette mounted a barge with a few dozen troops and arrived at Yorktown on March 14th, where he took command of all Continental and militia forces in Virginia, replacing General von Steuben.[9] The fifty-one-year-old Prussian had to swallow his pride when he relinquished his command to the twenty-four-year-old Frenchman, but he had no choice since Lafayette outranked him.

General von Steuben informed Lafayette that he would soon have five thousand Virginia militia assembled to lay siege to the British base. Lafayette was confident that with his Continentals, the militia, and the guns of Detouches' fleet, he could conduct a successful siege. However, there was still no sign of the French fleet.[10]

THE CONTINENTAL CONGRESS, PHILADELPHIA

While Greene and Cornwallis played fox and hound in the Carolinas and Lafayette prepared to dislodge the British from Virginia, Congress struggled to deal with the faltering war effort on the home front and abroad. The failure of the states to support their troops in the field resulted in the weakening and inactivity of the army in the north. Nationalists in Congress pushed for "emergency" war powers for the central government to enforce revenue-raising measures, but they lacked a majority to pass such legislation. With bankruptcy looming on the horizon, Congress again turned to France for more loans and military support, but the French government was wavering on giving more support to the Americans.

Congress appointed a young South Carolinian, Colonel John Laurens, as special envoy to appeal for more French loans and military support. Laurens was one of Washington's most trusted aides, and the Commander-in-Chief stressed to him the urgency of acquiring powerful French naval support. Washington was still focused on driving the British from New York, and this could only be accomplished by achieving naval superiority off the northeast coast. He knew that Rochambeau would not commit his troops to a joint Franco-American offensive without the support of a powerful French fleet. After receiving Washington's guidance, Laurens set sail for France in January.

While pressure on the French government to provide more support continued on both sides of the Atlantic, Congress increased the pressure on Maryland to ratify the Articles of Confederation. Maryland was the last remaining holdout among the thirteen states, arguing that Virginia would first have to relinquish its disputed western land claims. Under intense pressure from the other states and the French minister, the dispute between Maryland and Virginia was finally settled. After five years of debate and haggling, Congress approved the Articles of Confederation on March 1st, 1781; however, ratification by the states was still required. The Articles provided a constitutional foundation for the United States of America, but it did little to strengthen the central government. The new country remained a confederation of states in which sovereignty resided in the states rather than in their union. The confederation did, however, provide for the establishment of cabinet system that included Secretaries of War, Finance, and Foreign Affairs. While these positions held only limited powers, they provided for a more coherent and coordinated management of the war effort.

The new Secretary of Finance, Robert Morris, was quick to point out to Congress and the Commander-in-Chief that the treasury of the fledgling republic remained empty because the states continued to refuse to approve new taxes.[11] An amendment allowing Congress to impose a five percent duty on imports into the country would not be added to the Articles until after ratification by the states some months later. In the near term, financial support for the war effort would have to come from France, where Benjamin Franklin and others were attempting to arrange for yet another French loan.

THE FRENCH FOREIGN MINISTRY—VERSAILLES, FRANCE
January–March 1781

Efforts to secure additional French assistance for the American war effort made little progress during January and February of 1781. Despite the best efforts of American diplomats Benjamin Franklin and John Adams, the requests from Generals Washington and Rochambeau for more assistance to support a campaign in 1781 went unanswered during the early winter months. During the first three years of the alliance, France had little to show for its outlays of funds, arms, and manpower. The 1780 campaigns had cost the French one hundred and fifty million livres, and Washington and Rochambeau's plans for 1781 would likely cost much more. Rochambeau had sent his son back to France to present the generals' requests formulated at the Hartford Conference of 1780, but the French response was long delayed. Vergennes, the French foreign minister, initially gave a cool response to the requests, but he was not ready to abandon the cause completely. Although he had proposed a summit of European nations to discuss a settlement of the war, he wanted to negotiate from a position of strength rather than weakness.

On the 9th of March, the French government finally responded to the specific proposals formulated by Generals Washington and Rochambeau at the Hartford Conference. The request for ten thousand additional French troops was refused. Moreover, Rochambeau's request for naval transports to move the two thousand troops he left behind in France to North America was also denied. Taking a different course, the French did agree to provide Washington with money so that he could strengthen his own command by raising additional American volunteers. Accordingly, six million livres were to be placed at Washington's disposal as a gift rather than a loan. As a bonus, Vergennes revealed that Admiral Comte de Grasse's powerful fleet had been sent orders to sail to the coast of North America later in the year to cooperate with the French and American commands in an unspecified joint campaign against the British.

As Rochambeau's son departed for America with the French promises of further assistance, John Laurens arrived on French soil to present the case for additional financial aid. Many in Congress had lost confidence in Benjamin Franklin's ability to secure more aid, and he barely survived an attempt to recall him. Laurens was given instructions by the Congress to deliver a request to the French for a loan of twenty-five million livres. When Laurens delivered the American request for yet another loan, Vergennes was obliged to decline. The French treasury was nearing the breaking point. However, neither the young John Laurens nor the aged American ambassador, Franklin, were prepared to walk away empty handed. The pair began a two-month lobbying campaign to secure whatever they could from the French government. In large measure, the American campaign during the summer of 1781 depended on their efforts.

7

WE FIGHT, GET BEAT,
AND FIGHT AGAIN

"The country to a wide extent around, waste and rolling, was covered with lofty trees and thick shrubby underwood. Narrow tangled glades wound between the hills and desolated spots of forsaken cultivation, and presenting, far as the eye could trace them, somewhat livelier vegetation, dripped their scant rills into a larger stream and a darker valley, that crossed the great Salisbury road, about two miles from the courthouse. The melancholy horror, the wild sterility, and the lonely aspect of the scene, seemed ready to overawe the rage, and to welcome the fears of men."

—Henry Lee
The Campaign of 1781 in the Carolinas

March 14–April 10

For the first time since he assumed command of the southern army, General Greene prepared to face his adversary with a numerically superior force. Reinforced by Continentals from Virginia and militia units from North Carolina, Greene's southern army numbered approximately 4,400 men.[1] Of that total, forty percent were battle-hardened Continentals and Virginia militia. The remaining sixty percent were North Carolina militiamen, who had never faced British regulars in close combat. Although Greene knew he had at least a two to one advantage over Cornwallis, he also knew that the outcome of any future battle was heavily dependent on the performance his two brigades of untested North Carolinans. The Rhode Islander also knew that the terrain on which he chose to give battle was of prime importance. He found the ground he was looking for in the rugged countryside surrounding Guilford Courthouse.

The Guilford Courthouse building was the centerpiece of an isolated backwoods farming community of about one hundred residents. The small village surrounding the courthouse sat on high ground astride a rough wagon road that ran southwest toward Salisbury. A few acres surrounding the village were cleared of trees, but the low ground to the southwest was mainly heavily wooded with thick underbrush. An approaching enemy following the narrow wagon road would pass through a wooded valley, however the ground at the far end of the valley was clear with cornfields stretching about two hundred yards on both sides of the road.

Greene correctly assumed that the British would approach Guilford Courthouse from the southwest following the Great Salisbury wagon road. After reconnoitering the approaches to the Courthouse, Greene concluded that Cornwallis's column would move into linear battle formations after it reached the cleared cornfields at the far end of the valley. After advancing across the fields, the British would have to continue another half a mile through a wooded valley and climb the slopes to the high ground where the village was situated. Executing this maneuver in the rugged terrain, all the while under American fire, would be a daunting challenge even for Cornwallis's well-trained army.

Greene studied Morgan's tactics at the battle of Cowpens, and modified Morgan's tactical plan to fit the ground at Guilford. Like the Virginian, Greene opted for a defense in depth employing three lines of defense with the militia defending the first two lines and Continentals forming the main defensive line behind the militia. He also used his horsemen supported by militia riflemen to protect his flanks, just as Morgan had done. However, unlike Morgan's deployments at the Cowpens, Greene made no provisions for a reserve force that could counterattack a British breakthrough of his main line of Continentals. There were other differences as well.

The ground that Greene chose for his defense differed significantly from Cowpens. The area between his first two lines and the third line was heavily wooded and much wider than the open ground at Cowpens. Moreover, the distance between the three lines was much greater. The distance from the forward most American positions to the main defensive position held by the Continentals was nearly a mile. Although the woods made it difficult for the British to maintain their formations, and mount effective bayonet charges, the woods and undergrowth afforded no easy withdrawal routes for the militia.

*   *   *

Shortly after dawn on March 14th, Greene marched his troops from their camp at Speedwell Iron Works, on Troublesome Creek, to Guilford Court-house, a distance of about twelve miles. Cornwallis's troops were encamped at a Quaker meeting house about ten miles to the southwest. By the after-noon of the 14th, Greene's troops had arrived at Guilford Courthouse, and began moving toward their assigned defensive positions.[2]

Two brigades of North Carolina militia, under Generals John Butler and Thomas Eaton marched southwest down the Salisbury road to where the woods on each side of the road gave way to the open cornfields. Eaton moved his brigade into position on the east side of the road, while Butler positioned his men in the field to the west. Two six-pound cannon were positioned between the two brigades sighting down the road. Colonel Washington's cavalry, Captain Robert Kirkwood's Delaware infantry com-pany, and Colonel Lynch's Virginia riflemen were positioned to support the North Carolina militia's right flank, while Lieutenant Colonel Henry Lee's Legion supported by Colonel Campbell's Virginia riflemen and a detachment of mounted militia covered the left flank.

About three hundred and fifty yards to the rear of the first line, two brigades of Virginia militia under Brigadier Generals Edward Stevens and Robert Lawson marched into the dense woods on either side of the road. Almost seven hundred yards to the rear of the Virginians, General Huger's Virginia Brigade of Continentals, and Colonel Otho Williams's Maryland Continentals formed on the open forward slope of a gently rising hill below the courthouse. The Virginians occupied the right side of the line and the Marylander's the left. Two-six-pound cannon were positioned on the road slightly to the front of the two Continental brigades. The Continental infantry and the artillery had excellent fields of fire to their front.

Greene had little doubt that the British would attack the following day, and in the hours before the battle he rode from regiment to regiment checking their positions and giving words of encouragement to the men. The Rhode Islander lacked Morgan's charisma and rapport with the

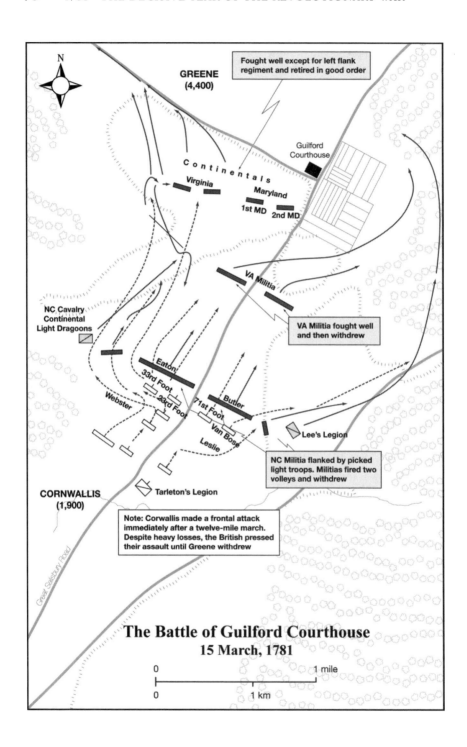

GREENE
(4,400)

Fought well except for left flank
regiment and retired in good order

Guilford
Courthouse

C o n t i n e n t a l s

Virginia

Maryland

1st MD   2nd MD

VA Militia

NC Cavalry
Continental
Light Dragoons

VA Militia fought well
and then withdrew

Eaton
33rd Foot
23rd Foot
71st Foot   Butler
Webster   Van Bose
Leslie   Lee's Legion

NC Militia flanked by picked
light troops. Militias fired two
volleys and withdrew

CORNWALLIS
(1,900)

Tarleton's Legion

Note: Corwallis made a frontal attack
immediately after a twelve-mile march.
Despite heavy losses, the British pressed
their assault until Greene withdrew

Great Salisbury Road

The Battle of Guilford Courthouse
15 March, 1781

0   1 mile

0   1 km

militiamen, but his calm presence and optimism allayed the fears of many of his men.

Nightfall brought on a chilly rain, and the men gathered around smoldering campfires trying to stay warm as they ate their evening meal. After wrapping themselves in their threadbare blankets, the soldiers tried to catch a few hours sleep between their shifts on guard duty. By dawn the rain had stopped and the day broke clear and cold. A light frost quickly disappeared under the first rays of sunlight, but the ground remained damp and spongy.

By the time the Americans rolled out of their soggy blankets and stretched their limbs, the British had already marched several miles through the chilly pre-dawn darkness toward Guilford Courthouse. With food in short supply, Cornwallis had not issued his men a breakfast ration. Shortly after seven o'clock, an advance guard of Lieutenant Colonel Tarleton's dragoons met head on with Henry Lee's horsemen who had ridden forward to give early warning of a British approach. A few men on each side were wounded in the clash, and after a failed attempt to interpose his cavalry between Tarleton's dragoons and the main British column, Lee ordered his men to withdraw back toward the American lines.[3]

The North Carolina and Virginia militia assigned to the first and second lines heard the firing as the cavalry skirmished to their front, and the militia officers ordered their men to fall into ranks and march to their assigned positions. After loading their weapons, the North Carolinians in the first battle line stood behind a zigzag split rail fence with the edge of the woods to their backs. On the second battle line, Virginians were ordered to firing positions behind trees that covered the valley landscape. Standing nervously at the ready, the militiamen on the first line could hear the picket fire to their front as the British neared their position. As the American and British cannon roared, the militiamen rested their rifle barrels on the split rail fence to steady their aims. About 1:30 P.M., the North Carolina militiamen saw British and Hessian soldiers entering the valley to their front and deploying into line of battle.

*   *   *

Major General Alexander Leslie commanded the British right wing that included the German Regiment von Bose, the British 71st Regiment (Frazer's Highlanders), and the 1st Guards Battalion. Leslie's troops coolly marched through the woods toward the clearing on the right side of the Salisbury wagon road amid the beating of drums and the shrill blaring of fifes. The North Carolina militiamen on Greene's first line watched in awe as Leslie's troops emerged from the tree line on the opposite end of the fields in well-dressed battle formations, and began to march straight toward them.

As Leslie's troops filed to the right, Lieutenant Colonel James Webster's left wing began taking up positions to the left of the road. The 33d and 23d Regiments formed to the front while the Brigadier General O'Hara's elite Grenadier Guards and 2d Battalion Guards formed to their rear. Cornwallis kept his reserve, the Jaegers and the light infantry of the Guards, concealed in the tree line to the left of the road behind Webster's left wing. Tarleton's horsemen, also in reserve, remained on the road behind the attacking formations. Cornwallis ensured that Tarleton understood he was not to enter the battle until he was ordered to do so.

As the British and American artillerymen exchanged shots, the British regiments dressed their ranks and began marching forward with their colors unfurled, their drums rolling, and bayonets glistening in the early afternoon sunlight. The Highlanders, Hessians and Guards formations marched down a soggy slope, crossed a creek, and continued up a slope toward the Americans. Mid-field fences slowed the advance, but the ranks were quickly reformed after the men crossed each one. William Campbell's Virginia riflemen on the far left flank opened with well-aimed rifle fire on the Hessians and British as soon as they came into view. North Carolina riflemen in Butler's brigade also joined in the fire when the British line was about 100 yards from their position. The Virginian and North Carolina riflemen chose their targets carefully, aiming at the men with silver gorgets at their throats, the distinctive badges worn by British officers. Both the Highlanders and the Hessians suffered casualties from the rifle fire. Ensign Dugald Stewart of the Highlanders wrote, "One-half of our Highlanders fell on that spot." Sergeant Koch of the Bose Regiment reported that, "About a 100 yards from the enemy line, they delivered a general fire and 180 men of our von Bose Regiment immediately fell."[4] The attrition of Cornwallis's army had begun.

The British and Hessian formations faltered momentarily before dressing their lines and returning fire. Then, they stepped over their dead and wounded and continued their attack. Nineteen-year-old Nathan Slade of Caswell County testified that the enemy approached, ". . . within eighty to a hundred yards of us when they made their first fire." The first volley of British musket fire undoubtedly resulted in some casualties, but most of Butler's militiamen, "stood firm until after the second fire."[5] After the second British volley, Butler's North Carolinians broke and fled in disorder. Slade and a few of his comrades endured a third volley before withdrawing. Henry Lee, whose cavalry was guarding the American left flank, observed what was happening and rode to intercept and rally the fleeing militiamen, but to no avail. As Butler and his men fled in disorder, the wounded militiamen were left to the mercy of the British and Hessians. Some were bayoneted where they had fallen while others were taken prisoner. Benedict Watkins, who suffered a head wound, and seven of his comrades were among the more fortunate. Watkins group was taken prisoner by the British, but managed to escape the night after the battle.[6]

While the fighting raged south of the road, a similar scene was playing out north of it. Lieutenant Colonel Webster ordered his lead regiments forward a few minutes after Leslie's men stepped off. Captain Thomas Saumarez commanding the left wing of the Fusilier Regiment wrote in his memoirs that, ". . . they advanced upon a ploughed field, which was very muddy from the rain that fell the day before."[7]

Eaton's North Carolina brigade held their fire until the British were within effective range before delivering their first volley of musket and rifle fire. Saumarez described the American volley as "a most galling and destructive fire . . ."[8] The British line recoiled for several seconds before closing ranks and firing their own volley. The Fusiliers then charged the American line hoping to break it before the militiamen could reload, but it was too late. Eaton's men let loose with a second volley at the charging troops, momentarily halting their charge. When the British regulars quickly regrouped and resumed their advance, almost all of Eaton's line broke and fled into the dense woods to the rear.[9] Some stopped at the second line, but many fled the battlefield. Among those who fled was seventeen-year-old John Warren serving in William Linton's militia regiment that was assigned to Eaton's command. Warren recalled, "Colonel Linton and his men broke and left the field in disorder." Warren fled to his home in Halifax County where he later rejoined his militia unit.[10] Westwood Armistead, a twenty-year-old militiaman from Northhampton County, testified that "his whole company fled., but again Rendezvoused at Troublesome Iron Works . . ."[11] As most of the American first line crumbled before the British onslaught, Captain Anthony Singleton quickly ordered the withdrawal of his two six pound cannon to support the American third line.

Benjamin Williams's Warren County militia on the northern flank of Eaton's brigade held their position longer than Eaton's other regiments, holding up the advance of the British 33rd Regiment. The 33rd was also receiving enfilading fire from Virginia and Delaware Continentals guarding the American right flank. Surveying the action, the British left wing commander, Lt. Colonel Webster, ordered his Jaegers forward to assist the 33rd in dealing with the Continental flank guard. As the Jaegers advanced, the remainder of Eaton's men broke and fled for their lives.

While the Jaegers dislodged the American right flank guard, the Regiment von Bose and the 1st Battalion Guards, having broken the left of the militia line, turned to confront Lee's Legion, Campbell's Virginians, and a company of Virginia Continentals that guarded the American left flank. The ensuing fight evolved into what has been called "The Battle Within a Battle," since it was fought in a hilly wooded area to the southeast of the main British attack on the second and third American defensive lines.[12]

When the 1st Guards Battalion turned to attack the American left, Lee and Campbell withdrew slowly along a road running southeast. As the Guards pursued Lee, they left their own left flank exposed to Stuart's Virginia riflemen. The Virginians unleashed a heavy fire on the Guards, driving them back to a wooded hill where they made a stand and repulsed the Virginians. No sooner had the Guards fended off the Virginians than a second line of Americans appeared on the right of the Guards' position. After being hit from the front and flank, the Guards, some of the best troops in the British army, were on the verge of collapse with all of their officers either killed or wounded. Only the timely arrival of the Hessians saved the Guards battalion from complete annihilation.

The Virginians at first thought that the blue coated Hessians were American Continentals, but when the Hessians opened fire they realized their mistake. The Hessians, assisted by the survivors of the Guards battalion, launched an attack against the Virginians, driving them into the thick woods. In the confused fighting that followed, the British and Hessians eventually found themselves under attack from several directions as Campbell's riflemen, Lee's Legion infantry, and Wallace's Virginia Continentals arrived on the scene. British and Hessian accounts agree that they were hit from all sides. The fighting went on for more than thirty minutes with heavy casualties on both sides. When Cornwallis heard the heavy firing on his right flank, he ordered Tarleton and part of his cavalry to ride to determine the situation on that flank. The horsemen arrived in the nick of time to reinforce the beleaguered Guards and Hessians. Many of the Virginia riflemen and Continentals were cut down by the British cavalry, and Tarleton was able to rescue a number of British and Hessian prisoners. The Virginians gave way to the British cavalry, withdrawing deep into the dense woods after delivering some parting shots at Tarleton's legionnaires. Lt. Colonel Tarleton may have been one of the last casualties. At least one participant in the fighting reported that the Green Dragoon "had the misfortune to lose two fingers on his right hand by a shot from a rifleman" in the flank fighting.[13] The British suffered numerous casualties in the fighting on the right flank, which contributed nothing to the main British attack.

General Nathaniel Greene was not in a position where he could personally observe the performance of the North Carolina militia on the first line, but instead relied on reports from Lieutenant Colonel Lee who was in a position to observe the action near the American left flank. Lee's reports were disparaging of the performance of the North Carolina militia, and the low numbers of men killed and wounded supported his reports. A large number of North Carolina militiamen were also reported as missing after the battle, further attesting to their poor performance on the American first line. Although many of the North Carolinians admitted that their companies did flee in panic as the British closed on their positions, British and Hessian soldiers recalled that their units suffered a significant number of casualties before they broke the American first line.[14] Undoubtedly, some militia units on the first line fought poorly, but others stood their ground and fought well.

* * *

After breaking the Americans' first line, the British wasted no time in advancing into the woods toward their second line, defended by the Virginia militia. First the British had to traverse 400 yards of rough wooded country. It was impossible for the various British units to maintain their well-ordered formations and maintain contact with the units on their flanks while moving through the woods and underbrush. Formations quickly broke apart, reducing the Redcoats' ability to deliver volley fire and mount bayonet charges. Although they were not able to observe the fighting on the first line, the Virginians were well aware of the results. They heard the heavy exchange of musket and rifle fire, and the screams of the wounded echoed through the hills and ravines. Moments later, panic-stricken North Carolina militiamen came crashing through the underbrush toward their positions with the British hot on their heels. Many of the militiamen had discarded their weapons and equipment as they fled the first line. Few halted to assist the Virginians in defending the second line.

Two brigades of Virginians were deployed on the second line; one north of the Salisbury Road and the other to the south. Brigadier General Edward Stevens's brigade, composed of four regiments, mostly from the lower Shenandoah Valley, was deployed south of the road, while Brigadier General Robert Lawson's brigade of three militia regiments from central and eastern Virginia held positions to the north. Continental infantry companies from Delaware and Virginia, reinforced by Continental and North Carolina cavalry, anchored the northern flank of the second American defensive line.

The British attacked the second line in much the same order of battle as the first, with the exception of the Regiment von Bose and 1st Guards Battalion. The aforementioned units continued their own battle with the Americans well off the British right flank. As the British approached the American second line, the Jaegers and Guards light infantry moved up to protect the left flank of Eaton's brigade, and the Grenadier Guards and 2d Battalion Guards pushed forward along the Salisbury road between Eaton's brigade and Butler's brigade.

North of the road, American Brigadier Charles Lawson ordered his two northernmost regiments forward to engage the British, hoping to overlap the Fusiliers' left flank. Lawson was an experienced former Continental officer, who thought he saw an opportunity to flank the British line, but he was unaware that the British 33rd Regiment was moving forward on the Fusiliers' left flank, but at a slower pace. As the Americans moved forward, they were also surprised to see the Grenadier Guards and 2nd

Battalion Guards moving up fast on the right of the Fusiliers. Despite his years of battle experience, the thirty-six-year-old Lawson's order to advance was a catastrophic mistake. In the confusion that followed, Lawson lost control of the battle north of the road. His regiments and companies were quickly dispersed in the woods. Platoon and squad leaders took control of the fighting in the dense underbrush. Lawson tried desperately to reorganize a cohesive defense to withstand the British onslaught, and nearly lost his life when his horse was shot from under him. The small groups of Virginia militiamen fought valiantly, and withdrew only when their ammunition was expended. The British also experienced a breakdown in unit cohesion, and soon expended most of their ammunition, forcing them to rely on their bayonets.

Seeing the confusion and stiff resistance by the rebels north of the road, Cornwallis himself rode forward to encourage his men. He too narrowly escaped death when his horse was shot from under him. Several of his officers were not as fortunate. Among them was Brigadier General Charles O'Hara, who took a ball through his thigh, forcing him to temporarily relinquish command of the Guards Brigade.

The American regulars guarding the northernmost flank under Colonel Washington's command were also under strong attack by the Jaegers, the Guards light infantry, and the 33rd Foot. As the scattered remnants of Lawson's brigade began to fall back, Washington and his Continental officers ordered their men to withdraw back to the third line. The American regulars made a successful fighting withdrawal under heavy pressure from the British.

South of the Salisbury road, the British were having a tougher time dislodging Brigadier General Edward Stevens's brigade of Virginia militia. The depleted ranks of the 71st Highlanders and 2nd Battalion of the Guards were making slow progress against the Virginians. As they moved forward in the woods and underbrush, their units became separated, and companies broke down into isolated squads and platoons, each fighting their own small but fierce engagements.

The Virginians put up a fierce resistance, giving ground slowly and exacting a heavy toll on the British. However when their commander, Brigadier Stevens, took a ball through his thigh, they began to give way. The northern regiments of Stevens's brigade closest to the road were the first to retreat under heavy pressure from the Guards. The southern regiments commanded by Colonel George Moffet and Colonel Samuel McDowell were under less pressure and held their positions longer, but were eventually forced to pull back as well.

Cornwallis had succeeded in rolling up Greene's first two lines, but the defense in depth had worked. The North Carolina and Virginia militias had given way, but they had exacted a heavy toll on Cornwallis' outnumbered force. The British now faced an even tougher challenge with Greene's main defensive line.

*   *   *

The Continentals manning the third defensive line heard the musket, rifle, and cannon fire to their front, but were unable to see the ebb and flow of the fighting in the woods. The fearful looks on the faces of the panic-stricken militiamen who withdrew from the fighting did not disturb the seasoned regulars. Greene had carefully selected the ground for his third and final defensive line. Two brigades of Virginia Continentals under the command of General Issac Huger held the American right, while two brigades of Maryland Continentals under Colonel Otho Williams defended the left of the line.

Two of Captain Singleton's six-pound cannon were positioned to fire down the Salisbury Road, the only high-speed avenue of approach into the American line. The other two six-pounders were positioned to the right front of the Virginia Continentals to provide enfilading fires across the American front.

Colonel Washington's cavalry protected the Continentals' left flank from a position south of the road. Washington's horsemen were ideally positioned to counterattack any British breakthrough of the American line. Delaware and Virginia Continentals, and Virginia riflemen who withdrew from the second line protected the Americans' right flank.

The cleared ground to the front of the American position dropped off into a narrow, steep-sided valley with some large gullies running from the high ground into the valley. Since the gullies were not cleared of underbrush, they served to slow any British advance, but did provide some concealment for the British attackers. Despite the uneven terrain, the ground generally favored the American defenders.

The weakest point in the American line was on the extreme left flank where the Salisbury Road entered the defensive position. Here Greene positioned the recently reorganized 2nd Maryland Regiment. The right of the regiment's line faced west and was located some distance from the 1st Maryland Regiment. The two Maryland regiments had no visual contact with each other due to a copse of trees between the units. The left of the 2nd Maryland's line faced south, paralleling the Salisbury Road almost as far as the Courthouse. While a number of the rank and file of the 2nd Maryland were battle-hardened veterans, a number of the officers were newly appointed to their commands as a result of a recent reorganization, and many of the regiment's non-commissioned officers had been reassigned to fill shortages in the 1st Maryland. Those factors were to prove critical in the fighting along the third American line.

The first British troops to emerge from the tangled woods belonged to the 33rd Foot, the Jaegers, and the Guards light infantry. The survivors of the fierce, confused fighting on the second line paused on the southern lip of a natural arena that was cleared of trees and underbrush for cultivation. Opposite them, they could see the Continentals standing in ranks on the northern lip of the vale. The tough fighting in the woods had brought on an adrenalin rush among the troops, and their commander, Lieutenant Colonel Webster, made no efforts to restrain his men. Rather than waiting for the Guards Brigade and Leslie's Brigade to emerge from the woods to launch a coordinated attack against the entire American line, Webster led his units down the slope of the vale, and then charged up the other side into the guns of Colonel Gunby's 1st Maryland regiment and two companies of Delaware Continentals. The American regulars held their fire until the British were within one hundred feet of their line. Then, on command, they fired a murderous volley that shattered Webster's command. Finley's two six-pounders added to the slaughter, firing case shot into the broken infantry ranks. Lieutenant Colonel Webster was wounded when a ball slammed into his knee, but he remained on the field. Under relentless fire, the survivors fell back in disorder, leaving their dead and seriously wounded on the slope. The repulse of Webster's brigade might have been the turning point in the battle had Greene followed up with an attack on the disassembled British units, but the American commander remained cautious. In keeping with his strategy, Greene refused any impromptu action that might risk the destruction of his army, even when the odds were seemingly in his favor. Despite the collapse of Webster's brigade, it soon became apparent that there was still plenty of fight left in Cornwallis's army.

As Webster attempted to reform the remnants of his brigade, General O'Hara's 2nd Guards Battalion emerged from the woods on the American left. The twice-wounded O'Hara had relinquished his command to his deputy, Lieutenant Colonel James Stuart, prior to the attack on the third line. The Guards, like the men of the 33rd Foot, were full of fury and anxious to get at the Continentals. Like Webster, Stuart was eager to attack the Americans on the opposite side of the vale. Rapidly reforming his Guards as they emerged from the woods, he ordered his men down the slope, guiding on the Salisbury Road to his right. Charging forward with fixed bayonets, the Guards headed directly for Singleton's two six-pounders on the Salisbury Road, and the 2nd Maryland's angled position just north of the road. The sight of the enraged Guards dashing towards them with bayonets flashing in the sun proved too much for the men of the 2nd Maryland. They broke and ran without firing a volley.

The Guards quickly captured Singleton's guns and began to pursue the Marylanders. On the right, the 1st Maryland was initially unaware that the 2nd Maryland had fled; their view was blocked by a copse of trees. When a staff officer rode up to inform Colonel Gunby what had happened, the Colonel ordered his men to face about and march forward to engage the Guards' left flank and rear. When the Guards saw the men of the 1st Maryland coming toward them from the left, they attempted to change their front to face the new threat. It was a complicated maneuver, even for a well-trained unit like the Guards. Nonetheless the highly disciplined battalion began the maneuver. Some of the Guards platoons managed to fire a volley at the Marylanders, buying time for the remaining units to take up their new positions. The British volley slowed, but did not stop the American assault. Colonel Gumby's horse was shot from under him as he was leading the attack, and command devolved to Lieutenant Colonel John Howard.

As the Marylanders advanced toward the Guards, trading volleys at close range, a bugle call echoed across the field. The ever-alert Colonel Washington saw his opportunity to charge the Guards from the rear. The dragoons galloped into the fray, recapturing Singleton's guns and trampling a number of Guardsmen. Once the horsemen charged through the British ranks, they wheeled their mounts around and charged into the ranks a second time, sabering some and trampling others under their horses' hooves. One of Washington's cavalrymen was a Virginian, Peter Francisco, who enlisted in the American army at the age of sixteen. Francisco stood a full head taller than the average American soldier of his day, and weighed more than 250 pounds. He was seriously wounded at the battles of Monmouth and Stony Point, and his exploits in combat were legendary throughout the army. He was in the midst of the fighting as Washington's dragoons charged into the British Guards, cutting down at least four men with his broad sword before s Guardsman pinned his leg to his horse with a bayonet. After receiving a second bayonet wound, he turned his horse and rode toward the American lines where he fell from his mount and passed out from loss of blood.[15]

Meanwhile, the Marylanders continued exchanging fire with the Guards at near pointblank range before charging their lines with fixed bayonets. Desperate hand-to-hand fighting ensued with slashing and stabbing bayonets, swinging rifles, and pointblank firing. The Guards' acting commander, Lieutenant Colonel Stuart, was killed during a sword fight with a young Captain from the 1st Maryland.[16] The Marylanders and Washington's dragoons were destroying the Guards with their combined assault.[17] Observing the fight, Cornwallis ordered his artillery officer, Lieutenant John McLeod, to fire into the melee of Continentals, Dragoons, and Guardsmen.[18] The British three-pounders fired into the entangled mass of brawling Britons and Americans, tearing apart flesh and bone. Those men who were not felled by the grapeshot scattered in all directions. Whether Cornwallis intended to drive off Washington's dragoons, or to deliberately sacrifice some of his own troops in order to win the day is a matter of conjecture. Regardless of his intent, the end result was that Washington's dragoons were driven off, and the melee ended with the Guards and Continentals dispersed and reforming. The twice-wounded General O'Hara then reassumed command and rallied his Guards. The timely arrival of the Grenadier Guards' company saved the day for the battalion. As the 1st Maryland reformed to continue the fight, the British 23rd Foot and 71st Highlanders arrived on their front and flank, forcing the proud Marylanders to withdraw in good order.

General Greene knew that the 2nd Maryland was broken and unlikely to regroup to withstand a coordinated British attack. He also knew that the 1st Maryland was no longer capable of withstanding a frontal and flank assault by both the Fusiliers and Highlanders. Greene therefore ordered a general retreat from the third line, abandoning his artillery and relinquishing the field to the British. Greene's main concern was the preservation of his army to fight another day. He knew that Cornwallis would declare victory, since his army held the field at the end of the day, but Greene also knew that it was a Pyrrhic victory for the British.

The American army retreated in good order to the west on the Reedy Fork Road, marching about three miles before halting to allow stragglers to catch up. The British were too badly damaged to mount an effective pursuit. Greene's men then continued to march through the cold rainy night and into daylight until they reached their old encampment at Speedwell Ironworks on Troublesome Creek. A number of North Carolina militia who had fled from the British on the first line had already made their way to the ironworks. The ever-prudent Greene had his men prepare for a renewed British attack, even though he considered it a remote possibility. There were other matters to attend to as well, such as caring for the wounded, burying those who expired during the march, and procuring provisions for his exhausted troops. Greene also appointed Colonel Otho Williams as temporary Adjutant General to complete the task of compiling casualty lists for each unit that fought at Guilford Courthouse.

According to the lists compiled by Williams, the Continentals defending the third line sustained the heaviest losses of the battle. The combined losses of the Maryland, Delaware, and Virginia regulars were 51 killed, 95 wounded, and 151 missing. Washington's cavalry and Lee's Partisan Legion had combined losses of 6 killed, 16 wounded and 10 missing.[19] In all, Greene lost about twenty percent of his Continentals in the battle, however, many of the wounded would recover and rejoin their units in the following weeks. Despite those losses, Greene's army remained an effective fighting force. His battle-hardened Continentals, the core of his army, remained an effective fighting force capable of conducting offensive operations against the British and Loyalists in the Carolinas in the coming months.

Losses in the North Carolina and Virginia militia units were much more problematical, since many of the militiamen who were reported as missing simply fled to their homes after leaving the field. Suffice to say that the militia losses, excluding those reported missing, were significantly less than the Continentals. Otho Williams reported militia losses as 22 killed, 73 wounded, and 885 missing. Total American casualties for the battle including both Continentals and militias totaled 264 killed and wounded, or a six percent casualty rate. The British losses were much heavier.

In a March 17th letter to Lord Germain, Cornwallis reported that his army lost 93 killed, 413 wounded, and 26 missing.[20] Assuming that Cornwallis accurately reported his casualties, his losses amounted to a 28 percent casualty rate. The Guards alone lost more than 50 percent of their men. After the battle, Cornwallis had just 1,400 troops who were capable of marching and firing a musket. Additionally, both his field grade and company grade officers' ranks were decimated. Lieutenant Colonel James Stuart, the 2nd Guards battalion commander, lay dead on the field, and Lieutenant Colonel James Webster of the 23rd Fusiliers was mortally wounded. Brigadier General Charles O'Hara was also seriously wounded and unfit for field command. Those commanders were irreplaceable, as were the dozens of fallen officers of lesser rank.

General Cornwallis's army was spent after more than 600 miles of marching without adequate rations, tents, and a sufficient number of wagons to carry supplies and the sick and wounded. Moreover, the British were more than three hundred miles from Charleston, and over two hundred miles from the Wilmington, where they could be assured of rest, supplies, and reinforcements. Loyalist militia support in North Carolina had not materialized as promised, and without that support Cornwallis could not afford another battle with the American army. The British winter campaign in the Carolinas ended as a strategic failure at Guilford Courthouse on March 15, 1781.

*   *   *

The day after the battle, the French fleet under the command of Admiral Rene Detouches that had sailed from Newport, Rhode Island arrived off the Capes of Virginia to assist Lafayette in a joint naval and ground attack to dislodge Arnold's force from Portsmouth. This was the second French naval expedition dispatched to dislodge the British from Portsmouth. A month earlier, a French naval squadron under Captain Arnaud de Tilly had arrived off Hampton Roads to launch a combined naval and land assault on Portsmouth. However, when de Tilly learned that only some 3,000 poorly trained Virginia militia were available to launch a ground assault on the base, he decided not to risk his ships in an attack that had little chance of success, and he therefore returned to Newport. When General Washington learned of the failure of the French naval effort, he made an arduous 200-mile journey from his New Windsor headquarters to Newport, to convince the French commanders to make another attempt to deal with Arnold's force in Virginia. Washington's personal pleas were successful, and General Rochambeau and Admiral de Touches agreed to dispatch a much stronger fleet, along with 1,100 French ground troops to Virginia. In turn, Washington promised to send a Continental Brigade under General Lafayette to Virginia to bolster the militia.

The Allied plan called for the French fleet to sail south to Virginia, enter Chesapeake Bay and then sail north up the bay to rendezvous with Lafayette at Annapolis. After taking the Continental troops aboard the French transports, the fleet would then sail back down the bay to Portsmouth. The Continentals, the French ground troops, and the Virginia militia would then launch a ground assault on Portsmouth, while the French fleet pounded Arnold's fortifications with cannon fire. However, the plan went awry before the French fleet arrived off the Virginia Capes.

Unbeknownst to Admiral Chevalier Detouches, the commander of the French fleet, a British fleet under the command of Admiral Marriot Arbuthnot had raced south from New York, arriving off the Virginia Capes ahead of the French. When the French arrived, Detouches was shocked to see the British fleet, equal in size to his own, lined-up and ready to give battle at the entrance to Hampton Roads.

Admiral Detouches deployed his eight ships of the line in two parallel columns to confront the British and make a run for the bay. The British, with a slight advantage in cannon, were deployed in a perpendicular line at the entrance of the bay to keep the French from entering. When the French made their run for the bay, the British moved swiftly to intercept them. When both fleets were within range of each other, fire and smoke erupted from the gun ports as cannon balls flew across the waves slamming into the hulls and rigging of the opposing ships. The French gunners damaged three British ships, and the British salvo did considerable damage to two French vessels. Outgunned and unwilling to risk another run for the bay, Detouches let his fleet drift north out of range of the British guns. The British chose not to pursue.

While neither side could claim victory in the engagement, the British base at Portsmouth was no longer threatened from the sea. When Lafayette and the American militia commanders learned that the British fleet had driven off the French, they realized that a successful siege of the base was no longer possible. Arnold and his force were no longer in imminent danger. Ten days later another British fleet arrived off Portsmouth. On board the British ships were 2,200 British troops under the command of Major General William Phillips, who had been sent by General Clinton to replace Arnold as commander of British forces in Virginia. With the addition of Phillips's troops, the British had some 4,500 men on the ground in Virginia, the largest British force assembled in Virginia since the beginning of the war.

*   *   *

After a three-day hiatus, Cornwallis's army departed Guilford Courthouse on the 18th of March, and proceeded to the Quaker community at New Garden, where the troops rested for two additional days. During the interlude, Cornwallis issued a proclamation to the citizens of North Carolina announcing his complete victory and encouraging Loyalists to rise up and take control of their communities for the Crown. In fact, the battle had changed nothing except for the further weakening of the Cornwallis's army. The North Carolina militia and partisan bands were not destroyed and remained active in their communities, and Nathaniel Greene's army was still very much intact.

Belying the words of his own proclamation, Cornwallis then began a slow tedious hundred-mile march to the village of Cross Creek (modern day Fayetteville), bypassing the town of Hillsborough, where a month earlier he had proclaimed his success in driving Greene's army from the state. His direction of march signaled his intent to leave the backcountry of North Carolina for good.

At Cross Creek, Cornwallis hoped to gather subsistence for his army, and hopefully meet reinforcements marching from Wilmington. He found neither. Although the Loyalists living in the Cross Creek area had gathered supplies for Cornwallis's army, five hundred North Carolina militiamen rode into Cross Creek ahead of the British and burned most of the stores on hand and carried off the rest. When the British arrived at Cross Creek, they found that little remained of the public stores, and foraging parties sent into the countryside returned empty handed. Adding to his woes, Cornwallis learned that no reinforcements were marching from Wilmington to join his army.

With his army on the verge of starvation, and his 400 sick and wounded dying off by the day, Cornwallis was left with two choices. He could either march southeast for ninety miles to reach the British occupied seaport at Wilmington, North Carolina, or march southwestward for 120 miles to reach and reinforce the endangered British base at Camden, South Carolina. Cornwallis chose to march to Wilmington, possibly out of concern for his men, but more likely he had had enough of the inhospitable interior of the Carolinas. While a march to Camden made more strategic sense, it also meant crossing two major rivers and numerous swampy branches and tributaries, whereas the road to Wilmington generally paralleled the Cape Fear River and the terrain was less hilly and easier to traverse.

Before his arrival at Cross Creek, Cornwallis had hoped to ferry his sick and wounded down the Cape Fear River to Wilmington on the coast. Much to his disappointment, he learned that the river was narrow with high banks offering ideal positions for rebel ambushes and snipers. Therefore, on Sunday, April 1st , after a one-day rest at Cross Creek, Cornwallis led his depleted, weary army on an overland march toward Wilmington. After a six-day slog through rebel-infested territory, Cornwallis's lead units reached the safe haven of Wilmington on the 7th of April. Once General Greene, who was trailing Cornwallis's army, was satisfied that his opponent intended to reach Wilmington, he turned his army and marched toward South Carolina determined to drive the newly exposed British garrisons from their outposts in that state.

* * *

There is little doubt that the accomplished professional soldier Lord Cornwallis was out-generaled by the unassuming former Quaker and foundry-owner from Rhode Island, Nathaniel Greene. The failure of the British strategy in the Carolinas began in London where Lord North vastly overestimated Loyalist support in the southern American colonies, and therefore refused to allocate sufficient numbers of British troops to the region. Many of the reinforcements that did arrive in the Carolinas were not sent to reinforce Cornwallis as he pursued Greene's army. Some 5,000 troops under the command of Lord Rawdon garrisoned the seaports of Charleston, Wilmington, and the interior bases in South Carolina. Loyalist militia units could have made up for the shortfall in British troop strength, but Cornwallis never made a sustained effort to recruit, train, and adequately equip Loyalist militia after Ferguson's defeat at Kings Mountain. On the other hand, both Morgan and Greene worked closely with local militia and partisan leaders, and employed their units effectively.

Strategically, Cornwallis focused on Greene's southern Continental army as the American center-of-gravity for his campaign. At the same time, he underestimated the threats posed by American irregulars to his supply and communication lines as he marched deep into the interior of the Carolinas. Furthermore, he underestimated the operational mobility of Greene's army and the American militias. Another failure in the British strategy was the failure to synchronize Cornwallis's campaign with Arnold's operations in Virginia. Conversely, Greene received both logistical support and reinforcements from Virginia throughout the campaign.

Greene demonstrated throughout the campaign that he was a strategic thinker who had a keen appreciation for the importance of maneuver and logistics. Nathaniel Greene knew how to keep one step ahead of the British, preparing in advance his supplies and boats, and he gave battle only on ground of his own choosing. Once committed to battle, Greene fought resolutely, but refused to risk the annihilation of his army. Washington's decision to appoint Nathaniel Greene to command the American Southern Department was indeed a wise choice.

PART 2

No Spring nor Summer Rest

"We have pursued them to the Eutaw's."

—General Nathaniel Greene
September 11, 1781

8

EVERYTHING HAS CHANGED

Across southern Virginia and the Carolinas, the fields and forests were greening and the flowering dogwoods and azaleas were turning the landscape a snowy white, pink, or red, a sure sign that winter was over and a new campaign season was about to begin. More than six hundred miles to the north, only the faintest signs of spring almost invisible to the human eye were appearing in the Hudson valley. Even though April had begun, the gloom of late winter still held sway at Washington's headquarters in New Windsor.

ARMY HEADQUARTERS—NEW WINDSOR, NEW YORK
April 1781

The news that French Admiral Detouches had failed to enter Hampton Roads to join Lafayette in a land and sea attack on Arnold's base at Portsmouth angered Washington, and lowered his expectations of French cooperation in his own campaign. The Commander-in-Chief remained adamant that the only way to win the war was to launch a campaign to drive the British from New York. In two separate letters written to his chief of intelligence, Benjamin Tallmadge, during April of 1781, Washington requested details of the British "strength on York, Long, and Staten Islands, specifying the several corps and their distributions." He also pressed Tallmadge for information on "arrivals, embarkations, preparations for movements, alterations of positions, situations of posts, fortifications, garrisons, strengths and weaknesses of each, distribution and strength of corps, and, in general, every thing which can be interesting and important for us to know."[1]

Although intelligence was essential in planning for an attack on New York, Washington knew that without French monetary and troop support, he lacked the means to undertake the campaign. In an April letter to John Laurens, who was in Paris soliciting additional French assistance, Washington wrote, "that without a foreign loan, our present force, which is but the remnant of an army, cannot be kept together this campaign, much less will it be increased and in readiness for another."[2]

Despite his obsession with New York, Washington realized that Greene's operations in the Carolinas and Lafayette's efforts in Virginia were necessary for political reasons. It was unthinkable that the southern states could be ceded to the British. Washington therefore ordered General Anthony Wayne's six regiments of the Pennsylvania Line, some 1,000 men in all, to march south to reinforce Lafayette in Virginia. Notwithstanding this commitment, he remained obdurate in his belief that future American and French efforts should be directed at New York.

NEWPORT, RHODE ISLAND
April–May 1781

The French commander, Lieutenant General Comte de Rochambeau, remained unenthusiastic about a campaign directed against New York, and waited for news of reinforcements and materials at his headquarters in Newport, Rhode Island. It had been more than six months since he had sent his twenty-six-year-old son back to France to solicit more troops and supplies to support a major summer campaign in 1781. When his son finally returned in mid-May, the general learned that the French government had decided not to commit major ground reinforcements to America, but did agree to a 6,000,000-livre gift to the Continental army. Although the French government refused to ship more ground forces to Newport, French Admiral Comte de Grasse was ordered to move his fleet from the Caribbean to North America by mid to late summer to support a joint American-French campaign. Based on these developments, Rochambeau requested a conference with Washington, and both agreed to meet in Wethersfield, Connecticut on the 21st of May to finalize plans for a summer campaign.

THE SOUTHERN THEATER
Spring 1781

While Washington and Rochambeau considered their options for a summer campaign, Generals Cornwallis and Greene laid respective plans of their own, and by the end of April they had set them in motion. On the 7th of April, Greene marched his men down the Cape Fear River toward Wilmington. By threatening Wilmington, Greene hoped to deter Cornwallis from marching into South Carolina to reunite with Lord Rawdon's force at Camden. However, the American maneuver was a deliberate feint. Greene had already made a decision to return to South Carolina to drive the British from the state. After that, he intended to drive them from Georgia. Greene was not convinced that Cornwallis would attempt to follow him into South Carolina with his depleted army, but if he did, the Americans still held a strategic advantage in that state. Although the British had nearly 8,000 troops in South Carolina and Georgia, they were spread widely apart. Large numbers of troops were committed to protecting the seaports at Charleston and Savannah, and others were scattered across the countryside protecting small bases in the interior. Those bases and the lines of communication between them were under constant threat of attacks by guerilla and militia forces led by Generals Marion and Sumter, and Colonel Pickens. The initiative clearly rested with the Americans, who were capable of striking at will with their highly mobile irregular troops.

With only 1,450 Continentals under his command, the success of Greene's campaign to drive the British from the interior of South Carolina was heavily dependent on the cooperation of the state militia units and partisan bands. Those forces became an integral part of his campaign plan. He assigned Brigadier General Francis Marion—known as the "Swamp Fox"—primary responsibility for threatening the British lines of communication and posts between Camden and Charleston, while Brigadier General Thomas Sumter, with three regiments of South Carolina regulars, was responsible for the area between Camden and Ninety Six. Colonel Andrew Pickens, commanding the militia in the western part of the state, was responsible for interdicting supplies headed for the British posts at Ninety Six and Augusta. With the British supply and communication lines under constant threat by partisans and militia, Greene planned to use his Continentals and regular state troops to selectively attack the main

British posts in the interior, forcing the British garrisons to withdraw to Charleston.

Greene chose as his first objective the British garrison and supply base at Camden in the northeast quadrant of the state. Cornwallis's deputy in South Carolina, twenty-six-year-old Brigadier General Lord Francis Rawdon, considered Camden his primary base, and he assumed personal command of its 900 British and Loyalist troops. Although Greene had a numerical advantage over Rawdon's force at Camden, he was concerned that reinforcements might reach the British before he launched an attack. Of particular concern was the Loyalist force garrisoning Fort Watson on the Santee River, only 60 miles to the south. Greene therefore assigned the mission of capturing the post to the partisan leader Francis Marion. He attached Lieutenant Colonel Henry "Lighthorse Harry" Lee's Legion, and a company of Maryland Continentals to assist in the attack. Marion's partisans and the regulars rendezvoused at Black River on April 14th, and laid siege to Fort Watson the following day. After a five-day siege, the garrison surrendered to the Americans on April 23d.

While the siege of Fort Watson was in progress, General Greene and his Continentals arrived in the Camden area on April 20th. Prior to their arrival, the British troops constructed a ring of redoubts that blocked the main avenues of approach to the town. Greene did not have a sufficient number of troops to launch attacks on the redoubts, or mount a siege. He therefore positioned his army along a pine-covered ridge known as Hobkirk's Hill. The ridgeline ran east to west about one and a half miles from the town. After occupying Hobkirk's Hill, Greene hoped that the overconfident Lord Rawdon would leave his fortifications and attack the American position.

Greene chose an excellent piece of terrain to defend. The ground between the hill and the town was heavily wooded with thick undergrowth. Hobkirk's Hill itself was covered with timber and flanked on the left by an impassable swamp. The American position on the hill also blocked the main road leading to the Waxhaws and the North Carolina border.

Greene formed his defensive line with General Isaac Huger's brigade of two regiments of Virginia Continentals on the right of the road, and Colonel Otho Williams's brigade of Maryland Continentals on the left of it. The American artillery was positioned in the center covering the road.

Captain Robert Kirkwood's light infantry picketed the front of the American position, and a second line of North Carolina militia was posted behind the main line. Colonel Washington's cavalry was on call to circle behind the British attacking force and sweep up its rear. Greene's defensive plan made excellent use of the terrain, but the execution of the plan depended on the performance of the commanders and their troops in the heat of battle.

Although he was outnumbered almost two to one, the aggressive Lord Rawdon could not ignore the threat posed by the Americans in close proximity to his base. He gained some information about the defenses on Hobkirk's Hill from an American deserter, but the information was not entirely accurate. The deserter told Rawdon that the Americans had no artillery positioned on the hill. As a result, the British commander decided to attack without his own artillery support. Rawdon planned a surprise attack on the position using some 900 troops.

Just before dawn on April 25th, Rawdon's force, comprised of the 63d Regiment of Foot, his own regiment (the Volunteers of Ireland), the King's American Regiment, the New York Volunteers, and the South Carolina Royalists, marched toward Hobkirk's Hill. The column arrived at the base of the hill around 11:00 am. The Americans were preoccupied with preparations for their noon meal, as the British regiments skirted the swamp on the American left, and started up the ridgeline. The British lost the element of surprise when the American pickets spotted Rawdon's men as they moved into attack formations in the woods to their front. Alerted by the picket fire, Greene's commanders shouted orders for their men to rush to their assigned positions to receive the attack.

Greene observed the British regiments as they deployed into attack formations, and began advancing up the ridgeline. Noticing that Rawdon's regiments were advancing on a narrow front, Greene saw an opportunity to seize the initiative. He quickly ordered his left and right flank regiments to outflank the attackers, while Colonel Washington led his cavalry to the right to gain the British rear and complete the encirclement. However, Washington's dragoons swung too far to the right to get behind Rawdon's fast moving attacking regiments. Washington's horsemen did manage to capture a number of prisoners; however, they were mostly noncombatant medical personnel, wounded, and commissaries. However, the dragoons were too far in the British rear to engage in the heavy fighting that was erupting on Hobkirk's Hill.

Responding to General Greene's orders, Lieutenant Colonel Benjamin Ford's 2nd Maryland Regiment quickly moved forward on the left, while Lieutenant Colonel Richard Campbell's Virginia regiment attempted to envelop the British right flank. After Ford and Campbell's regiments and Washington's cavalry were in motion, Greene thought he saw an opportunity for an easy victory, and promptly ordered Colonel John Gunby's 1st Maryland, and Lieutenant Colonel Samuel Hawes' 2nd Virginia to charge down the hill into the front of the attacking regiments. At that moment, the unforeseen happened. The American frontal attack stalled when Captain William Beatty who was leading two companies on the 1st Maryland's right was shot and killed. Colonel Gunby then ordered the regiment to fall back to a position where it could reform before continuing the attack. Almost simultaneously, Lieutenant Colonel Ford commanding the 2nd Maryland Regiment was seriously wounded while leading an assault on the British right flank. With their commander out of the fight, and their sister regiment moving toward the rear, the 2nd Maryland followed suit. The disorder and withdrawal of the Maryland line regiments left the flanks of the two Virginia regiments exposed, and they too were soon obliged to fall back. Lord Rawdon saw the confusion in the American ranks, and pushed his regiments forward to seize the high ground before the Americans could reform their defensive line.

After observing the general disorder and confusion among his Continentals, Greene ordered a general withdrawal. The withdrawal was orderly enough to discourage an immediate British pursuit, and the eventual return of Washington's cavalry forestalled any follow-up British attacks. The artillery, ammunition wagons, and baggage were all saved from capture during the retreat, but there was little doubt that Rawdon's small disciplined force had won a brilliant tactical victory, albeit at a high cost. British losses in killed and wounded were twice those of the Americans. Greene withdrew only about three miles from the battlefield, and the British withdrew back to Camden, leaving only a company of dragoons at Hobkirk's Hill. Upon their return, Washington's cavalry easily drove off the British dragoons.

After returning to Camden, Rawdon found that his victory at Hobkirk's Hill had gained him nothing. The Americans soon returned to occupy the same positions on the hill as before, and the South Carolina militia and partisans under Thomas Sumter and Francis Marion, supported by Henry Lee's Legion, continued to disrupt his supply and communication lines with Charleston. By early May, Lord Rawdon was convinced that the British post at Camden was untenable, and on the 9th of May the British abandoned it and marched to Moncks Corner, only thirty-five miles from Charleston. Despite losing a battle, General Greene had once again achieved strategic success by wresting control of the northeastern portion of South Carolina from the British.

* * *

On April 25th General Cornwallis departed Wilmington with some 1,600 troops, all that remained of his once formidable army. Rather than marching to reinforce Lord Rawdon at Camden, the British southern theater commander turned north, marching his army through the coastal lowlands toward Virginia. Cornwallis was fully aware that by marching toward Virginia, he was abandoning his mission of pacifying the Carolinas, in violation of General Clinton's orders. Those orders were never rescinded or modified in subsequent directives from General Clinton. Justifying his decision, Cornwallis later complained that he had received no guidance from Clinton since he departed Winnsboro in January of 1781. While British communications between Clinton's headquarters in New York and Cornwallis's army in the field in the Carolinas were difficult, Cornwallis took full advantage of the situation to exercise independent command. Furthermore, he carefully took measures to allay any future criticism of his actions.

Before departing Wilmington, Cornwallis wrote carefully worded letters to General Clinton and Lord Germain in London to justify his actions. Germain, a former General who was Secretary of State for the American Department in Lord North's cabinet, was a strong supporter of Cornwallis. In his April 18th letter to Lord Germain, Cornwallis wrote that he was, "in daily expectation of seeing the reinforcements from Europe, and of receiving the Commander-in-Chief's directions for further operations of the campaign."[3] Five days later Cornwallis wrote two letters, one to Lord Germain and one to General Clinton, in which he painstakingly attempted to justify his abandonment of South Carolina. In his April 23rd letter to

Clinton, he wrote, "Neither my cavalry nor infantry are in readiness to move," further adding, "I must however begin my march tomorrow," referring to his move toward Virginia. In the same letter he acknowledged his "anxiety" over the situation in South Carolina, but added that if Greene returned to North Carolina, which was highly unlikely, he would not be able to join General Phillips in Virginia.[4] Cornwallis's letter to Lord Germain on the same date was apparently an attempt to gain approbation for his decision from a higher authority than Clinton. In the letter, Cornwallis acknowledged the threat posed by Greene's army to the British at Camden, but then added that he had warned Lord Rawdon of the threat. He then attempted to justify his refusal to return to South Carolina by adding that due to the lack of "forage and subsistence . . . and the difficulty in passing the Pedee (river) when opposed by an enemy render it impossible for me to give immediate assistance."[5] He further wrote that while Greene was occupied in South Carolina, he was "seizing the opportunity" to march to Virginia, even though the march from Wilmington, North Carolina to Petersburg, Virginia was even more difficult than a march to Camden. To reach Petersburg, Cornwallis's army had to march more than 250 miles across the swampy fever-infested lowlands of North Carolina and Virginia; a march that required the crossing of five major rivers. In addition, most of the countryside along the route of march was in rebel hands, and offered little subsistence for an army on the march.

Cornwallis was fully aware that he was ceding control of the interiors of North and South Carolina, as well as Georgia, to the rebels against the wishes and orders of the British Commander-in-Chief, General Clinton. Moreover, his assumption that Virginia was the key to the success of the British southern strategy proved to be incorrect and presumptuous. The interior of Virginia was as inhospitable to an invader as the other southern states, and reinforcing Virginia with Continental and French troops was far less challenging than reinforcing Greene's army in South Carolina. As the southern theater commander, Lord Cornwallis was subordinate to General Clinton, the British Commander-in-Chief in North America, and it was not his responsibility to make decisions impacting British grand strategy without prior approval from his superior. Lord Cornwallis's unilateral decision to march his army to Virginia set in motion a chain of events that would ultimately lead to disaster.

* * *

As Greene attempted to drive the British from Camden, and Cornwallis began his ill-fated march to Virginia, the young Marquis de Lafayette struggled to keep supplies and reinforcements flowing southward to General Greene's army. Lafayette's adversary, Major General William Phillips, had an intimate knowledge of Virginia, having been a loosely held prisoner of war at Charlottesville after the British surrender at Saratoga. Before his exchange, Phillips had made the acquaintance of many members of the state's elite in Charlottesville, including Governor Thomas Jefferson. Unlike Arnold, Phillips had the respect of his officers and men, and was dedicated to selfless service to his King and country. He was also quite capable of keeping Benedict Arnold on a tight leash, focused on British interests rather than his own. Together, the two generals had a combined force of 4,500 men, more than enough to secure Portsmouth and mount operations into the interior. Those operations were intended to disrupt militia and Continental recruitment efforts, undermine and disrupt rebel local and state governments, and confiscate or destroy supplies intended for use by the rebel army. High on the British priority list of targets was Petersburg. The town was a gathering and transit point for Virginians who had enlisted for service in the Continental Army in the Carolinas. It was also a storage and transshipment area for weapons, ammunition, and supplies destined for Greene's use.

On April 24th, General Phillips sailed up the James River toward Richmond with a force of 2,500 men, threatening another attack on the capital. Instead, he landed at City Point, and marched to capture Petersburg. Brigadier General Peter Muhlenberg's Virginia's militia shadowed the British from the south bank of the James as they moved up the river, and were able to reach Petersburg first. Together with Muhlenberg's men, General von Steuben had gathered a small number of local militia to resist the British assault. Outnumbered by more than two to one, von Steuben knew that his force of one thousand militia could not hold the town for long. However, he was determined to delay the British until the military hardware and supplies were removed from the town.

Shortly after noon on April 25th, the British arrived on the outskirts of Petersburg, and then launched an immediate assault on the town. To General Phillips's surprise, the Virginia militiamen offered stiff resistance, beating back three assaults on the town. After three hours of heavy fighting, General von Steuben ordered the Virginians to withdraw across the Appomattox River. As the militiamen withdrew across the bridge they pulled up the planks on the bridge rendering it unsafe to cross. The Americans then occupied Colonial Heights, where they regrouped and prepared to march to join Lafayette's Continentals at Richmond. Other than some stores of tobacco, Phillips found nothing of significant value in Petersburg. Von Steuben had managed to remove almost all of the military stores. After sending Arnold to scour the countryside for the missing supplies and equipment, Phillips tarried in the Petersburg area for several days before turning his army toward Richmond on the 28th of April.

Arriving at the outskirts of Richmond on the 29th of April, Phillips was shocked to see the glimmer of Continental bayonets on Shockhoe Hill. General Lafayette had force-marched 1,500 American Continentals from Annapolis to defend Virginia's capital. To reach Richmond ahead of the British, Lafayette had to complete the march without his slow moving artillery. After his arrival, the General deployed his force on a wide front in positions that were clearly visible to the approaching British; thereby making his force appear much larger than it was. The ruse worked. Uncertain of the size of Lafayette's force, Phillips declined to give battle and ordered his army back to the British ships waiting on the James River. His intent was to return to the British base at Portsmouth, but before the flotilla reached the base Phillips became seriously ill. When his flagship anchored off Burwell's Ferry near Williamsburg, the fever-ridden Phillips received a letter from Cornwallis calling for a juncture of their two armies at Petersburg. Phillips immediately ordered his flotilla to reverse course and sail up the Appomattox River toward Petersburg.

Lieutenant Colonel Banastre Tarleton led the advance guard of Cornwallis's army as it marched north toward Petersburg. Other than a few minor skirmishes with militia, the march was uneventful. Having learned the importance of boats during his pursuit of Greene's army, Cornwallis gave specific orders to Tarleton to seize as many boats as possible as the army approached each major river. Cornwallis also mounted two boats on wagons in his supply train to expedite the river crossings. As the army crossed into Virginia, Cornwallis was perplexed since he had not received any response to the messages he had sent forward by couriers to Phillips.

Unbeknownst to Cornwallis, Phillips was lying comatose at his latest head-quarters in Petersburg, dying of typhoid fever. Cornwallis learned of his friend and colleague's death shortly before reaching the town.

After his juncture with the British force at Petersburg on April 20th, and with more reinforcements on the way from New York, Cornwallis would soon have some 7,000 troops to oppose Lafayette's meager force of 1,200 Continentals. The Frenchman wisely kept his distance, waiting for the British to make their next move.

*   *   *

The day after Cornwallis's army arrived in Petersburg, a major conference was underway in Wethersfield, Connecticut. The meeting between Generals Washington and Rochambeau and their staffs was intended to negotiate a joint strategy for the summer and fall campaigns. French Admiral Comte de Barras, the new commander of the French naval squadron in Rhode Island, accompanied Rochambeau to Wethersfield. Also present was Connecticut's governor, Jonathan Trumbull, a trusted friend and advisor to Washington. After the ceremonial formalities honoring the chiefs, the negotiations began in earnest. Rochambeau set a positive tone for the meeting by informing Washington of France's six-million-livre gift to the American Army. The generals then presented and discussed their preferred strategies for defeating the British in North America. Washington argued strongly for a campaign to retake New York. He insisted that General Clinton's army defending the city was seriously weak-ened after sending reinforcements to Virginia and the Carolinas. Rocham-beau, however, remained unconvinced that a campaign against New York offered any chance of success. The Frenchman was seven years older than Washington, had served with distinction in France's European wars, and Washington listened attentively to his arguments. Speaking through his interpreter, Rochambeau proposed a major campaign against the British in Virginia, arguing that such a campaign would not be expected by the British, and could be prosecuted with or without French naval superiority. At that moment, the Frenchman chose not to reveal to Washington that Admiral Comte de Grasse's fleet had been ordered to sail north from the Caribbean to North America. The fleet was expected to arrive in mid to late summer. The French government suggested that a joint American-

French attack on Nova Scotia should be considered, but left the final decision to Rochambeau and Washington on how best to employ their ground and naval forces.

After three days of at times heated discussions, General Rochambeau was still unable to convince Washington that a campaign directed against New York offered little chance of success. Nonetheless, the Frenchman had been directed by Versailles to allow Washington to make the final decision on allied strategy. Therefore, he acceded to Washington's preference for a campaign to liberate New York, despite his own preference for a campaign in Virginia. At the end of the three-day conference, General Rochambeau agreed to move his army to New York as soon as possible. As a conciliatory gesture to the French, Washington made one concession. In a letter dated May 23rd, 1781, to Chevalier De La Luzerne, the French Minister to America, Washington recommended that the French fleet in the West Indies "should run immediately to Sandy Hook," to facilitate a joint attack on New York, but then added, "or any other, which may be thought more advisable."[6] It was all the opening Rochambeau needed. At the conclusion of the conference, Rochambeau forwarded a copy of the conference minutes to Admiral de Grasse, adding his own personal note requesting that the Admiral bring his fleet to the Chesapeake, and not to New York.[7]

SOUTH CAROLINA

As Cornwallis marched north toward Richmond, and Washington and Rochambeau debated grand strategy, General Greene continued his campaign against the British and Loyalist outposts in South Carolina. The British had constructed and garrisoned a line of forts, strategic towns, and ferry crossings across the breadth of the state from Georgetown in the east to Augusta just over the Georgia border in the west. In between were the British forts and garrisons at Orangeburg, Camden, Fort Watson, Fort Motte, Fort Granby, and Ninety Six. The outposts and supply depots were intended to protect the British lines of communications between Charleston and the interior, and support the Loyalist forces scattered across the state. The numbers of troops garrisoning each outpost were relatively small, mainly in the low hundreds, however much effort had been expended in fortifying the posts. The larger forts were defended by infantry supported by artillery, and could only be captured through siege operations.

After the fall of Fort Watson, and even before the British evacuation of Camden, General Greene laid plans to attack the other outposts using his own Continentals and the state militia units. Francis Marion was assigned responsibility for capturing Fort Motte, a major supply depot near the spot where the Congaree and Wateree rivers merge to form the Santee River. One hundred and fifty British infantry defended the fort, which was protected by a stockade, a ditch, and abatis. To insure success, Greene attached Lieutenant Colonel Henry Lee's 300 regulars to Marion's force that numbered around 150 men. Marion and Lee arrived in the area on the 8th of May and began digging approaches to the fort. The British held out for four days before surrendering on the 12th of May,

Orangeburg, a fortified town and supply base some 50 miles south of Fort Ganby was the next to fall. Defended by a garrison of less than one hundred men, the town quickly surrendered to a force of 350 partisans led by Colonel Sumter on May 11th, after a one-day siege. While Sumter's men were evacuating supplies and prisoners from Orangeburg, Marion and Lee were marching from Fort Motte to their next target, Fort Granby, near present-day Columbia, South Carolina. Arriving on the evening of May 14th, the Americans demonstrated their strength the next morning by unleashing volleys of musket fire and an artillery barrage. Concerned that Lord Rawdon was marching to relieve the fort, Lee decided to offer generous surrender terms to the fort's commander. The commander accepted the offer, and the fort was surrendered at noon on the 15th of May. The garrison of 60 British regulars and 280 Loyalists were allowed to withdraw to Charleston, taking their private property and baggage with them, including some goods plundered from the local area. The Americans confiscated a number of other stores including significant numbers of weapons, powder, cartridges, and shot.

After the American victories at Fort Watson, Fort Ganby, Fort Motte, and Orangeburg, General Greene turned his attention to the British post at Ninety Six in the northwest quadrant of the state, some 65 miles north of Augusta, Georgia, and one-hundred miles west of Camden. Ninety Six was heavily fortified and defended by about 500 Loyalist militia. It was the most important post in South Carolina's interior still in British hands. Loyalists outnumbered the Patriots by more than five to one in the area around Ninety Six. Therefore, General Greene decided to commit the major portion of his army to its capture, while Henry Lee's Legion and General Pickens's militia moved against the British at Augusta. If the Americans succeeded in this phase of the campaign, the British presence in South Carolina and Georgia would be limited to their enclaves in the port cities of Charleston and Savannah.

On May 17th, General Greene's army began a grueling march across the backcountry of South Carolina to reach Ninety Six. Greene's weary veterans trudged along the narrow country roads and trails, traversing pine-covered hills and valleys and fording chest-deep streams and rivers. It was a challenging march for the battle hardened Continentals, who toted their heavy loads of weapons, ammunition, and other equipment, but they completed the hundred-mile march in five days, arriving at Ninety Six on the 22d of May.

On arrival, the Americans found a fortified village surrounded by an imposing stockade. The village had connecting covered trenches, bunkers, and abatis with sharpened timber stakes. Within the village were two strongpoints, the Star Fort and Fort Holmes, which protected the village's only water supply. Some 500 Loyalist troops manned the fortifications. After a reconnaissance of the impressive fortifications, Greene and his chief engineer, Thaddeus Kosciuskzo, concluded that Ninety Six could not be carried by an immediate direct assault. Despite his concern that Lord Rawdon would attempt to reinforce the threatened outpost, Greene decided to mount a siege. Lacking proper siege equipment, however, Kosciuskzo was forced to improvise using materials on hand, and timber from the surrounding forests.

During the next three weeks, the Americans dug approach trenches and parallels, threw up earthworks to protect a three-cannon battery, and even attempted to dig mines under the stockade walls. Cannon and musket fire and occasional well-timed sorties by Loyalists sallying forth from the fort often interrupted the siege operations.

While Greene continued his siege at Ninety Six, 1,600 American troops led by General Pickens and Colonel Lee marched against the British at Augusta, Georgia. The British had constructed three forts to defend Augusta, Forts Galphin, Cornwallis, and Grierson. On the morning of May 18th, Lee's mounted militia lured a group of enemy militia out of the front gate of Fort Galphin. When the Loyalists began to pursue Lee's mounted men, his Legion infantry, who were concealed in the woods near the fort, charged the open gate and took the fort without a single casualty, capturing 126 prisoners.

On the evening of May 21st, Lee crossed the Savannah River and moved toward Augusta. There he joined with General Pickens and Colonel Elijah Clarke to take the two remaining British forts. Fort Cornwallis was situated in the middle of the town, and Fort Grierson was a half-mile up the river. The Americans constructed artillery batteries midway between the two forts. Lee, Pickens, and Clarke decided to attack the weaker of them, Fort Grierson, first. The attack began on May 23rd and the fort fell quickly after a coordinated attack by Georgia militia, North Carolina Continentals, and Lee's Legion. The Loyalist defenders lost thirty killed and dozens of wounded, while the Americans suffered only light casualties.

The Americans next laid siege to Fort Cornwallis, the last British bastion protecting Augusta. On the 31st of May, siege preparations were complete and a summons to surrender was sent to the British commander, Lieutenant Colonel Browne. The fort's commander at first refused the American terms, but after four days of bombardment by artillery, he asked for a truce and offered to open negotiations. The terms of surrender were agreed on the 4th of June; however, since that day was the King's birthday, Browne postponed the surrender to the following day. The next morning at 8 a.m., Browne's 300 troops marched out of the fort and surrendered their arms. The Americans then marched in and raised their flag. Augusta was in American hands.[8]

Meanwhile the siege of Ninety Six continued. When, General Greene learned that Lord Rawdon was marching with a 2,000-man force to relieve the garrison, he sent dispatches to militia leaders Brigadier Generals Sumter and Marion, requesting that they do everything possible to delay Rawdon's column. After Greene learned that Sumter and Marion were unable to block Rawdon's approach, he decided on one last effort to take the fort by storm.

Reinforced by Lieutenant Colonel Henry Lee's wing of the army, which had just forced the surrender of British garrison at Augusta, Greene mounted an all-out attack on Ninety Six on the 18th of June. After a heavy artillery barrage, the Americans launched a two-pronged attack on the two forts at Ninety Six. Lee's Legion infantry, reinforced by North Carolina and Delaware Continentals, assaulted Fort Holmes, and Colonel Richard Campbell's Virginia and Maryland Continentals attacked the Star Fort, the principal fortification at Ninety Six. Lee's troops successfully crossed the moat surrounding Fort Holmes, and after an hour of close-in fighting managed to force their way into the fort and overwhelm the defenders.

Protected by two blockhouses and a twelve-foot high stockade surrounded by a deep ditch, the Star Fort was a much more formidable bastion. The fort's defenders stood on a parapet protected by a three-foot wall of sandbags. Thus protected, the Loyalists could fire down at the attackers in the ditch before they could scale the walls of the stockade. Greene selected two lieutenants, one from the Maryland Line and one from the Virginia Line, to lead the "forlorn hope" detachment into the ditch to begin the assault. They were supported by a group of Continentals carrying hooks on long poles to pull down the sandbags protecting the men on the parapet, and ax men to cut down the abatis and fascines in the ditch. Greene wrote, "A furious cannonade preluded the attack. They entered the enemy's ditch, and made every exertion to get down the sand bags . . . under a galling fire."[9]

Immediately after the Americans entered the ditch, a party of Loyalists emerged from the fort with fixed bayonets, and took the fight to the Americans who were struggling in the ditch. General Greene saw that his men were getting the worse of it and called off the attack. The Continentals lost forty men killed and wounded, including the two officers who led the assault. When he learned that Lord Rawdon's relief column was within a few miles of the town, Greene ordered an end to the twenty-eight-day siege. Once again, General Greene withdrew when he faced with a stronger British force, preserving his army to fight another day. The British pursued the Americans and overtook Greene's rear guard. However, Lee's Legion fought a successful action ending the pursuit. The British troops, many of whom were newly arrived from Great Britain, were simply worn out and suffering greatly from the near hundred-degree heat after the forty-mile pursuit. Lord Rawdon then marched his exhausted troops back to Ninety Six. After assessing the damages to the fortifications, he decided to abandon the post. The British departed Ninety Six for Charleston on the 29th of June, leaving a small force of troops behind to guard the Loyalists while they gathered their belongings and families in preparation for a march to

Charleston. On the 8th of July, the British destroyed the fortifications at Ninety Six and escorted the Loyalists and their families to the coast.

With the evacuation of Ninety Six, and successful operations against Augusta and Georgetown, the Americans controlled the interior of South Carolina, except for the area surrounding Charleston. There remained only two British outposts near Charleston, one at Dorchester and another at Monck's Corner. After his return to Charleston, Lord Rawdon was ill and exhausted from the hard campaigning. His health continued to decline, and he was forced to relinquish command and return to England. When the British and their Tory allies retired to Charleston to languish in the summer heat and humidity of that coastal city, the American army marched to the high hills of the Santee to rest and recuperate. The hills provided some relief from the soaring temperatures and humidity.

Although General Greene's army still had one more major battle to fight, it was clear that the Americans had thwarted British efforts to keep the Carolinas and Georgia as colonies. After six months of hard campaigning that included marching hundreds of miles across three states, fighting numerous skirmishes and several pitched battles with some of the finest British regiments, Greene's small southern army accomplished what most thought impossible: they had driven the British from the interiors of the Carolinas and Georgia. The British were left holding only the costal seaports of Wilmington, Charleston, and Savannah. Their outposts in the backcountry were gone, and their Tory militias and sympathizers were demoralized and in disarray. During the first six months of 1781, the Americans captured more than 3,500 British and Loyalist prisoners. General Nathaniel Greene, with only six years of military experience behind him, outgeneraled the best of Great Britain's officer corps.

VIRGINIA

After departing the Carolinas, Lord Cornwallis focused his attention on a new campaign in Virginia. With his own troops that had marched from the Carolinas and those from Arnold's and Phillips's commands, the British commander had a significant numerical advantage over his adversary, General Lafayette. Cornwallis set his army in motion in late May, marching from Petersburg to the south bank of the James, while Lieutenant Colonel Tarleton's Legion patrolled west along the Appomattox River. With a brigade of Guards securing the south bank of the James, Cornwallis's mile-long column began crossing the river on the 24th of May. Numerous flatboats and an assortment of other river craft were commandeered to ferry troops, supply wagons, and artillery to the northern shore. The army's horses swam the river behind the boats, guided by ropes. Despite the high winds, the crossing was completed in less than three days. After the river crossing, the British reoccupied Arnold's former encampment site on the Byrd Plantation at Westover.

After establishing his headquarters at the Byrd mansion, Cornwallis finalized his plans for a summer campaign. Anticipating General Clinton's concern for the security of the British base at Portsmouth, Cornwallis sought to assure his superior that he was attentive to that concern. He knew that he had already pushed Clinton's patience to the limit by leaving the Carolinas. He therefore sent General Leslie with the 17th Regiment along with two German battalions of the Ansbach Regiment to reinforce the base.

Meanwhile, Cornwallis proceeded to launch his own campaign in Virginia. It was designed to disrupt the functioning of local and state rebel governments, and to forestall the recruitment of additional Virginia militia. The plan also targeted the Virginia economy. Commanders were ordered to destroy or confiscate all agricultural products considered excess to individual family needs. This included not only food products, but also tobacco, the mainstay of the tidewater economy. Cornwallis also intended to drive Lafayette from Richmond, and prevent the Americans from linking up with General Wayne, who was marching toward Virginia with the reorganized Pennsylvania Line. The British commander hoped to force Lafayette into battle, but he did not intend to engage in a long pursuit of his adversary as he had done in the Carolinas. Instead, he planned to make maximum use of Tarleton's cavalry and Colonel Simcoe's light infantry to screen Lafayette's movements, and keep the rebel government on the run, capturing as many public officials as possible. His orders were that no paroles were to be granted to rebel political officials before he personally interviewed them.

As he prepared to launch his Virginia campaign, Cornwallis remained concerned about the vulnerability of the British base at Portsmouth. He voiced his concerns in a letter to General Clinton, writing, "The objections to Portsmouth are, that it cannot be made strong without an army to defend it, that it is remarkably unhealthy, and can give no protection to a ship of the line." In the same letter, he wrote that he was, "inclined to think well of York" [Yorktown] as an alternative site for a base.[10] Yorktown was situated on a bluff overlooking the York River opposite Gloucester Point, where the river narrowed to a half mile in width. At that point, the river was still navigable for deep draft ships of the line. To reach the proposed base from the sea, ships had to enter Chesapeake Bay, and then sail north to the mouth of the York River. Cornwallis believed the site was more defensible than Portsmouth, and was a healthier encampment for his troops. Benedict Arnold, who was about to return to New York, disagreed, arguing that Yorktown sat on at rather narrow peninsula that could easily be sealed off by the Americans and their French allies. Deferring a final decision on the matter, Cornwallis set off to locate and destroy Lafayette and his Continentals.

*   *   *

The British departed Westover on the 27th of May, and camped that evening near White Oak Swamp, just fifteen miles from Richmond. Later the same evening, British spies rode into camp reporting that Lafayette had abandoned Richmond and was marching north. Lafayette knew that his small force of 1,800 men was no match for Cornwallis's army, which outnumbered his force by almost six to one. Moreover, he knew that most of Richmond's citizens had already fled the city, and the legislature had relocated to the relative safety of Albemarle County. Additionally, few supplies and stores of military or commercial value remained in the city. He therefore concluded that Richmond no longer had any significant military or political value.

Lafayette made sure that the evacuation of the city's defenses was accomplished in an orderly and professional manner to forestall any panic among the militia and the few remaining citizens. Brigadier General Thomas Nelson Jr., who would succeed Thomas Jefferson as governor of Virginia, led the American withdrawal, riding at the head of his Tidewater brigade of Virginia militia. Brigadier General Peter Muhlenberg, who led the remainder of the Virginia militia, followed him. Last to depart were Lafayette's well-armed and splendidly uniformed Continental regiments.

The Americans marched north out of the capital in high spirits, keeping step with the beating of drums.

Although Lafayette's force was vastly outnumbered in men and horses, the American troops proved quite capable of stealing a march on the British. The Americans marched north toward Fredericksburg, some fifty-five miles away, where they hoped to rendezvous with General Anthony Wayne's Pennsylvanians. Lafayette's rather small force, unencumbered with large numbers of wagons and baggage, moved swiftly through the familiar hilly terrain north of Richmond, staying one step ahead Cornwallis's army. The Americans soon crossed the South and North Anna rivers and camped near the Mattapony River, thirty miles south of Fredericksburg. Lieutenant Colonel Tarleton's legionnaires, riding well ahead of the lumbering British column, skirmished with Lafayette's pickets, but soon withdrew to the British camp on the North Anna when Lafayette's men "stood to arms," daring Tarleton's green jacketed dragoons to attack.

Realizing that he could not overtake the Americans before they reached Fredericksburg, and concerned about an imminent link-up between Lafayette and Wayne's columns, Cornwallis decided to end his pursuit of Lafayette, and retire toward Richmond. The British commander was unaware that General Wayne was still far off, trying to reach the Potomac River and cross into Virginia.

After the January mutiny of the Pennsylvania Line, and subsequent discharge of a significant number of men, recruiting officers scoured the towns and countryside to fill the ranks of the remaining regiments. However, discontent was still rampant among those soldiers who were not discharged. Wayne quickly identified the most serious troublemakers, and in early May convened a court martial before beginning his march. Seven men were sentenced to die by firing squad, and each Pennsylvania regiment was marched past the bodies at the place of execution. Ebenezer Denny wrote in his journal that, "This was a an awful exhibition. The Seven objects were seen by the troops just as they had sunk or fell under the fire."[11] It was a hard but effective lesson. The Pennsylvania troops knew that Wayne was not going to tolerate any further disobedience or mutinous behavior.

General Wayne's six regiments of the Pennsylvania Line, totaling about 800 men, departed York, Pennsylvania on the 15th of May. The march south soon turned into a nightmare. As the men moved south into Maryland, torrential rainstorms flooded the roads, turning them into quagmires. There was no way for the men to dry out, and the column was barely able to march fifteen miles a day. A frustrated Wayne pushed his men even harder, starting each day's march well before dawn. River and stream crossings slowed the march even more. During one five-day period, Wayne's column covered a mere fifty miles. The Pennsylvania regiments finally reached the Virginia side of the Potomac on the 5th of June, and after a one-day rest they set off for Fredericksburg some fifty miles away. The weather turned sunny and the temperatures continued to rise, lifting the Pennsylvanians' spirits as they marched further south. On the 10th of June, more than a week after Cornwallis gave up his pursuit of Lafayette, Wayne's scouts located Lafayette's army camped on the Rapidan River.

While the Pennsylvanians were still on the march, Cornwallis received intelligence that the Virginia Assembly was about to convene in Charlottesville to vote on new tax legislation to fund a large draft of new militiamen. Another intelligence report indicated that Baron von Steuben, leading a force of Virginia militia, was moving to secure a Continental store of cannon, small arms, and munitions located at Point of Fork, some thirty-five miles southeast of Charlottesville. Cornwallis ordered Tarleton's dragoons and mounted infantry to march on Charlottesville to disrupt the legislature and take as many political prisoners as possible, including the outgoing governor, Thomas Jefferson. He also ordered Colonel Simcoe's light infantry, jaegers, and rangers to move against von Steuben at Point of Fork. Both forces were to strike simultaneously, and Tarleton had orders to support Simcoe after completing his mission in Charlottesville.

Realizing that the success of his mission depended on surprise and speed, Tarleton's mounted force departed Cornwallis's camp on the North Anna early on the 3rd of June. Tarleton's horsemen raced toward Charlottesville, seizing fresh, well-bred mounts from farms along the way. The horsemen were permitted only one break during their advance, stopping at a tavern for a breakfast meal on the 4th of June. John Jouett, a captain in the Virginia militia, happened to spot the British as they entered the tavern, and galloped by a shorter route to Charlottesville to warn Jefferson and the assemblymen. Forewarned, the Speaker quickly adjourned the Assembly before it could elect a governor to succeed Jefferson, and the legislators were ordered to reconvene in Staunton, Virginia on the western side of the Blue Ridge. His term having expired, Jefferson hastened to his estate at Monticello to move his family to safety. Bundling his wife and two daughters into a carriage, he instructed the coachman to take them southwest, out of harms way, to an estate called Enniscorthy, fourteen miles from Charlottesville. Jefferson decided to remain behind at Monticello as long as possible.

Tarleton's dragoons soon charged into Charlottesville, scooping up the few assemblymen who had lingered too long. The British horsemen looted the town, destroying military supplies and burning public records. Thousands of the British prisoners of war who were held in a compound near Charlottesville were evacuated prior to the raiders' arrival. Another group of British dragoons galloped off to Jefferson's country estate at Monticello hoping to capture the famous American.

Jefferson was loading his saddlebags with his most valuable papers and family treasures when a Virginia militia lieutenant galloped up to warn him that the British were already riding up the winding road leading to his hilltop mansion. Wasting no time, Jefferson put his spurs to his favorite thoroughbred stallion, Caractacus. Jumping over hedges and fences, he soon reached the nearby woods and bridle paths. He followed the same road taken by the carriage that carried his wife and daughters to safety. It was one of the most dramatic and narrowest escapes of the war. The British dragoons looted Jefferson's wine cellar, and scared the dickens out of the estate's few remaining slaves, but they did not destroy or plunder the home. Since he no longer had any official status, his term as governor having expired, Jefferson placed priority on the safety of his family. After overtaking their carriage, he escorted his wife and daughters to the home of a friend some forty miles to the southwest of Charlottesville, well out of British reach.

Lieutenant Colonel Simcoe's mission to capture the armaments guarded by General von Steuben's militia was somewhat more successful than Tarleton's raid on Charlottesville. Surprised by the sudden appearance of the British, von Steuben ordered the poorly trained militia to withdraw, leaving behind a 30-man rear guard. Simcoe's men promptly killed or captured the entire rear guard, and destroyed the materials in the depot. The British pushed the American heavy cannon into the Rivanna River.

After destroying the depot, Simcoe's force rejoined Cornwallis's main army.

As Jefferson fled with his family, Cornwallis marched west to another Jefferson-owned plantation, Elk Hill, located about thirty miles southeast of Charlottesville. Cornwallis's army, numbering around 7,000 men, established camp in the corn and tobacco fields around the manor house where their commander established his headquarters. After establishing camp, Cornwallis sent raiding parties across the Piedmont to forage for food and plunder, and terrorize the citizenry. Having suffered little during the first six years of the war, the citizens of Virginia suddenly found themselves at the epicenter of the conflict.

As the Virginia Assembly convened in Staunton, frontier militiamen gathered to defend the gaps in the Blue Ridge to prevent the British raiders from ravaging the Shenandoah Valley. The British never ventured across the Blue Ridge, but they showed no restraint in ravaging the countryside around Elk Hill. Barns filled with hay and corn were burned, livestock was stolen, and young horses were slaughtered to prevent their future use by the American cavalry. In addition, hundreds of slaves were persuaded to leave their owner's plantations and follow the British army, hoping to gain their freedom.

When Cornwallis learned that Wayne's Pennsylvanians had joined Lafayette's army, he began a withdrawal toward Richmond. By the 16th of June, the British were once again marching into the capitol. Still short of cavalry and awaiting more reinforcements from the north, Lafayette kept his distance from the British. Meanwhile, Brigadier Generals Daniel Morgan and William Campbell were marching to join Lafayette's force, bringing with them nearly 600 experienced Virginia riflemen, all mounted. With his army growing in numbers by the day, Lafayette knew that time was on his side, and he waited for Cornwallis to make the next move.

While Cornwallis claimed that his campaign was a huge success, based on the quantities of military stores and tobacco that he had either destroyed or captured, he had achieved little of strategic value. In fact, the campaign had made the British situation even worse. As a result of Cornwallis's invasion, Virginia mobilized increasing numbers of militia, and the number of new enlistments continued to rise. With the addition of new militia, Lafayette's strength continued to grow. Moreover, Cornwallis's campaign had failed to stop the flow of supplies and troops to Greene's army in South

Carolina. Making matters worse, Cornwallis soon received orders from General Clinton to send 3,000 troops, almost half of his army, to New York. He had no choice but to comply. On the 21st of June, Cornwallis departed Richmond and marched his army in the sweltering June heat toward Williamsburg on the low-lying Tidewater peninsula.

PEACE NEGOTIATIONS

As the tempo of military operations continued to increase during the first six months of 1781, the Continental Congress debated a very divisive issue: under what terms and conditions would America agree to open peace negotiations with Britain? Congress began discussions of the issue in February, at the prompting of the French Minister to the United States, Chevalier de la Luzerne, who was acting on the orders of France's Foreign Minister, Vergennes.

France and her allies were struggling to find a way out of the seemingly endless and expensive war, and there was open talk in European capitals of a peace conference between the belligerents. Russia and Austria offered to act as the mediators. Britain had sent diplomatic signals to the French indicating that Britain might accept a peace agreement if they could retain the American colonies that were under control of British troops at the time of the conference. Such an agreement would have meant that the United States might lose its southern states, leaving the new nation with only the New England and Middle Atlantic states. Britain might also have demanded control of New York City. While the Continental Congress had earlier rejected the idea of ceding any of the thirteen states to Britain, some delegates from the northern states appeared to be wavering on the issue.

Open discussions of the question heightened the suspicions and distrust of the southern delegates. The southerners feared that after six years of sacrifice of their states' blood and treasure, they were about to be sold out by their fellow Americans. The delegates representing the southern states knew that if their states were ceded to Britain they would all be forced into permanent exile, along with all southern Patriots who had actively supported the rebellion. Adding to their suspicions was the fact that John Adams, a New Englander, would be the American negotiator at the peace conference. To allay the apprehensions of the southern delegates and to demonstrate solidarity, Congress voted on the 15th of June to appoint a five-member peace-negotiating committee that included John Adams, but also added Benjamin Franklin, John Jay, and southerners Henry Laurens and Thomas Jefferson. Additionally, Congress instructed the members to stand firm on the issues of complete independence and national sovereignty for the United States, including all the territory of the thirteen states. Although peace negotiations would not begin for another year, Congress sent a clear message to the French that America would never accept the loss of any of its territory to the British as a condition of any peace settlement.

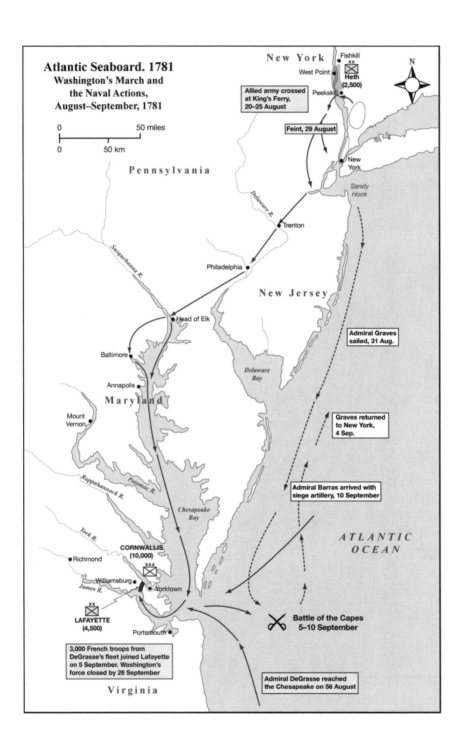

Atlantic Seaboard. 1781
Washington's March and
the Naval Actions,
August–September, 1781

0   50 miles

0   50 km

New York

Fishkill

West Point

Heth
(2,500)

Peekskill

Allied army crossed
at King's Ferry,
20–25 August

Feint, 29 August

New
York

Sandy
Hook

N

Pennsylvania

Delaware R.

Trenton

Philadelphia

Susquehanna R.

New Jersey

Head of Elk

Baltimore

*Delaware
Bay*

Annapolis

Admiral Graves
sailed, 31 Aug.

Maryland

Mount
Vernon

Graves returned
to New York,
4 Sep.

Rappahannock R.

Potomac R.

*Chesapeake
Bay*

Admiral Barras arrived with
siege artillery, 10 September

York R.

ATLANTIC
OCEAN

CORNWALLIS
(10,000)

Richmond

Williamsburg

James R.

Yorktown

LAFAYETTE
(4,500)

Portsmouth

Battle of the Capes
5–10 September

3,000 French troops from
DeGrasse's fleet joined Lafayette
on 5 September. Washington's
force closed by 26 September

Admiral DeGrasse reached
the Chesapeake on 56 August

Virginia

9

THE LION SLEEPS AT YORKTOWN

"In the afternoon, marched through the city of Philadelphia. The streets being extremely dirty and the weather warm and dry, we raised a dust like a smothering snow storm blinding our eyes and covering our bodies with it…Our line of march, including appendages and attendants extended nearly two miles. The general officers and their aids in rich military uniform, mounted on noble steeds elegantly caparisoned, were followed by their servants and baggage. In the rear of every brigade were several field pieces, accompanied by ammunition carriages. The soldiers marched in slow and solemn step, regulated by the drum and fife."
—James Thatcher, *A Military Journal During the American Revolutionary War, from 1775 to 1783*

When Cornwallis's army departed Richmond on the 13th of June, Lafayette shadowed his adversary at a respectful distance. By that time, Lafayette's army had grown to about 6,000 men, including 2,500 regulars, with the rest being Virginia militia, many of whom were mounted.[1] Keeping a distance of about eighteen to twenty miles between his main force and the British, and his advance guard closer yet, Lafayette waited for an opportune moment to strike a first blow at his enemies.

As Cornwallis approached Williamsburg, the former colonial capital, Lafayette learned that Lieutenant Colonel Simcoe's Queen's Rangers, reinforced by a force of Hessian jaegers, were returning from a foraging expedition along the Chickahominy River. Lafayette ordered General

Wayne to intercept the foragers before they returned to Williamsburg. Eager for a fight after his long march from Pennsylvania, General Wayne ordered Colonel Richard Butler's Pennsylvania regiment, reinforced with 120 mounted Virginia riflemen, to intercept and destroy Simcoe's force.

After a moonlit night march along the wooded lanes of the Tidewater, Butler caught up with Simcoe's regiment at Spencer's Ordinary, a nondescript tavern about six miles northwest of Williamsburg, on the morning of June 26th. Simcoe's troops had halted at the tavern to rest, feed their horses, and round up more cattle to join the herd they had already seized during their raid. Butler's advance guard struck first at one of Simcoe's foraging parties. After hearing the firing, Simcoe's cavalrymen leapt into their saddles and charged the American advance guard. In the melee that followed, several Americans were unhorsed by the saber-wielding British and subsequently taken prisoner. When Colonel Butler's Pennsylvania infantry began to arrive, Simcoe ordered his jaegers and light infantry to confront the Americans, while the cattle herd was driven off toward Williamsburg. When the British commander learned from a prisoner that Lafayette's main body was not far off, he hastily ordered his men to withdraw. Meanwhile, when Colonel Butler learned that British reinforcements were within two miles of the Ordinary, he ordered his troops to disengage and rejoin the main American force at Tyre's Plantation. Both sides claimed victory after the skirmish. Reports of losses on both sides vary, but a safe estimate would put the total casualties on each side at less than one hundred men. As a result of the skirmish, however, Cornwallis realized that Lafayette was no longer too weak and timid to strike at his army. Therefore, he formulated a plan to lure the young Frenchman into a trap.

In order to comply with General Clinton's latest orders to send 3,000 troops to New York, Cornwallis had to first cross the James River to reach Portsmouth, where ships waited to transfer the troops. Cornwallis knew that the river crossing would present an ideal opportunity for Lafayette to attack, since the British forces would be split and on both sides of the river during the crossing. Knowing that Lafayette would likely strike after most the British troops were across the river, Cornwallis devised a clever trap for the Americans.

On the 6th of July, Cornwallis marched his army toward a crossing site at Green Spring, near the site of the 17th-century settlement at

Jamestown. He then ordered Lieutenant Colonel Simcoe to begin the crossing, while the larger part of the army remained hidden in the surrounding forest. Lafayette's scouts soon spotted Simcoe's regiment strung out across the river, and reported that the main force of redcoats was crossing. Then, several slaves employed by the British were sent into the American lines to misinform Lafayette on the British dispositions. The slaves reported that most of Cornwallis's army had already crossed the James. Cornwallis's ruse worked like a charm. Lafayette took the bait, and ordered General Wayne and his Pennsylvania regiments to attack what he believed were Cornwallis's rear guards at the crossing site.

Dusk was fast approaching when Wayne's Pennsylvanians began to cross the narrow causeway that led to the site. British infantry lay hidden in the swampy cypress forestland on both sides of the causeway prepared to spring the ambush. Muzzle flashes and black powder smoke soon erupted from the surrounding woodlands. Wayne's men were strung out along the causeway and had little room to maneuver. Wayne saw that there was no route of escape, and led an assault on the main British encampment. His men came within few dozen yards of the British lines, temporarily throwing the enemy off balance. Lafayette realized that Wayne was trapped, and rushed forward with reinforcements. The furious fighting continued after sunset.

Josiah Adkins, a Connecticut Continental soldier, whose brigade rushed to reinforce Wayne's men, recorded in his diary, "The enemy were more than 6 times our number. . . . This notwithstanding, our troops behaved well fighting with great spirit & bravery." Continuing, he wrote, "The infantry were oft broke; but as oft rallied & form'd at a word: While the Pennsylvanians, when broken cou'd not be form'd again for action; by which they lost their *field-piece*, & we the ground."[2] Under the covering fire of the reinforcing regiments, most of Wayne's men managed to slip away in the fast approaching darkness, but two artillery pieces were left behind and captured by the British. Lafayette had two horses shot from under him, but he finally restored order among his regiments, and withdrew about five miles from the crossing site. In the twilight battle, the Americans lost twenty-eight men killed, ninety-nine wounded, and another twelve missing. The British lost about half that number. Despite his heavy losses, Lafayette tried to put a positive spin on the near disaster. Once

Cornwallis completed crossing to the south side of the James the following day, the Marquis boasted that he had chased the British across.[3]

After his army was safely across the James, Cornwallis marched the main column toward Suffolk, while Tarleton's Legion conducted a raid to Prince Edward Courthouse and New London located in Bedford County. The purpose of the raid was to destroy stores of arms, ammunition, clothing, and corn that were to be sent to Greene's army in South Carolina. During the 400-mile raid deep into southeastern Virginia, Tarleton's raiders found that most of the stores had already been shipped away. Tarleton later wrote that the quantities of stores destroyed were outweighed by, ". . . the loss of men and horses by the excessive heat of the climate."[4] Tarleton's raiders returned to Suffolk on the 24th of July, reuniting with Cornwallis's army. The British then marched on to their base at Portsmouth, and Virginians breathed a sigh of relief. For the first time in six months, most of the state was free of British invaders. In little more than four weeks, Cornwallis had relinquished control of the major portion of the state to the Americans. His army sat isolated within the defenses of their Portsmouth base on Hampton Roads. Given Lafayette's growing numbers, and his orders from General Clinton to send almost half his troops to New York, Cornwallis's options were limited. Having stretched General Clinton's patience to the limit by abandoning the Carolinas, he could not afford to challenge his Commander-in-Chief again. Henceforth, he had to comply with General Clinton's orders to the best of his ability, or face relief from command. Lord Cornwallis was no longer master of his own fate

WHITE PLAINS, NEW YORK

While Cornwallis prepared to cross the James on the 6th of July, some five hundred miles to the north, the American and French armies were united near White Plains, New York. After a grueling eighteen-day, 200-mile march across Rhode Island and Connecticut, General Rochambeau's French expeditionary force of 5,500 regulars marched into newly established camps in the lower Hudson valley. Rochambeau's regiments were among the finest in the French army. Equipped with the latest weapons, and clad in splendid uniforms of white broadcloth trimmed with green, and white pantaloons, they marched and paraded with an air of discipline and professionalism. Many of the French troops were combat veterans, and their commanders were superb and highly respected leaders.

On the day after his arrival, General Rochambeau reviewed Washington's army. A French commissary officer recorded his own impressions of the Continental force: "The soldiers marched pretty well, but they handled their arms badly. There were some fine looking men; also many who were small and thin, and even some children twelve or thirteen years old. They have no uniforms and in general are badly clad."[5]

Over the next several weeks the allies became acquainted, visiting each other's camps. Generals Washington and Rochambeau continued to debate strategy. Washington continued to insist on an attack against New York. Prior to his departure from Rhode Island, Rochambeau wrote Washington to inform him that Admiral de Grasse's West Indian fleet was scheduled to arrive off the American coast in late summer. The French general wanted to know where Washington intended the employ the fleet. Washington's response was ambiguous, suggesting that Admiral de Grasse should make his own decision based on the whereabouts of the British fleet.[6] Since Washington did not insist that the French sail to the waters off New York, Rochambeau seized the opportunity to advance his own grand strategy for ending the war. After receiving Washington's response, Rochambeau wrote to Admiral de Grasse recommending that he sail to Virginia rather than New York. On the 14th of August, de Grasse wrote that that he had departed the West Indies and would comply with Rochambeau's suggestion.

Washington did not reproach his French counterparts for undermining his preferred strategy, but instead accepted the *fait accompli*. The Commander-in-Chief agreed that the American and French forces would march south to Virginia under his personal command. In his return letter to Admiral de Grasse, Washington wrote, ". . . we have determined to remove the whole of the French Army and as large a detachment of the American as can be spared to Chesapeake; to meet Your Excellency there."[7] One of the most remarkable feats in American and French military history began on the 19th of August, when some 4,000 French troops and 3,000 Americans departed their camps in New York, and began their 450-mile journey south to Yorktown where they had a date with destiny.

Moving the combined American and French armies from New York to the Tidewater required an extraordinary effort in planning and execution. Washington's chief engineer, French Brigadier General Luis Du

Portail, planned an initial allocation of 3,106 horses and 2,132 oxen for the allied army's use during the campaign. Additionally, supplies and provisions were needed at points along the route; men and horses had to be fed. The commander-in-chief made a number of requisitions that had to be met to meet the combined army's needs. He requested that three hundred barrels of flour, three hundred barrels of salt meat, and ten hogsheads of rum be pre-positioned at the Head of Elk for the subsistence of the troops on their way down the bay. Boats to carry seven thousand men, artillery, and supplies down the Chesapeake were also required.[8] In addition to subsistence and transportation, Washington also requested sufficient funds to disburse one month's pay for the American troops before departing the Head of Elk. This was a solemn promise that had been made to the troops. Washington relied heavily on the newly appointed Superintendent of Finance, Robert Morris, to meet the army's needs.

Although he had only been in office for two months, Morris was determined to do everything within his power to remedy the poor condition of the army. One of his first actions after assuming the office in June was to arrange for the delivery of two thousand barrels of flour for Washington's starving army. In early August, Morris made a personal visit to Washington's headquarters at Dobb's Ferry to determine firsthand the army's needs. Morris held meetings with both Washington and Rochambeau to determine quantities and types of supplies and other arrangements that were required for the campaign in Virginia. He then returned to Philadelphia and began to make arrangements with the states and other public and private agencies to fulfill his promises. It was Morris's idea to rely heavily on private contractors to procure and deliver supplies and arrange transportation for the army as it moved south. Although Congress had authorized Morris to contract for the army's sustenance and transport, there were no funds available to pay the contractors. Therefore, he was forced to use some of his private funds and credit to pay for the services. When his personal resources ran out, contracting officers had to rely on the willingness of individuals and firms to accept interest-bearing Continental and state loan certificates, and promissory notes that would be paid at some future date.

Robert Morris had many plans for the organization of the nation's finances, but he gave first priority to moving the American and French armies from New York to Virginia, and provisioning them during what was expected to be a long campaign. Without his immediate attention and dedication to solving the army's logistical problems, it is doubtful that the allied army would have reached Virginia in time to achieve a decisive victory at Yorktown.

With Morris in charge of procuring supplies and transportation, Washington's Quartermaster General, Colonel Thomas Pickering, and his staff were busy reconnoitering and selecting roads, bridges, ferry crossings, fording sites, and campsites for the American and French forces. After Washington informed his staff of the precise date when the army would begin marching south, Pickering and his staff had only four days lead time to begin their daunting task of selecting the best routes of march for the American and French units. Once the movement began, the Quartermaster General or his deputy would issue each day's marching order, no later than 4:00 a.m. The order included specific instructions for each marching unit, prescribing roads, crossing sites, and camp sites that were to be used. Since Washington's Continentals had spent years marching across New Jersey, southeastern Pennsylvania, Maryland, and Delaware, and were very familiar with the roads, only a minimum of instructions and details were necessary. On the other hand, special attention and detailed instructions had to be given to the French units that had no familiarity with the geography and terrain.

Although most of the Continentals marched south, Washington knew that he could not leave the strategic Hudson corridor unguarded. A sufficient number of troops had to remain to prevent the British from launching an offensive from their secure base in New York City, or an offensive down Lake Champlain into the heart of the Hudson Valley. He therefore left General William Alexander (known as Lord Stirling) with a small force at Saratoga, and General William Heath with 4,000 men spread across the fortifications in the Hudson Highlands.[9]

*   *   *

When General Clinton learned that General Rochambeau's force had departed Rhode Island and was marching to link up with Washington's army north of New York City, he wrote to Cornwallis ordering him to send three thousand of his troops to New York, "with all possible dispatch."[10]

Clinton further directed Cornwallis to stay put in Virginia with his remaining troops, and locate and fortify a secure base that was readily accessible to the British navy. During the following weeks, Clinton wrote a series of letters to Cornwallis, each changing the orders given in the previous communication. One letter written in late June directed Cornwallis to take his army to Philadelphia to conduct raids on supply depots before marching on to New York. Within a week, he received three additional letters, each with conflicting orders. The first one directed that Cornwallis send an additional two thousand men directly to New York, while keeping the remainder in Virginia to build and defend a secure naval base on the Chesapeake. The next dispatch indicated that he should remain in Virginia with his entire army. Cornwallis was appalled by his superior's indecisiveness, but knew that he had to comply with the most recent directives that he had received. Fortunately, only a few transports were moored at Portsmouth so only a few hundred troops were able to sail north in compliance with Clinton's directives.

Clinton's lack of decisiveness was likely the result of the developing situation around New York. He also received conflicting advice from his senior staff and commanders, including Benedict Arnold who wanted to lead an attack on Philadelphia. Clinton also knew that as long as Cornwallis remained in Virginia, Lafayette's two thousand Continentals would remain to protect that state. If Cornwallis withdrew from Virginia, Lafayette would, in all probability, march north to join Washington and Rochambeau in an attack on New York. Moreover, the politically astute General Clinton realized that if he recalled Cornwallis and his army to New York, he would likely become the scapegoat for a failed British southern strategy and the loss of the Crown's southern colonies.

Clinton's directives to Cornwallis also restricted his operations in Virginia, and precluded his return to the Carolinas. The British Commander-in-Chief made it clear that Cornwallis's mission was to build and fortify a naval base on the Chesapeake, and be prepared to immediately sail to reinforce New York. Although Clinton suggested that Old Point Comfort might be the best location for a naval base, he left the final decision to Cornwallis.

During late July, Cornwallis ordered his engineers and navy advisors to examine Old Point Comfort and the channels adjoining it to determine its suitability for a base. Point Comfort is a narrow strip of land on the northern side of the entrance to Hampton Roads. The engineers examined the soil and scoured the surrounding terrain for building materials, while naval experts took soundings and surveyed the width of the channel and anchorage. The engineers and naval officers reported that there were major concerns with the site. First, an enemy fleet could easily lay off the channel, out of range of shore batteries, and blockade the base. The navy officers were also concerned about the shoals and sandbars near the main channel. After making his own trip to Old Point Comfort, Cornwallis decided that Yorktown, a village situated on a high bluff overlooking the York River was a better site for a base.[11] The river narrowed at Yorktown, but the channel had sufficient depth to accommodate the British men-of-war, and two marshes on both flanks of the town made any land attack difficult. Gloucester Point, a narrow neck of land that protruded into the river directly opposite Yorktown, was also a perfect site for a battery and fort. Since the river narrowed to less than a mile at Yorktown, Gloucester also offered a potential escape route for Cornwallis's army if the Americans sealed off the Yorktown peninsula.

* * *

On the 29th of July, Cornwallis set sail from Portsmouth with the 80th Regiment of Foot, leaving Brigadier General O'Hara behind to complete the evacuation of the town. After a four-day voyage, the British transports unloaded the troops of the 80th Regiment at both Yorktown on the south bank of the York River and at Gloucester Point on the opposite shore. During the following week, additional regiments arrived, and work on the fortifications began.[12] The evacuation of Portsmouth was completed by the third week of August. In addition to the troops, a large number of Loyalist refugees and liberated slaves were transported to Yorktown.

Cornwallis wrote to Clinton on the 22nd of August, estimating that it would take at least six weeks to put Yorktown and Gloucester, "in a tolerable state of defence." He also expressed concern about his army's lack of artillery, complaining that he had only four 18-pound cannon and one 24-pounder to defend the bases at Yorktown and Gloucester. In addition, he pleaded for more arms and provisions for his troops and refugees.[13]

Almost overnight, the small, sleepy tobacco port of Yorktown was transformed into an army camp with more than 7,000 troops and 1,000 refugees. The village's few dozen houses, its courthouse, and several churches were soon occupied by soldiers and refugees, with the senior British officers establishing their headquarters in the area's few mansions.

British work parties labored day and night felling trees in the surrounding forests, and constructing earthworks, redoubts, bunkers, and magazines. African-American laborers conscripted from Virginia plantations were assigned the toughest tasks such as digging lengthy trenches and wide ditches, throwing up earthworks and berms, and manhandling and shaping logs for the stockades, abatis, and fascines. The extreme August heat and smothering humidity took a heavy toll on all the workers. Despite the brutal conditions, British officers supervising the work pushed the men hard, and administered harsh punishments on those they considered slackers and potential deserters. Cornwallis knew that his army had no time to spare.

While Cornwallis redeployed his army from Portsmouth to Yorktown, Lafayette concentrated the American forces at Malvern Hill on the James River on the south of the peninsula, from where he closely monitored the British troop deployments. Washington wrote Lafayette on the 15th of August, directing him to keep Cornwallis pinned down and not let him slip away and return to the Carolinas.[14] Lafayette remained vigilant, keeping the British under close surveillance. His scouts and spies around Portsmouth and Yorktown provided precise information on troop movements down to the regimental and battalion level, as well as the progress being made on the fortifications at Yorktown and Gloucester. Lafayette was also diligent in quickly reporting the latest intelligence to General Washington.[15]

* * *

After departing their camps near White Plains, the American and French troops marched to Kings Ferry, where they began crossing the Hudson. It took six days to ferry all of the American and French troops and their accompanying wagons and artillery across the river. For the next several days, the armies marched in two columns, a few miles apart, in the direction of Newark. Detachments of Continentals stationed in northern New Jersey joined the army along the way, swelling its ranks. Civilians from the small towns and farms turned out to catch a glimpse of troops as they

Nathaniel Greene. Major General Nathaniel Greene commanded American forces in the Southern Theater during 1781, and was largely responsible for thwarting the British southern strategy. *Courtesy of the National Archives and Records Administration*

Benjamin Lincoln. Major General Benjamin Lincoln was compelled to surrender American forces at Charleston, South Carolina in 1780, but later commanded the American Right Wing at Yorktown and accepted the British surrender on October 19th 1781. *Courtesy of the National Archives and Records Administration*

Anthony Wayne. Major General Anthony Wayne commanded the Pennsylvania Line during the mutiny of January 1781, and later marched his command to Virginia during the Yorktown campaign. *Courtesy of the National Archives and Records Administration*

Thomas Jefferson. During his term as Governor of Virginia, Jefferson narrowly escaped capture by British forces during a raid on Charlottesville. *Courtesy of the National Archives and Records Administration*

Robert Morris. Known as the financier of the American Revolution, Morris's efforts to procure supplies, transport, and pay for the troops was instrumental in the success of the Yorktown campaign. *Courtesy of the National Archives and Records Administration*

Lord Cornwallis. General Cornwallis led the British Southern campaign during 1781, and surrendered his command at Yorktown, Virginia on October 19, 1781. *Courtesy of the National Archives and Records Administration*

Banastre Tarleton. Lieutenant Colonel Tarleton commanded British forces at the Battle of the Cowpens where he suffered a decisive defeat. Tarleton narrowly escaped capture and fled the battlefield with less that 250 of his men. *Courtesy of the National Archives and Records Administration*

Compte de Rochambeau. Lieutenant General compte de Rochambeau commanded French forces in America during 1781, and led the Left (French) Wing at Yorktown during the siege. *Courtesy of the National Archives and Records Administration*

Baron von Steuben. Major General von Steuben was Inspector General of the American Army and commanded the Second (Center) Division during the siege of Yorktown. *Courtesy of the National Archives and Records Administration*

Henry, "Light Horse Harry," Lee. Lieutenant Colonel Lee's Legionnaires were assigned to the southern theater of war during 1781, and fought at the battles of Guilford Court House, Augusta, Ninety Six, and Eutaw Springs. *Courtesy of the National Archives and Records Administration*

Daniel Morgan. Brigadier General Daniel Morgan commanded American forces at the battle of the Cowpens in January 1781, decisively defeating British forces commanded by Lieutenant Colonel Tarleton. *Courtesy of the National Archives and Records Administration*

Continental soldiers. *Courtesy of the Army Art Collection, US Army Center of Military History*

Continental officers of Nathaniel Greene's southern army.
Courtesy of the Army Art Collection, US Army Center of Military History

William Augustine Washington. Colonel Washington led the American mounted forces during the Battle of the Cowpens where he routed the mounted British forces.
Courtesy of the National Archives and Records Administration

The Continental Line, Guilford Courthouse.
Courtesy of the Army Art Collection, US Army Center of Military History

General Washington waves to French General Rochambeau aboard ship on the Delaware River during the deployment to Yorktown. *Courtesy of the Army Art Collection, US Army Center of Military History*

Battle of the Virginia Capes. *Courtesy of the US Navy*

Yorktown prior to the siege. *Courtesy of the Colonial National Historical Park, NPS*

View of the west end of Mainstreet, Yorktown. *Courtesy of the Colonial National Historical Park, NPS*

Preparation of siege materials, Yorktown. *Courtesy of the Colonial National Historical Park, NPS*

American troops construct earthworks and fortifications, Yorktown.
Courtesy of the Colonial National Historical Park, NPS

General Washington meets with his senior American and French commanders at his field headquarters during the siege of Yorktown. *Courtesy of the Colonial National Historical Park, NPS*

American troops digging the first parallel under the cover of darkness during the siege of Yorktown. *Courtesy of the Colonial National Historical Park, NPS*

British officers observe allied siege line from a British artillery battery in the Hornwork during the siege of Yorktown. *Courtesy of the Colonial National Historical Park, NPS*

The American Battery, Yorktown. *Courtesy of the Colonial National Military Park, NPS*

French artillery park at Yorktown. Siege artillery was parked behind the allied lines until fortified artillery battery positions were constructed along the siege lines.
Courtesy of the Colonial National Historical Park, NPS

The Grand French Battery, Yorktown. *Courtesy of the Colonial National Historical Park, NPS*

Redoubt 9 Yorktown, Virginia. This redoubt was captured by French grenadiers and chasseurs from the Regiment Gatenois and Regiment Royal Deux Ponts on October 12, 1781. *Courtesy of the Colonial National Historical Park, NPS*

General Washington receives French officers at his Mount Vernon plantation during the deployment of allied forces from New York to Yorktown, Virginia. *Courtesy of the National Archives and Records Administration*

Moore House, Yorktown. British and allied officers met at the Moore House met to negotiate the final terms for the British surrender. *Courtesy of the Colonial National Historical Park, NPS*

The home of Governor Thomas Nelson, Yorktown.
Courtesy of the Colonial National Historical Park, NPS

Capture of Yorktown. *Courtesy of the National Archives and Records Administration*

The Battle of Eutaw Springs. Colonel William Washington's cavalry assaults the British strongpoint around the Roche Plantation house.
Courtesy of the National Archives and Records Administration

British troops march to surrender their arms during the Yorktown surrender ceremony.
Courtesy of the Colonial National Historical Park, NPS

The Surrender Road, Yorktown. *Courtesy of the Colonial National Historical Park, NPS*

marched along the dusty roads. There is little doubt that there were Tories and British spies among them, who promptly reported on the progress of the armies and their direction of march.

Washington kept the final destination of the allied troops under a veil of secrecy, entrusting the information only to a small handful of trusted staff officers and his most senior commanders. To deceive the British, Washington developed an elaborate deception plan. He had an extensive encampment laid out in New Jersey opposite Staten Island. Large ovens for baking were constructed to give the impression that a large body of troops would soon occupy the camp.[16] Washington also ordered boats to be built to give the impression that he intended to ferry the allied troops to Staten Island. Additionally, false rumors and misinformation were leaked to the troops knowing full well that British spies and informants would pass what they heard on to Clinton's headquarters in New York. Washington's headquarters also fabricated correspondence which outlined bogus plans for a siege of New York, and made sure that the British intercepted these false dispatches.[17] British officers on Staten Island stared through their telescopes at the opposite shore, closely monitoring and reporting the enemy activity to General Clinton's headquarters. Generals Washington and Rochambeau conducted their own reconnaissance of British defenses around New York a week before their troops departed their camps along the lower Hudson, and the activities of the two commanders did not go unnoticed by the British.

At Clinton's headquarters, British intelligence officer Major Oliver DeLancey, Jr. and his staff worked day and night trying to pull together numerous reports from his spies and agents, and from the British outposts in New York and New Jersey. Clinton also received reports from the British navy concerning the movement of French ships off the Atlantic coast and in the Caribbean. He even knew that Admiral de Grasse's fleet was preparing to sail north from the West Indies in late summer. There were, however, some things that Clinton did not know. He didn't know precisely how many French ships would sail north, nor did he know their destination. Also, though he knew that Washington and Rochambeau's troops were on the move, he was unaware of their final destination. For the most part, the British Commander-in-Chief made prudent decisions during the summer months of 1781, with one major exception. When Clinton learned that the Allied troops had changed direction and were marching south toward Trenton and Philadelphia, he still had sufficient time to either reinforce Cornwallis's army at Yorktown or evacuate the British troops from Virginia. He did neither.

*   *   *

By the 30th of August, the vanguard of the allied army was within a dozen miles of the Jersey shoreline opposite Staten Island. Most of the American and French troops assumed that they were about to lay siege to the British garrison there prior to launching an attack on Manhattan. However, when the American and French columns turned south, marching through the New Jersey countryside in the direction of Philadelphia, there was little doubt among the troops that they were headed for Virginia.

The Continental and French troops soon settled into a daily routine while on the march. Each day's movement typically began around 4:00 a.m., and the troops marched until they reached their next bivouac site. Usually the campsites could be reached by early afternoon. Thus, the troops were spared from marching during the hottest time of the day. After reaching the bivouacs, the soldiers were issued their daily rations, and were afforded sufficient time to prepare and consume their main meal of the day before erecting their tents or shelters for the night.

On the afternoon of September 2nd, American troops marched through the city of Philadelphia. James Thatcher, a surgeon in the American army, wrote in his journal that, "The streets being extremely dirty and the weather warm and dry, we raised a dust like a smothering snow storm, blinding our eyes and covering our bodies with it."[18] The senior officers and their staffs rode ahead of their units dressed in their finest uniforms, followed by their personal servants and baggage. The soldiers, many of them barefoot and clad in a mix of tattered military and homespun clothing, marched at "a slow and solemn step, regulated by the fife and drum."[19] Artillery field pieces and ammunition wagons rolled along in the rear of each brigade. Bringing up the rear of the two-mile column was a long train of wagons carrying tents, provisions, and other baggage, along with a few hundred camp followers, mostly soldiers' wives and children.

The following day the French troops paraded through the city, led by a complete marching band. Compared to the Americans, the French were well turned out, dressed in their uniforms of white broadcloth faced with green. The citizens of Philadelphia flocked into the streets to catch a glimpse of the elegantly attired French regulars. The French passed in review before the President and members of the Continental Congress and their own Minister from the Court of France to America, Anne-César de la Luzerne, before marching to their camps near the Schuylkill River.

While in Philadelphia, Washington accepted an invitation from Robert Morris to establish headquarters at his home on Market Street. During his stay, Washington was updated on the arrangements Morris had made for provisioning and transporting the army to Virginia. It had only been nine days since Morris had departed Washington's headquarters in New York, but during that period he had already arranged with Delaware and Maryland to provide fresh beef, salt, rum, salt beef, and salt pork, as the army passed through those states. Morris had also urged Virginia to furnish subsistence for the troops upon their arrival, and appointed an agent at Baltimore to secure boats and supplies to be placed at Washington's disposal. In addition, the financier was continuing to make arrangements to secure funds to pay the Continental troops from the northern states.[20]

After a day's rest, the allied armies crossed the Schuylkill and continued their march, passing through Wilmington, Delaware before continuing on to Head of Elk, Maryland. While he was in Wilmington a mounted courier found Washington and delivered the news the Commander-in-Chief had longed to hear. Admiral de Grasse had arrived at the mouth of the Chesapeake Bay with a fleet of thirty-six ships of the line on the 29th of August. On board the ships were over three thousand more French troops, who would soon land and join Lafayette's command. Washington was so thrilled by the news that he galloped off to Chester on the Delaware River to deliver the news personally to General Rochambeau. Rather than move overland from Philadelphia to Delaware, the French commander opted to sail down the Delaware River. As his ship was passing Chester, Rochambeau and his staff were startled to see the American Commander-in-Chief standing on the shoreline waving his hat and white handkerchief. When Rochambeau disembarked to confer with his American counterpart, Washington uncharacteristically embraced the Frenchman before passing on the good news that Admiral de Grasse's fleet was in Virginia's waters.

Upon his arrival at the mouth of the Chesapeake Bay on August 29th,

Admiral de Grasse sent boats and sloops carrying the 3,100 fresh French troops to the James River. The troops disembarked at Green Springs and joined Lafayette's force. The landings were completed on September 3rd. Meanwhile, Admiral de Grasse's fleet remained off Hampton Roads await-ing the arrival of French Admiral de Barras's squadron from the north. De Barras had sailed from Newport, Rhode Island on August 25th, with the French siege train embarked. When the British learned that de Barras's squadron had departed Newport, British Admiral Graves set sail from New York hoping to intercept the French ships before they reached the Chesa-peake. Graves was unaware that de Grasse's fleet had already arrived in the Chesapeake from the West Indies.

When the British fleet arrived off Virginia's Cape Henry at the entrance to the Chesapeake on the 5th of September, Admiral Graves was startled to see the sails of a French fleet of twenty-six ships anchored just inside the Bay. The French outnumbered and outgunned the British, and could have easily prevented them from entering the Chesapeake, but Admiral de Grasse chose instead to sail out to engage the British fleet at sea. He was concerned that Admiral de Barras's squadron would not be able to slip past the British fleet and enter the Bay.

Admiral De Grasse ordered his fleet to weigh anchor about noon, and all hands were ordered to prepare for action. The fleet was underway in less than an hour. As the French ships sailed toward the mouth of the Chesapeake, Admiral Graves ordered his nineteen warships to sail south-west toward Cape Henry, where they formed a line of battle to engage the French as they exited the Chesapeake. There followed the largest and most important naval battle of the American Revolution. Nineteen British and twenty-four French ships were engaged. The battle raged for four hours with furious cannonades that damaged most of the ships on both sides. A shift in wind direction during the battle made it difficult to maintain the battle lines, but both sides suffered significant damage to their ships and crews. The French gunners were particularly accurate in targeting the British masts, topsails, and rigging. The firing continued until around 6:30 p.m. No ships were taken or sunk, but several were severely damaged, including the British 74-gun *Terrible*, which had to be burned because she was no longer seaworthy. Casualties on both sides were horrific. Approxi-mately 200 French sailors were killed or wounded, while the British suffered some 350 casualties. During the sea battle, Admiral Barras's squadron arrived with the army's siege equipment on board, and slipped unnoticed into Chesapeake Bay. At the conclusion of the engagement, the French maintained their advantage in ships and guns, and after a week of maneuvering in the Atlantic off the Virginia Capes, neither side was able to gain an advantage. Finally, unable to reengage the British fleet, Admiral de Grasse ordered his ships back to the entrance of the Chesapeake, and on September 14th Admiral Graves ordered his battered fleet to set sail for New York.

Although neither the French nor the British fleets were able to score a decisive victory in the Battle of the Capes, the final outcome was nonetheless a strategic victory for the allies. Cornwallis's army was effectively isolated, with a still powerful French fleet standing by to prevent any British reinforcements or supplies from reaching Yorktown. Moreover, Admiral de Barras was able to deliver the heavy artillery required for siege operations. The stage was almost set for the climactic battle of the war.

*   *   *

While the British and French fleets battled off the Virginia Capes, General Clinton decided to launch a raid against New London, Connecticut. His reasons were twofold: first, New London was an active base for American privateers that prowled the waters off the New England and New York coasts; and second, Clinton hoped the raid would distract the American and French forces that were en route toward Virginia. Clinton selected Benedict Arnold to lead the expedition to Connecticut. After his return to New York in June, Arnold had proposed a number of expeditions, primarily directed against economic targets that would bring the Americans to sue for peace at any price. Clinton rejected most of Arnold's schemes, but finally authorized the raid on New London, which was a scant twelve miles from Arnold's home town of Norwich.

Arnold's force of 1,700 men sailed from New York and moved up Long Island Sound, arriving off the mouth of the Thames River on the morning of September 6th. At dawn, Arnold sent 800 troops ashore to attack New London town, while the remainder of the troops landed on the opposite side of the river to attack Fort Griswold on Groton Heights. As the British approached, Colonel William Ledyard, the American militia commander at New London, sent out an order for all militia in the surrounding area to assemble and confront the intruders. He then proceeded to check on the two forts that defended the town.

Fort Trumbull was located in New London, but there were only two dozen men to defend it. Ledyard ordered the fort's commander to fire one volley at the British, and then spike the cannon before abandoning the post. The British troops who entered the town met little resistance and began setting fire to supplies that were stockpiled in warehouses along the waterfront. A store of gunpowder in one of the warehouses exploded, and the flames from the blast soon spread to the center of the town. More than 140 buildings and homes were burned.

As the town burned, Colonel Ledyard made his way across the river to Fort Griswold, which sat on high ground overlooking the harbor. On that day only some 160 militiamen garrisoned the fort; however, Ledyard was confident that additional militia units were on the way to reinforce the garrison. When the British commander, Lieutenant Colonel Edmund Eyre, arrived at the fort with his column, he sent a message demanding that the Americans surrender. After holding a council of war with his officers, Ledyard refused the British offer and ordered his men to prepare to receive the assault. The British attacked the fort from two sides, and the assaulting troops were met with a hail of musket and cannon fire. Lieutenant Colonel Eyre, who personally led the attack on the south side of the fort, was badly wounded in the chest. On the east side, Major William Montgomery was killed as his men attempted to scale the walls. Despite the stiff resistance of the Americans, the greater number of British attackers began to prevail. Soon British infantrymen managed to scale the fort's walls, and hand-to-hand fighting began inside the fort. As the struggle continued, the British managed to open the front gate of the fort, and more troops poured in. In an attempt to prevent a full-scale massacre, Colonel Ledyard ordered his men to lay down their arms and surrender. The British, however, gave no quarter to the Americans. Ledyard and a number of his men were killed as they attempted to surrender. After capturing the fort and destroying its magazine, the British troops reboarded their transports and departed the area before the arrival of militia reinforcements.

The Americans lost 85 killed and 60 wounded in the battle for Fort Griswold, but British casualties were high as well. Arnold reported his total losses as 51 killed and 142 wounded. The bloody raid reinforced the hatred and distain that his former countrymen held for Benedict Arnold, but it did little lasting damage. The town of New London was rebuilt, and American privateers soon resumed their operations against British shipping in the sea lanes off the Atlantic coast. Moreover, Arnold's raid failed to distract Washington from his primary objective, the destruction of Cornwallis's army at Yorktown. Upon his return to New York, Arnold, fearing for his own safety and that of his family, petitioned General Clinton for permission to move to England. Clinton initially denied the request, but later gave his permission. Benedict Arnold and his family set sail for England, never to return to his native country.

* * *

After receiving the news of the arrival of the French fleet, the American and French troops under Washington and Rochambeau were ordered to step up their pace to reach Head of Elk, Maryland, near where the Elk River flows into Chesapeake Bay. An assortment of some eighty American and French ships and vessels of various types were waiting at Head of Elk to ferry the troops, baggage, cannons, mortars, and other ordnance down the Chesapeake to Virginia.

When the American troops learned they were about to embark for Virginia, there were rumors that some of the Continental troops might refuse to proceed until they received their promised one-month's pay. Washington was on the scene, and quickly sent off a letter to Robert Morris in Philadelphia, writing, "Every day discovers to me the increasing necessity of some money for the troops. I wish it to come, on the wings of speed."[21] After reading Washington's letter, Morris promptly dispatched Philip Audibert, Deputy Paymaster of the United States, to the Head of Elk, armed with a letter addressed to General Rochambeau. Morris's letter authorized the paymaster to receive French money on behalf of the United States, and promised that the money would be repaid by October 1st. Rochambeau had enough money in his war chest to cover most of the payment. He had the funds delivered to the American paymasters in kegs with the tops removed, so the troops could see that each keg was filled with French silver half crowns. Although Rochambeau had dispersed 144,000 livres to the Americans, Washington still needed $6,500 to complete payment of all his troops. Robert Morris managed to raise the money by using his own personal funds and credit, and borrowing from his friends. Every Continental soldier headed south received one-month's pay in hard currency, rather than the nearly worthless Continental paper money, and there was no further talk of mutiny.

On the 8th of September, the first contingent, consisting of 1,450 Continentals, was completely loaded and prepared to sail south, and the second division began boarding the remaining vessels. However, only 350 New Jersey troops and around 1,200 French troops could be accommodated on the remaining ships. The remainder of the troops, some 4,000 French plus their artillery, and approximately 1,000 Continentals marched overland to Baltimore, where additional transports had arrived. Rochambeau's second in command, Baron de Viomenil, refused to have his men board the transports, however, as he judged them to be unseaworthy. Instead, he decided to march his troops overland to Virginia. The Americans, on the other hand, boarded the transports and set sail down the Chesapeake on the 17th of September.[22]

On the same day that the transports carrying the Americans departed Baltimore, Baron de Viomenil received word that transports sent by Admiral de Grasse had arrived at Annapolis to carry most of his men south. The French troops then changed their direction and headed for Annapolis, where they were loaded onto nine French transports and accompanying warships. The convoy set sail from Annapolis on the afternoon of September 21st and arrived in the York River a day later. While most of the American and French forces sailed down the Chesapeake to the Tidewater, the supply train with some 1,500 horses, 800 oxen, and 220 wagons moved overland to Virginia escorted by cavalry units.[23]

On the evening of September 19th, the first Continentals came ashore at Archer's Hope on the James River, and marched to Williamsburg where they encamped behind the College of William and Mary. Four days later the French grenadiers and chasseurs landed at Burwell's Ferry, a mile below College Creek, and set up their camp near Williamsburg.

As September passed, more Allied troops arrived, and the British worked day and night on their fortifications at Yorktown and Gloucester. Cornwallis remained confident that he would be reinforced by troops from New York, but he worried that the French ships guarding the mouth of the York River would block any attempt to land the reinforcements. He therefore approved a plan to send fire ships downriver to set the French ships ablaze.

Shortly after midnight on September 22nd, the British fire ships, manned with skeleton crews and loaded with sulfur, tar, and rosin, sailed down the York River toward the guard ships. Two hours later, the crews of the fire ships sighted the French vessels and began to move silently toward them. Surprise was lost when the crew on one of the British ships set their vessel afire prematurely, alerting the French. Drummers on the French ships signaled their sailors to general quarters, and the watch officers quickly ordered their men to cut their anchor cables and set sail. Two of the French ships easily outdistanced the fire ships, but the third one only narrowly escaped. The ship suffered structural damage, and several French sailors were badly burned.

As the French ships sailed further down the bay, the crews of the fire ships abandoned their burning vessels, and rowed toward the shoreline. The fire ships continued to burn down to the waterline, and the burning hulks could be seen from Yorktown and far out into the Chesapeake where the main French fleet remained on station. While the mission was largely a failure, the French ships guarding the mouth of the York River began to take up new stations several miles further down the river.[24]

British spies continued to report the numbers of American and French troops arriving on the Peninsula, and Cornwallis knew that his opposition was growing by the day. He had under his command around 5,500 British, German, and Loyalist troops and sailors before the siege began. There were also between 1,500 and 2,000 African-Americans who were impressed by the British to work on the fortifications.[25] Although the British troops belonged to some of the most elite units of the British Army, they were no match for the pure numbers of allied troops that would soon be arrayed against them.

By the 26th of September, all of the American and French troops that had made the journey south were camped around Williamsburg, some thirty-eight days after they had marched out of their New York encampments. Rather than sail with their troops down the Chesapeake, Washington, Rochambeau and their principal staff officers rode ahead, arriving at Williamsburg on the 14th of September. Washington's party enjoyed a four-day break along the way, during which Washington played host to Rochambeau at his Mount Vernon estate near Alexandria, Virginia. It was the Commander-in-Chief's first visit to his home in more than six years.

After arriving at Williamsburg, Washington and Rochambeau took time to visit each arriving regiment. The two commanders also reconnoitered the routes to Yorktown, and met with Admiral de Grasse aboard his flagship, the *Ville de Paris*. The French admiral was ten years older than Washington, and a few inches taller. When the six-foot Washington boarded the Admiral's flagship, the Frenchman greeted him cheerfully, exclaiming in French, "*Mon cher petit general,*" much to the amusement of the French sailors and officers within earshot. Putting his vanity aside, Washington gave no hint that he understood, or took offense at the Admiral's greeting. The meeting between the ground and naval commanders was a productive one, and Washington got most of what he wanted. Admiral de Grasse agreed to remain in the Chesapeake until the end of October, allowing six weeks for the allied army to destroy or force the surrender of Cornwallis's army. In addition, Admiral de Grasse agreed to send ships up the York River past Yorktown to shut off any flow of supplies to Cornwallis. Washington made one more request. He asked Admiral de Grasse to sail to Charleston after his departure from the Chesapeake to assist in the liberation of that city. De Grasse informed Washington that he had orders from his government to return directly to the West Indies. After the conference, Washington knew that he had less than six weeks to bring his campaign to a successful conclusion.

As the last of the American and French troops poured into the Williamsburg area, Washington ordered the deployment of one thousand Virginia militiamen and a force of French cavalry and marines to the Gloucester peninsula to prevent any British breakout from that area. By the last week of September, some 19,000 American and French troops were making final preparations for the march to Yorktown.

10

WE HAVE PURSUED
THEM TO THE EUTAWS

"We marched to attack the enemy at four o'clock in the morning of the 8th. Our front line was composed of four small battalions of militia, two of North and two of South Carolina; our second line consisted of three small brigades of Continental troops, one of North Carolina, one of Virginia, and one of Maryland; Lieut. Col. Lee, with his Legion, covered our right flank; and Lieut. Col. (William) Henderson, with the State troops, our left. Lieut. Col. Washington, with his Cavalry and the Delaware troops, formed the body of reserve. Two three-pounders were in the front of our line, and two six-pounders with the second line. The Legion and the State troops formed our advanced guard, and were to retreat on our flanks when the enemy should form. We marched in this order to the attack."
—Nathaniel Greene

SOUTH CAROLINA—SUMMER 1781

After the siege of Ninety Six ended in mid-June, Nathaniel Greene's army rested and refitted in the hills of the Santee for the next six weeks. According to Colonel Richard Lee, "By the time Greene's army reached the high hills, nearly one half of the army was disabled by wounds or fever."[1] The hills border the north bank of the Wateree River, about twenty miles from where the confluence of the Congaree and Wateree Rivers form the Santee River. The hills are only around two hundred feet high, but that was enough to provide relief from the oppressive heat. The troops enjoyed balmy breezes by day and mild winds at night. Clear running springs and streams flowed through the hills, providing an adequate water supply for the troops, and groves of oak and chestnut trees provided shade from the midday sun. The Continental camps were clean and policed by the highly disciplined troops. Tents were pitched in orderly rows, latrines were dug properly, and trash was burned or buried. While a fair amount of time was allocated for rest and relaxation, the troops were drilled in early morning and evening sessions to avoid the mid-day heat as much as possible. Roll call formations were held four times.[2] The time spent in the high hills slowly restored the health and morale of the troops. Many of the men had come down with fevers and other ailments during the exhausting marches across the lowlands and swamps of South Carolina.

Greene took advantage of his time in the high hills to petition Washington and Congress, asking for more troops and supplies. He was convinced that the war would be won or lost in the Carolinas. Greene believed that Charleston was the key to victory in the south, and that it must be retaken as soon as possible. However, with only fifteen hundred Continental troops, and four to five hundred state troops, reinforced by perhaps another fifteen hundred militia, he did not have sufficient strength to mount a siege. By his own estimate, Greene thought that he would need another ten thousand troops to "reduce Charleston with certainty and dispatch."[3]

All the while, General Greene assumed that General Washington would launch an attack upon New York as soon as a French fleet arrived to support the American and French ground forces. After a successful attack on New York, Greene thought that the next major campaign should be directed against British-occupied Charleston. This would require the transfer of thousands of Continentals and French troops to the southern theater. He was dismissive of a campaign against Cornwallis's army in Virginia. In a letter to Washington, Greene wrote, "If the operations cannot be carried out in Virginia and here at the same time, I think Charleston must have the preference, as the greatest object."[4] In the interim, Greene's intention was to keep the British forces penned up in Charleston. He was determined to swiftly engage and defeat any British force that ventured out of the city.

* * *

While the Continental army recuperated in the high hills, South Carolina state troops and militia kept the pressure on the British. In general, the South Carolinians, and in particular Francis Marion's men, were, "habituated to the swamps of the Pedee and were less affected by the prevailing fever," and were quite capable of keeping the pressure on the British, during the dog days of summer.[5] General Greene, therefore ordered General Thomas Sumter, supported by General Marion and Lieutenant Colonel Lee's Legionnaires, to continue operations in the low country to deprive the British of supplies and safe havens.[6] On the 17th of July, Sumter ordered his forces to pursue a British raiding force commanded by Colonel John Coates. Lee's cavalry led the way followed by Sumter's and Marion's militias. Lee's cavalry caught up with the British at Quimby Bridge. His horsemen galloped across the bridge to Shubrick's plantation, where the British had set up a strong defensive position supported by a howitzer. Lee and Marion decided that the position was too strong to assault, and began to withdraw. When Sumter arrived with his infantry, he ignored the advice of Marion and Lee, and ordered an attack. The British repulsed the attack, and the Americans suffered heavy losses, but the British withdrew to Charleston after the short engagement.

While Greene's Continentals rested in the high hills, British troops suffered in the suffocating summer heat and humidity in the low country surrounding Charleston. One of the many soldiers who fell ill that summer was the British commander, Lord Rawdon. Worn out after six years of hard campaigning, the twenty-seven-year-old Rawdon was no longer able to endure the sweltering climate. In July, he was forced to give up command of British troops in the Carolinas and return to England. His replacement was the forty-two-year-old veteran, Lieutenant Colonel Alexander Stewart, who arrived from Ireland in early June. Stuart brought with him the 3d, 19th, and 30th Regiments of Foot.

After his arrival, Stewart was anxious to resume offensive military operations in the interior. However, heavy rains throughout the month of July restricted overland movement in South Carolina, and it was not until early August that British troops were able to venture out of Charleston in force. Lieutenant Colonel Stewart marched from Charleston in mid-August with some 2,200 troops, including four regiments of British regulars, in search of Greene's army. Stewart marched his troops to the south of the Congaree River near where Fort Motte had stood. From his camp on the Patriot Colonel Thompson's plantation, Stewart was within a dozen miles of Greene's camp in the high hills, but a large body of water, created by the heavy rains and flooding of the Wateree and Congaree Rivers, separated the two armies.

When Greene learned that Stewart was within a few miles southeast of his camp, he saw an opportunity to pounce on his enemy. However, to get at the British, Greene had to cross either the Santee River or the Wateree River. The most direct route was to march downstream along the east bank of the Santee and cross at Nelson's Ferry. However, the approaches to the ferry were flooded, and Greene decided to take an alternate route. His army would first march northwest crossing the Wateree near Camden, and then turn south toward the Congaree River. After his troops reached the Congaree, Greene planned to cross at Friday's Ferry, and then attack the British camp. It was a more circuitous route, but Greene saw it as an added advantage. By first marching toward Camden, it would appear that he was moving away from the British. Additionally, it would provide additional time for Francis Marion to assemble his troops and join in the battle.

After forcing the British from Georgetown, Marion moved to the lower Santee to keep the British from foraging in the area to supply their troops in Charleston. There were abundant quantities of rice on the large plantations in the lowlands near the coast. On the 20th of August, Marion marched his men to the Edisto River to prepare an ambush for a body of troops led by Loyalist Major Thomas Fraser, who had earlier captured Patriot Colonel Isaac Hayne. The British subsequently hanged Hayne, and Marion had sworn to avenge the martyred patriot. When he learned that Fraser was leading a force of cavalry, supported by infantry and artillery, on a foraging expedition near Colonel Hayne's plantation, Marion took action. He established an ambush position at the end of a long causeway, and had a few of his men lure the British cavalry into charging down the causeway outdistancing their infantry and artillery support. Fraser's horsemen rode right into Marion's ambush. After killing and driving off most of the British cavalry, the Americans turned their attention to Fraser's infantry and artillery. All of the artillerymen were either killed or wounded before they could bring their cannon to bear on Marion's men, and the infantry were scattered. The British losses were reported as 125 killed, along with a great number of wounded. Marion reported that he had only one private killed and two wounded in the fight.[7]

Before dawn on the 23d of August, Greene's army marched northwest out of the high hills toward Camden. The army moved at a slow but deliberate pace. Greene hoped to preserve the strength of his army and minimize heat-related injuries by marching in the early morning and evening hours. After reaching Camden, the army crossed the Wateree and continued south along the Congaree. As the army neared Friday's Ferry on August 27th, he learned that the British were no longer at Thompson's Plantation. They had marched back in the direction of Charleston, halting at Eutaw Springs some sixty miles from the city.

Like his predecessors, Lieutenant Colonel Stewart found the interior of South Carolina challenging and hostile. After marching almost to the center of the state, he had over-extended his supply lines and found it impossible to sustain his army with the scant resources in the interior. His army was also much weakened by sickness and the relentless summer heat. When Stewart learned that a supply convoy was marching from Charleston, and needed a 400-man escort from his command to provide security, he decided to shorten their route by moving his entire force fifty miles closer to Charleston.[8] Eutaw Springs was an ideal location for Stewart to rest his troops while he waited for the arrival of the supply convoy. The area had two fresh water springs, and sweet potatoes were in plentiful supply in the surrounding fields to supplement his army's meager supply of bread.

General Greene decided to follow the British to Eutaw Springs and attack them at that location. He was convinced that once he defeated Stewart, the troops garrisoning Charleston could not hold out for long. Greene's column reached Burdell's Plantation, just seven miles from Eutaw Springs, on the 7th of September. General Marion's force of militia and state troops had already arrived. That same evening, Greene ordered his troops to cook one day's rations, and he allocated each man a gill of rum.

Greene's feint toward Camden had lulled the British into a false sense of security, and they were completely unaware that a large American force was within striking distance of their camp. During the evening of September 7th, Greene and his subordinate commanders finalized a plan for a surprise attack on Stewart's camp early the next morning. Brigadier General Marion was intimately familiar with the swampy ground all along the Santee River, and Greene took his advice in planning the attack. Marion was a diminutive, taciturn, and somewhat introverted man, who held commissions in both the Continental Army and the South Carolina militia. He had been fighting the British since he was commissioned in 1775. After the American defeat at Camden, Marion took command of the Williamsburg militia, and launched a guerilla war against the British in the swamps of the Santee and Pee Dee Rivers. When General Greene returned with his army to South Carolina, Marion strongly supported Greene's strategies. Now, he was fully prepared to lead his brigade into battle under Greene's direct command at Eutaw Springs.

At 4:00 a.m. on September 8th, the American troops marched in four columns through the pre-dawn darkness toward the British camp. The night air was close and hot. Colonel Otho Williams, who commanded the Maryland Continentals, later wrote, "The troops were thus arranged in reference to the order of battle, in which they were to be formed on the field."[9] Four battalions of North and South Carolina militia formed the vanguard of the American army. Francis Marion was in overall command of the front line, and moved forward with one of the South Carolina battalions on the right flank, while General Pickens was posted with the other South Carolina battalion on the left. The center of the militia line consisted of two North Carolina battalions under the command of Colonel Malmady. The front line of militia advanced eastward on both sides of and paralleling the River Road. Three small brigades of Continentals, one each from North Carolina, Virginia, and Maryland, moved behind the militia under the overall command of General Sumner. Lt. Colonel Lee and his legion covered the right (southern) flank, and Lieutenant Colonel Henderson's State troops protected the American left flank. Colonel Washington's horsemen, reinforced by Captain Kirkwood's Delaware Continentals, formed the army's reserve. Two three-pounders under Lieutenant Gaines advanced with the front line of militia, and two six-pounders under Captain Browne moved with the Continentals in the second line.

During the approach march, Lee's Legion and Henderson's state troops moved on the flanks, and slightly ahead of the militia battalions in the first line. The British were at first unaware that the Americans were fast approaching their camp; however, complete surprise was lost when Lee's horsemen and Henderson's state troops encountered a small detachment of British cavalry. Two North Carolina conscripts had deserted during the night and entered the British lines warning Stewart of an imminent American attack.[10] After receiving the warning, Stewart sent a detachment of infantry and cavalry led by Major John Coffin to investigate, and warn the British foraging parties that were sent out each morning. In the misty predawn light, the British cavalry first mistook Lee's mounted legionnaires for local Patriot militia, and charged into their midst. It was a fatal mistake. Lee's men opened with a heavy fire, and the South Carolina infantrymen followed up with a bayonet charge. Four British cavalrymen were killed and several others were wounded. The survivors fled for their lives leaving the mostly unarmed foragers, who had been digging sweet potatoes, to the mercy of the Americans. Many of them were subsequently captured before they could reenter the British lines.

General Greene heard the firing, and thought that his army had made contact with the British advance guard. He quickly ordered Marion's militia battalions to form a line of battle, while Lee's legionnaires and supporting infantry withdrew and assumed their positions on the left and right flanks. Greene and his troops were unaware that they were still more than two miles from the British camp. The militia in the front line then advanced cautiously through the heavily wooded terrain, occasionally firing at panic-stricken British foraging parties. Alerted by the heavy firing, Stewart's troops abandoned their half-eaten breakfasts, and rushed into battle formations with their muskets, bayonets, and cartridge boxes. Officers calmly took their posts, while sergeants and corporals dressed the ranks. The long roll of drums reverberated throughout the camp as the regiments marched out of camp in the early morning sunlight. Colonel Stewart ordered a detachment of infantry to move forward about a mile from the camp to act as a delaying force while he formed his men and prepared for battle

The temperatures soared soon after daybreak, portending yet another sweltering day. As they moved cautiously through the dense woods, the Carolina militiamen squinted into the bright rays of sunlight that filtered through the tree branches. When the Americans approached the British line, they were met with volleys of musket fire. The British had established their defensive line in the woods about two hundred yards west of their camp. Their line extended from Eutaw Creek in the north to beyond the Congaree Road in the south. Behind the British line, the woods opened into cultivated fields. Near the head of a creek that flowed to the Santee River stood a large two-story brick plantation house owned by Patrick Roche. The house looked out over a cleared area of about eight acres. A pallisaded garden was behind the house at the edge of the springs. There were also several outbuildings and a barn on the property.[11] The house and the surrounding area became the center stage of the battleground over the next few hours.

With the sun at their backs, the British infantrymen continued firing at the American militiamen at short ranges, and the screams of the wounded and dying soon filled the air. A heavy cloud of black powder smoke hung low beneath the tree branches adding to the confusion and chaos of battle. Colonel Henderson's South Carolina state troops covering the American left flank came under a galling oblique fire from the British right defended by Major John Majoribanks's battalion. Colonel Henderson suffered a disabling wound causing some disorder in the ranks, but Colonel Wade Hampton, who succeeded to command, quickly restored order on the American left.

The Carolina militiamen on the American front line gave a good account of themselves, but the superior firepower of the British regulars began to take a heavy toll among the Americans. The center militia brigade soon began to yield ground. Greene observed that the attack was faltering and quickly ordered General Sumner's North Carolina Continentals forward to support the militia line. Nearly all of the North Carolina Continentals were new recruits with less than a month of regular service, but as Greene later wrote, "They fought with a degree of obstinacy that would do honour to the best of veterans."[12] Soon after the North Carolinians entered the fight, Greene sent Colonel Otho Williams's Marylanders and Colonel Campbell's Virginians into action. Both attacks stopped the British advance, and in Greene's words, "The enemy was routed in all quarters."[13] However, the battle was far from over.

The American troops pursued the redcoats as they fled in disorder back through their own campsite. Meanwhile, Lieutenant Colonel Lee's legionnaires swept around the British left flank, and attacked them from the rear.

Only on the British right was there any firm resistance to the American attack. British Major John Majoribanks, who commanded a composite battalion with companies from the elite 3rd, 19th, and 30th Regiments of Foot, managed to rally his troops and establish a strongpoint around the two-story brick plantation house. Majoribanks placed his best marksmen in the house, which was impenetrable to small arms fire. Firing from the windows, the British could cover the entire open area surrounding the house. The remainder of Majoribanks's troops took up positions in the outbuildings and the pallisaded garden, while others found firing positions in the surrounding woods and blackjack thickets next to Eutaw Creek.

From their excellent firing positions, the British were able to keep the Americans at bay, killing and wounding a significant number. Colonel Stewart was able to rally more British troops, and quickly ordered them to reinforce Majoribanks's battalion.

After viewing the strong resistance on his northern flank, General Greene ordered Colonel Washington and his cavalry to charge the British strongpoint. It was a suicide mission for cavalry. Washington's horsemen soon became entangled in the dense thickets south of Eutaw Creek, and the British infantry emptied many saddles. Then, in desperation, Washington tried to circle behind the house and gardens and attack Majoribanks's men from the rear, all the while under withering British fire. Washington rode at the head of his troops, and was easily recognizable to the British marksmen, who concentrated their fires on him. The colonel's horse was shot from under him, and he was pinned beneath the dying animal. A British infantryman then rushed forward and began to bayonet Washington in the chest before a British officer intervened. Washington was taken prisoner and later evacuated to Charleston under the protection of General Stewart, where he recovered from the wound.[14] Only about half of Washington's cavalrymen survived the galling fire of Majoribanks's men. Further attempts to dislodge the British from their strongpoint with infantry and artillery were similarly unsuccessful. When Greene ordered two of his six-pounders and two captured pieces forward to fire on the house, most of the artillerymen were killed or wounded before they could fire their cannon.

After several hours of tough fighting under a merciless sun, discipline among the American troops began to break down. Those who had overrun

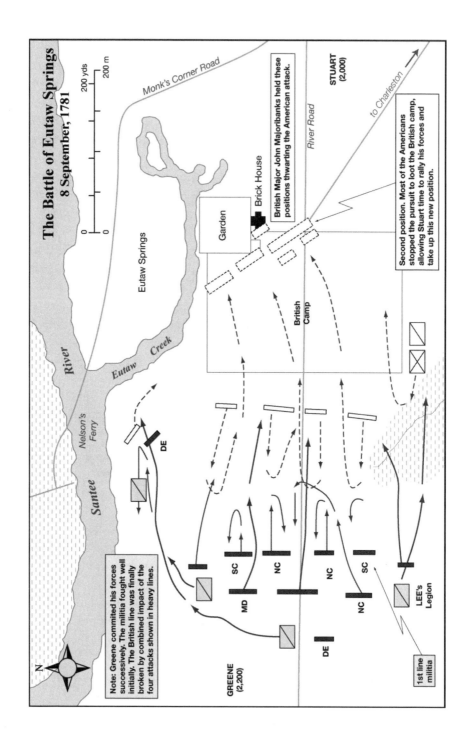

The Battle of Eutaw Springs
8 September, 1781

Monk's Corner Road

200 yds
200 m

0
0

Eutaw Springs

Garden

Brick House

British Major John Majoribanks held these
positions thwarting the American attack.

STUART
(2,000)

River Road

to Charleston

Second position. Most of the Americans
stopped the pursuit to loot the British camp,
allowing Stuart time to rally his forces and
take up this new position.

Santee   River

Nelson's
Ferry

Eutaw   Creek

British
Camp

DE

Note: Greene commited his forces
successively. The militia fought well
initially. The British line was finally
broken by combined impact of the
four attacks shown in heavy lines.

N

GREENE
(2,200)

MD

SC

NC

DE

NC

SC

NC

LEE's
Legion

1st line
militia

the British camp assumed that the battle was won, and began plundering the British stores of food, rum, and equipment. Despite the best efforts of their officers to restore order and renew the attack, the men continued to loot the camp. Soon the troops were too exhausted, and in some cases too drunk, to continue the fight. When the British launched a counterattack to recapture their camp, the stunned Americans were forced to withdraw. General Greene ordered his reserve battalion to cover the withdrawal. The unsuccessful assaults on Majoribanks's strongpoint, and the sweltering mid-day sun took the fight out of Greene's troops. After four hours of heavy fighting, Greene decided not to risk another attack and ordered his troops to withdraw to Burdell's Plantation. Once again, the Americans left the field in the hands of the British, who had paid dearly for the honor.

British losses at Eutaw Springs totaled 866 men, making it their most costly battle of the southern campaign. Colonel Stewart retreated from the battlefield toward Charleston the very next day, leaving behind 85 dead and more than 70 of his most seriously wounded, along with a large cache of supplies and weapons. In addition, the Americans had taken 430 prisoners during the fighting. The gallant British hero of the battle, Major John Majoribanks, died from his wounds in a slave cabin during the retreat, and his body was buried beside the road near Wantoot Plantation.

Overall, Greene's losses were fewer than the British. The Americans lost 561 men, including 119 killed in action, 382 wounded, and 60 captured. The Americans were able to recover all of their wounded except those who were under direct fire from the British strongpoint. However, numbers do not adequately describe the toll in suffering, pain, and loss endured by the American and British troops.

Eutaw Springs was the last battle of the war for thirty-year-old South Carolinian William Griffis. Born in the year 1751, Griffis first enlisted in the Army of the United States in 1776. He fought at Kings Mountain where he was wounded in the right shoulder and had a bayonet run through his leg. Griffis also fought in the battles of Ramsour's Mill, Cowpens, Ninety Six, and Guilford Courthouse, where he suffered a severe head wound. At Eutaw Springs he was wounded "in the lower portion of his bowels," and had to wear a truss for the rest of his life. Griffis had two brothers who fought at his side at Eutaw Springs; both were killed there. He was honorably discharged after the battle, having served for five years and having fought in almost every major battle fought in the Carolinas. At age eighty-five William Griffis was declared indigent and was awarded a pension as a Revolutionary War soldier. He had the scars to prove it.[15]

The battle also took a heavy toll on General Greene's major subordinate commanders. According to Lieutenant Colonel Henry Lee, he was one of only two regimental commanders who were unhurt in the battle. The other was Lieutenant Colonel Otho Williams, commanding the Maryland Continentals. The gallant cavalryman, Colonel William Washington, was wounded and taken prisoner. Lieutenant Colonels Howard and Henderson were wounded, and Lieutenant Colonel Campbell, commanding the Virginia Continentals, was killed. Lee later wrote that Campbell "received a ball in his breast, in the decisive charge which broke the British line."[16] The battle also took a heavy toll on the American junior officers. Six captains and five lieutenants were killed, and seven captains and twenty lieutenants were wounded. One of the bravest officers, Lieutenant Isaac Duval, who had been wounded leading the forlorn hope during the siege of Ninety Six, was killed at Eutaw Springs. According to one of Duval's men, the valiant lieutenant was shot, "as he mounted a captured cannon, took off his hat, and gave three cheers."[17]

* * *

When Stewart's shattered force began to withdraw toward Charleston on September 9th, General Greene followed with his army. Marion's militia and Lee's legionnaires led the way, harassing the British rear guard. However, Greene broke off the pursuit and returned to the high hills of the Santee after Colonel Stewart's column linked up with a British relief column led by Major McArthur on the morning of September 10th.

The battle of Eutaw Springs was the last great battle in the southern theater during the American Revolution. General Greene's strategic campaigns had driven the British from the interiors of the Carolinas back into their costal enclaves at Charleston and Savannah. After the battle of Eutaw Springs, the garrisons remaining in those cities were far too weak to resume offensive operations. Eutaw Springs did not, however, end of the bloodletting between the Patriot and Tory militias in the interior, or along the western frontiers of the Carolinas and Georgia. Bloody clashes and massacres continued for the duration of the war with the Patriots slowly gaining the upper hand.

The British continued their occupation of Savannah until July of 1782, and held on in Charleston until the following December. However, for all intents and purposes, North and South Carolina and Georgia were lost to the Crown for good after the battle of Eutaw Springs. Civil administration was restored under American governors, and legislatures were able to convene in relative safety after months of British occupation. Nathaniel Greene's strategic acumen and intellect were largely responsible for the American victory in the south. Although, he had superb commanders under him, men such as Daniel Morgan, William Washington, Henry Lee, Francis Marion, and Andrew Pickens, it was Greene's ability to make maximum effective use of the talents of these great leaders that led to final victory. While the troops that served under Nathaniel Greene were called upon to make monumental sacrifices, their general never wasted their lives needlessly, and he always looked after their needs to the best of his ability. General Washington's appointment of General Greene to command the American Southern Department was a stroke of genius, and was largely responsible for the ultimate failure of Britain's southern strategy.

PART 3

The Guns of Autumn

"I have the Honor to inform Congress, that a Reduction of the British Army under the Command of Lord Cornwallis, is most happily effected."

—General George Washington
October 19th, 1781

11

THE SIEGE OF YORKTOWN

17 October. "At daybreak the enemy bombardment resumed, more terribly strong than ever before. They fired from all positions without letup. Our command which was in the Hornwork, could hardly tolerate the enemy bombs, howitzers, and cannonballs any longer. There was nothing to be seen but bombs and cannonballs raining down on our entire line."

—Private Johann Conrad Dohla
Bayreuth Regiment, Yorktown, Virginia

After a twelve-day voyage down Chesapeake Bay and up the James River, Army Surgeon James Thatcher stepped ashore near Jamestown, Virginia on the 22nd of September. Transports loaded with French and American troops and artillery were arriving every day. From the landing place, the troops, followed by the wagons and artillery, marched through the town of Williamsburg to temporary camps on the outskirts of the town. The sleepy colonial capital and college town was bustling, as each arriving regiment paraded through the streets.

General Washington arrived in Williamsburg on September 14th and reviewed each brigade upon its arrival. The officers of each brigade then paid a courtesy call on the Commander-in-Chief at his headquarters. Twenty-year-old Ensign Ebenezer Denny of the Pennsylvania Line described meeting Washington at his headquarters in Williamsburg: "He stands in the door, takes everyman by the hand—the officers all pass in, receiving his salute and shake. This the first time I had seen the General."[1]

161

The red-haired ensign joined the Pennsylvania Line shortly after the January mutiny. Denny had a thirst for adventure that began in his early years. At age thirteen, he crossed the Allegheny Mountains alone, carrying important dispatches from Carlisle, Pennsylvania to Fort Pitt's commander, evading parties of hostile Indians along the way. Early in the war, he volunteered as a crewmember on an American privateer sailing out of Philadelphia to the West Indies. After joining the Pennsylvania Line, he marched to Virginia with General Wayne, and distinguished himself at Green Springs when Wayne's Pennsylvanians were lured into attacking Cornwallis's army as it prepared to cross the James. The young ensign took command of his company after all the other officers were wounded, and conducted an orderly withdrawal. Over the following weeks, he would be put to an even more severe test.

Another Pennsylvanian, Lieutenant William Feltman, was in his fifth year of service when he marched south with General Wayne to join General Lafayette in Virginia. Feltman participated in the defense of Philadelphia and spent the winter of 1777–78 at Valley Forge. He fought in the battle of Monmouth, and was present during the January mutiny of the Pennsylvania Line. Like Ensign Denny, Feltman fought at Green Springs and was wounded in the chest by a canister shot. After his recovery, Feltman rejoined his regiment and marched to Williamsburg, "a place he longed to see." He was curious about the French troops, and made it a point to visit their encampments on several occasions. He was impressed with their "soldierly appearance," and he later had the opportunity to meet General Rochambeau at Lafayette's headquarters. As the American and French troops continued to arrive at Williamsburg during the final days of September, Feltman found time to do some crabbing and play a game of billiards or two at one of the town's taverns. He was, however, anxious for a showdown with the British; he had a score to settle.[2]

Captain James Duncan arrived at Williamsburg on September 26th. The twenty-five-year-old Princeton graduate boarded one of the flat-bottom boats ferrying Connecticut Continentals from Head of Elk, Maryland to Virginia on September 15th. The flatboats ran into stormy weather off the mouth of the Rappahannock River, and several boats lost their masts and sails in the storm, delaying completion of the voyage. After arriving in Williamsburg, Duncan's company was assigned to Brigadier General

Moses Hazen's brigade in Lafayette's division. He had just two days to prepare his men for the march to Yorktown.[3]

Joseph Plumb Martin, of the Continental Corps of Sappers and Miners, landed near Jamestown after a long voyage down the Chesapeake in mid-September. A native of Massachusetts, Martin enlisted for the first time in June of 1776, at the age of fifteen. He later wrote that he enlisted because of the way the British had shot down his fellow Americans on Lexington green in 1775. Martin suffered the privations of the winter of 1777–78 at Valley Forge, marched through New Jersey, and fought at Monmouth Court House in June of 1778, and was present at the Morristown mutiny in May of 1780. As a nineteen-year-old Continental soldier, Martin would soon face an even greater challenge at Yorktown, but like most young enlisted men, he was more concerned with the gnawing hunger pains in his stomach than his own mortality.[4]

Twenty-five-year-old Sarah Osborn, wife of commissary Sergeant Aaron Osborn, accompanied Washington's army as a washerwoman and cook during the march south to Virginia. She sailed down the Chesapeake from Baltimore and landed near Jamestown, where she disembarked and traveled by horseback and wagon to Williamsburg, arriving two days before the army marched for Yorktown. Sarah was a strong woman who knew how to look after the men in her husband's company; she would need all of her strength in the coming weeks as one of the few female eyewitnesses at the siege of Yorktown.

*   *   *

Officers kept the newly arrived regiments under strict discipline. On the outskirts of the town, captains, under the watchful eyes of their colonels and generals, drilled the troops. General von Steuben, accompanied by his aides, was present at many of the drill sessions and maneuvers, casting a critical eye on the troops and vociferously critiquing their performance in a mixture of German and heavily accented English. In preparation for the coming battle, the army's Inspector General also ordered the inspection of all arms, accoutrements, and ammunition. By the 26th of September, the last of Washington and Rochambeau's troops had arrived in the Williamsburg area. The allied army numbered some 18,000 able-bodied men, all under General Washington's supreme command.[5]

The Commander-in-Chief organized the American and French units into two separate wings. The American Continentals and militia units were assigned to the right wing, which was organized into three divisions under the command of forty-eight-year-old Major General Benjamin Lincoln of Massachusetts. In addition to commanding the right wing, Lincoln also led the Third Division. Major General Lafayette commanded the First Division, and the Second Division was under the command of Major General von Steuben.

The left (French) wing of the allied army was commanded by Lieutenant General Comte de Rochambeau, and was organized into three brigades, each commanded by a French major general. Major General Antoine Charles de Houx, baron de Viomenil, commanded the Brigade Bourbonnois, and Major Generals Joseph Hyacinthe du Houx, compte de Viomenil, and Claude-Anne, marquis de Saint-Simon Montbleur, commanded the Brigade Soissonois and the Brigade D'Agenois, respectively. The left wing also had a separate infantry regiment and a cavalry regiment. The Regiment Touraine was led by Colonel Liamont, and Brigadier General Lauzun commanded the French Legion of cavalry.

Both the French and American wings had their own artillery, engineers (sappers and miners), and cavalry. The reserve, or second line of the army, was the militia division under the command of forty-two-year-old Brigadier General Thomas Nelson of Virginia. Nelson's militia division was composed of three Virginia brigades and Colonel Lewis's rifle corps. In addition to his military duties, Nelson was a signer of the Declaration of Independence, and the serving Governor of Virginia.

THE MARCH TO YORKTOWN

On September 27th, the allied army marched east from their camps around Williamsburg and camped for the night along the road leading to Yorktown. That evening, the Commander-in-Chief issued detailed orders for the 12-mile march to Yorktown. According to the orders, the march was scheduled to begin at 5:00 a.m. the following morning.

The American and French soldiers broke camp well before dawn on Friday, September 28th. After a cold breakfast, the troops assembled in marching order on the road leading to Yorktown. The march began before dawn with the American Continentals and French Troops formed in one long column. Leading the army was Lewis's Virginia corps of riflemen and Colonel Moylan's light dragoons. The army's reserve force, Nelson's militia, marched in a separate column behind the American and French regulars.

The day was oppressively hot and humid, and the dust raised by eighteen thousand marching troops made breathing difficult. The long column moved in fits and starts along the pine and cedar bordered road. Two miles east of Williamsburg, Nelson's militia turned right on the Harwood Mills Road and marched southeast to escort the army's supply train. The train had hundreds of horse- and oxen-drawn wagons full of provisions, supplies, tools, and other materials necessary for the siege.

The long column of American Continentals and French troops continued along the main Williamsburg-Yorktown Road until it reached the Halfway House Ordinary located near the midpoint between the two towns. A short distance past the Ordinary the road forked in three directions. At that point, the American and French forces split, with the French continuing on the main road that led directly to Yorktown, while the Americans took the center fork that led south toward Munford Bridge south of the objective.

By noon, the troops were drenched with sweat and a number of men fell out suffering from heat exhaustion and heat stroke. Many of the officers, whose mounts were needed to pull the supply wagons, marched on foot with their troops. After spending months in Rhode Island, the French troops were unaccustomed to the heat, and had to take frequent breaks during the march. One French officer wrote that, "We left nearly 800 soldiers in the rear."[6] Most of the American troops were more acclimatized, but still found it necessary to halt at least twice during the march, once for a noon meal.

Sergeant Joseph Plumb Martin, who marched with the Sappers and Miners, wrote in his memoir that his unit halted for a three-hour noon meal break. After the halt, Martin noticed that a nearby Pennsylvania unit had already lit a campfire, so he sauntered over to get some fire while his messmates made other preparations. While he chatted with the Pennsylvanians, he removed his waistcoat prior to lighting a piece of kindling in their fire. After returning, Martin noticed that someone had removed his pocket book from his waistcoat pocket. In all, he was out the pocketbook plus seven dollars, an enormous loss for any Continental soldier.[7]

Washington hoped to surprise the British by arriving at Yorktown before they could attempt a breakout, or intercept his army during the march. He therefore ordered that any attacks by British cavalry detachments and other screening units would be met with bayonets only, so as not to alarm the main British garrison. American and French advance guard units did encounter a few British cavalry detachments and pickets as they neared Yorktown, but there was no major British resistance during the approach.[8]

The French, having marched by the most direct route, arrived to within two miles of Yorktown by about 3:30 p.m. At that time, they encountered a British light infantry detachment that was guarding a working party. The British withdrew quickly, and a messenger galloped back to their outer works to warn that the allied army was fast approaching. Meanwhile, the French sent reconnaissance patrols forward to scout the enemy's defenses. As they emerged from the forest near the outermost British works, the French patrols were fired upon with grapeshot from a hidden battery and were forced to withdraw. Realizing that his troops were meeting increasing resistance, General Rochambeau sent his light artillery forward, supported by a group of mounted hussars. Reaching the advance guard's position, the guns unlimbered and swung into action, dispersing a group of British soldiers and killing a number of Lt. Colonel Tarleton's horses that were grazing in a field in front of the British works. The British outposts promptly withdrew to their Pigeon Hill redoubts that guarded a road running parallel to their outer works. The French light artillery continued to provide covering fire for reconnaissance patrols as they probed the British defenses. The scouts soon identified the major advance redoubts forward of the main British defensive line. Fusiliers Redoubt sat on a bluff overlooking the York River on the extreme right of the British defenses, and the Pigeon Hill redoubts sat astride the main road that ran west toward Williamsburg.

The American column moved along Grove Road that approached the Yorktown defenses from the southwest. The head of the column approached the British outer works shortly after the French. Here the Americans had a distinct advantage. Both the Commander-in-Chief, General Washington, and General Nelson, commander of the Virginia militia, were intimately familiar with Yorktown and the surrounding terrain. Washington's ancestors once owned much of the real estate in the area, and he had visited the area several times during his teenage years. Moreover, Yorktown was General Nelson's birthplace and former home. In addition to owning a home there, Nelson held title to hundreds of acres of farmland and forest-land in the countryside surrounding the town.

As the American column approached the British defenses, it veered off into an area known as Nelson's Quarter. Pushing forward, the column halted at Beaver Dam Creek, where the British had destroyed the bridges. Three squadrons of Tarleton's Legion were deployed about 300 yards to the Americans' front to oppose their advance. A section of four American light artillery pieces galloped to the front and took Tarleton's men under fire, while a party of engineers began to repair the bridges. Under heavy fire, Tarleton's cavalry quickly dispersed and withdrew toward Yorktown. During the night, the bridge repairs were completed, and General Muh-lenberg's light infantry rushed across before daylight. By the end of the fol-lowing day, August 29th, the entire American force had crossed the bridges, completing the investiture of Yorktown. During the crossings, the British fired occasional cannon shots at the Americans, costing one soldier his leg.[9] Captain John Davis of the Pennsylvania Line wrote in his journal that same day that, "This morning form'd a compleat investment round the Town and pitch'd our camp."[10] Sapper and miner Sergeant Martin, used more descriptive language to describe General Cornwallis's situation, "We had holed him and nothing remained but to dig him out."[11]

The British had worked hard to complete their fortifications, but they were still far from finished. The ground immediately in front of the inner works was cleared of trees and houses to provide open fields of fire, but work continued around the clock to improve the works themselves. The main line of defense consisted of a line of trenches and earthworks that formed a large arc around the town. Both ends of the arc were anchored on the river. Eight redoubts and eight artillery battery positions were spaced along the main defensive line. British seamen manned a ninth battery inside the perimeter. The cannon of that battery had been taken from British warships. Overall, the British had sixty-five cannon mounted on firing platforms within the nine fortified batteries. Two British frigates anchored in the York River provided additional fire support. Several addi-tional redoubts were situated a few hundred yards beyond the main British defensive line. Fusilier's Redoubt was located west of the town beyond York

Creek, on the extreme right. Redoubts 9 and 10 guarded the approaches to the extreme left of the main British line, and were located about five hundred yards east of the main fortifications. Two additional redoubts were located in an area known as Pigeon Hill. A distance of 250 yards separated the two Pigeon Hill redoubts, and each one guarded the main road that led west toward Williamsburg. Those two strategic redoubts were not as well constructed as the others, and were never fully manned by the British. Although there were weaknesses in the British defenses at Yorktown, both Washington and Rochambeau agreed that the fortifications were too formidable to be taken by an immediate direct assault.

THE SIEGE BEGINS

After the French and American troops deployed in front of the British outer-works, siege preparations began in earnest. Divisions and brigades consolidated their positions, and gaps between the brigades and divisions were closed or tightened to prevent a British breakout. The French, who had mastered siege warfare on the European continent, quickly erected three redoubts in their sector to protect against British sorties, and to cover all the roads leading into and out of Yorktown. Each redoubt accommodated 200 men and two four-pound cannon. To maintain communication between their brigades, the French cut swaths in the intervening woods and thickets to facilitate the patrolling of those gaps. French and American work parties were sent into the surrounding woods as soon the lines were established to cut timber and branches for fascines, gabions and abatis. Washington was concerned about the lack of expertise in siege warfare among the American units, and sent his chief engineer, French Brigadier General Du Portail, to oversee the construction of earthworks in each American brigade's sector. The fortifications consisted of a line of shallow trenches with firing parapets forward of each camp. Camp guards manned the trenches day and night to provide early warning of any British probing attacks.[12] Major Ebenezer Denny wrote in his journal, "Strong covering parties (whole regiments) moved from camp as soon as dark, and lay all night upon their arms between us and the enemy."[13]

As siege preparations continued, American and French reconnaissance patrols kept the British forward redoubts under constant surveillance, often exchanging shots with the defenders. Washington and Rochambeau also

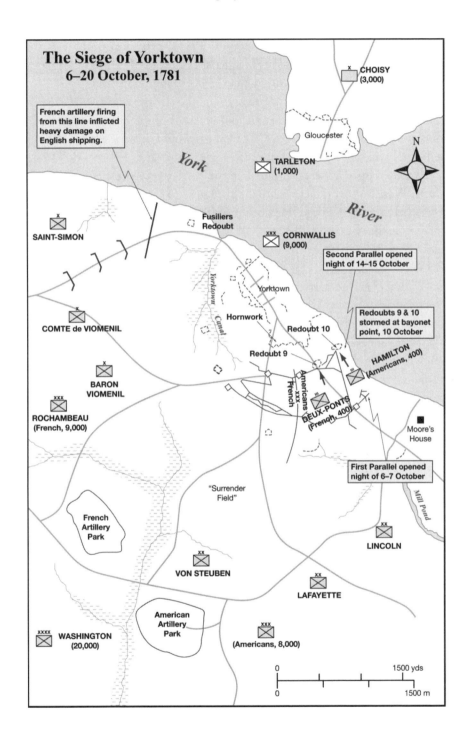

The Siege of Yorktown
6–20 October, 1781

CHOISY
(3,000)

French artillery firing from this line inflicted heavy damage on English shipping.

Gloucester

York

River

N

TARLETON
(1,000)

SAINT-SIMON

Fusiliers Redoubt

CORNWALLIS
(9,000)

Second Parallel opened night of 14–15 October

Yorktown Canal

Yorktown

COMTE de VIOMENIL

Hornwork

Redoubt 10

Redoubts 9 & 10 stormed at bayonet point, 10 October

Redoubt 9

Americans French

HAMILTON
(Americans, 400)

BARON VIOMENIL

DEUX-PONTS
(French, 400)

ROCHAMBEAU
(French, 9,000)

Moore's House

First Parallel opened night of 6–7 October

"Surrender Field"

Mill Pond

French Artillery Park

LINCOLN

VON STEUBEN

LAFAYETTE

American Artillery Park

WASHINGTON
(20,000)

(Americans, 8,000)

0   1500 yds

0   1500 m

came under fire during their inspection of the British positions.[14] Washington justified putting his own life at risk, claiming that the inspections were necessary for "determining a plan of attack and approach."[15]

Washington was also concerned about the British ships on station in the channel between Yorktown and Gloucester Point. He was convinced that at some point in the siege, Cornwallis would cross the river and attempt a breakout from the Gloucester peninsula, and Admiral de Grasse steadfastly refused to send his ships up the York River to destroy the British ships. Washington ordered Lauzun's Legion to Gloucester to reinforce Brigadier General George Weedon's 1,500 Virginia militia on the Gloucester peninsula, but he still wanted his heavy artillery moved forward as quickly as possible to begin a bombardment of the British works and the British ships.

When the allies arrived, Cornwallis knew immediately that his troops were spread too thin along the outer works to hold off the attackers. He therefore ordered the abandonment of all the outer works, with the exception of Fusiliers Redoubt and Redoubts 9 and 10. During the night of 29–30 September, the British abandoned most of their outer works. American and French patrols detected the movement, but by dawn most British troops manning the outer defenses had retired to the inner line.

On the morning of September 30th, Lieutenant Colonel Alexander Scammell, Washington's field officer of the day, rode forward to reconnoiter the abandoned fortifications. Schammel was 34 years old, a Harvard graduate, and an attorney in civilian life. Somehow he became separated from the picket guard that accompanied him, and he subsequently ran into a detachment of Tarleton's dragoons, who were covering the British withdrawal. Scammell was taken prisoner in the encounter.[17] It was later rumored that a British officer shot Scammell in the back after he was taken prisoner. Scammell's captors took him to Yorktown, where he was treated for his wound, and then he was issued a parole. He was subsequently evacuated to Williamsburg for further treatment of his wound, and died a few days later. Alexander Scammell was well liked and highly respected by his fellow officers and the troops he led. When details of the incident spread through the American lines, the officers and men were infuriated that the colonel had been shot after capture in clear violation of the rules of war.

*   *   *

The American and French troops moved quickly to occupy the abandoned British outer-works. The French also launched three ground attacks against the Fusiliers Redoubt, but were repulsed each time by defenders who were supported by the fire of the British frigate *Guadaloupe*, anchored in the York River. The star-shaped Fusilier's redoubt was the strongest of the British outer works. It sat near the edge of a high cliff overlooking the York River, and was protected by a ditch and two rows of abatis. The redoubt was defended by 150 troops from the 23rd Regiment of Welsh Fusiliers, and it remained in British hands throughout the siege.

As the Allies advanced toward the abandoned positions, British artillery kept up a steady fire, hoping to stall the advance, but the artillery had little effect. After entering the abandoned works, the troops began improving and modifying the fortifications. New firing apertures were dug facing the other direction. From the newly occupied fortifications, the Allies had an unobstructed view of the British defenses that were now within range of the American and French artillery. By moving forward, the allies were also able to shorten their own lines, thereby eliminating most of the gaps between the brigades and divisions, and making a potential breakout by the British more difficult.

Lord Cornwallis's decision to abandon the outer works may have been the result of a letter he received from New York reporting that three ships had sailed from Europe carrying reinforcements. Another letter stated that General Clinton planned to send a large fleet with a "considerable corps" to further reinforce the Yorktown garrison. According to the letter, the fleet was scheduled to depart New York on the 5th of October.[18] The abandonment of the outer works remained a matter of controversy in later years. Colonel Tarleton later wrote, ". . . the retreat to the fortifications of the town was a measure prematurely adopted."[19] Tarleton based his argument on the fact that the allied heavy artillery had yet to arrive, and the outer redoubts could not be taken without heavy bombardment. He further wrote that, "great time would have been gained by holding and disputing the ground inch by inch." And that Cornwallis's decision, "hastened the surrender of the British army."[20] Tarleton was correct on all counts. By abandoning his outer works, Cornwallis only tightened the noose around his army's neck.

*   *   *

On Monday, October 1st, Washington approved the final plan for the siege. The plan was primarily the work of his chief engineer, French Brigadier Du Portail, and was heavily influenced by the advice of General Rochambeau. The commander of the French forces was a veteran of fourteen European sieges, and was primarily responsible for convincing Washington to conduct a siege operation, rather than a series of direct attacks on the British defenses.

The plan for the construction of the first allied parallel made maximum use of the abandoned British fortifications. The parallel also called for the construction of four new infantry redoubts spaced at equal distances along the entire length of the line. A long series of trenches was also planned to connect the redoubts and batteries. The new parallel formed a large semicircular arc that was anchored on the steep bank of the York River on the far left, and stretched to Yorktown Creek ravine south of the town. The British defensive line was about half a mile in front the first allied parallel.

After Washington approved the siege plan, Brigadier General Henry Knox, American Chief of Artillery, and his French counterpart, Colonel Francois Marie d'Aboville, rode along the proposed line marking the positions for the American and French artillery batteries. The heavy siege artillery had not, as yet, arrived on the field. The heavy 18- and 24-pound siege guns and mortars were unloaded from vessels at Trebell's Landing on the James River, seven miles from Yorktown. From there, the heavy guns had to be dragged over a sandy road to the battlefield. A shortage of draft horses and oxen teams delayed the arrival of the heavy artillery and ordnance for several days.

As the artillerymen plotted their battery positions, Colonel Samuel Elbert, Superintendent of Materials for the Trenches, selected areas to create stockpiles. Fascines, gabions, and saucissons that were made behind the lines had to be moved forward to areas that were easily accessible to the troops who worked on the trenches and fortifications.

*   *   *

Within the British lines at Yorktown and Gloucester Point, living conditions among the troops and civilians worsened by the day. Anticipating a lengthy siege, the British commander ordered daily rations cut by a third.

Forage for the horses was also running low, and Cornwallis ordered the destruction of some 400 of the animals. The animal carcasses were then thrown into the York River.[21] Due to the cramped living conditions and lack of sanitation, diseases spread rapidly. The number of smallpox cases skyrocketed, both among the troops and among the numerous liberated slaves that moved with Cornwallis's army. Large numbers of African-Americans who were infected with smallpox were inhumanely forced to leave Yorktown. Many were left to die in the woods and along the roads on the Yorktown peninsula. The civilians who chose not to flee the town suffered as well. Many of the residents became homeless when callous British officers took over their dwellings. Others saw their homes torn down by the British troops, who used the timbers and wooden planking as fortification materials.

On Tuesday, October 2nd, the British unleashed their heaviest cannonade since the arrival of the allied army. Most of the fire was concentrated on the redoubts that were under construction. Surgeon James Thatcher wrote, "The enemy commenced a furious cannonade, but it does not deter our men from going on vigorously with their work."[22] The allies were unable to respond with counter-battery fires since their heavy artillery had yet to arrive, and their light three- and four-pound cannons did not have the range to reach the British batteries. The heavy cannonading continued for the next two days, but it did not deter Washington from making frequent visits to the front lines. During one visit, a shot struck the ground in front of the general and his party, spraying sand into their faces and filling a chaplain's tri-corner hat with dirt. Washington calmly turned to the chaplain and said, "You had better carry that home and show it to your wife and children."[23] Despite the heavy artillery fire, allied casualties were relatively light. However, some of the ordnance was deadly when it was on target. Thatcher wrote that one shot killed three men and mortally wounded another.

On Tuesday night, the British ships at anchor in the York River joined in the cannonading of the Allied lines. The purpose of the firing was to cover the crossing of Lieutenant Colonel Tarleton's legion and mounted infantry from Yorktown to Gloucester Point. Cornwallis wanted to strengthen the British force in the Gloucester peninsula for two reasons. First, he still considered the area his only remaining avenue of escape.

Secondly, he was concerned about the dwindling food supply for his men and the lack of forage for the army's horses. The Gloucester countryside was an excellent area for foraging, with an abundant supply of livestock, hay, and Indian corn.[24]

The British wasted no time in commencing foraging operations after Tarleton's arrival at Gloucester. The following morning, Lieutenant Colonel Dundas, commander of the British garrison, led the foraging detachments into the surrounding countryside, protected by Tarleton's legion and Simcoe's dragoons. By 10:00 a.m., the foraging parties had loaded their wagons with Indian corn, and rounded up a number of cattle and sheep. The foragers were headed back to the British lines at Gloucester when an officer of the Virginia militia spotted them. The officer sent word to General Choisy, the allied commander at Gloucester, who then ordered Brigadier General Lauzun and his Legionnaires to intercept the foragers. Choisy then followed the Legionnaires with Lieutenant Colonel John Mercer's select brigade of Virginia militia.

Lauzun's men soon overtook Tarleton's dragoons, who were providing the rear guard for the foraging party. Without hesitating, the French commander ordered his men to charge. Tarleton, in turn, ordered a countercharge, and a clash of cavalry ensued. Lauzun wrote, "Tarleton saw me and rode towards me with pistol raised. We were about to fight single handed between the two troops when his horse was thrown."[25] Tarleton was unhorsed and narrowly escaped death when Lauzun's lancers spotted him. In the nick of time, a party of his own dragoons rode to rescue their commander. After remounting, Tarleton led a series of unsuccessful charges against Lauzun's horsemen before withdrawing to the cover of the woods. Lauzun's Legionnaires followed at a safe distance until they encountered a line of dismounted Light Dragoons supported by a group of Welch Fusiliers that had just arrived on the scene. Outnumbered and outgunned, Lauzun ordered his men to exit the woods and withdraw to the rear. There the Legionnaires met Mercer's Virginia militia brigade and a battalion of Continentals. The combined forces then formed a line of battle with the militia and Continental infantry advancing in front. When Tarleton learned that Lauzun's force had been reinforced with American infantry, he quickly withdrew toward Gloucester Point. Losses on both sides were less than 50 killed and wounded.

Washington hailed the action as a "brilliant success." At the strategic level, he was correct. The day after the battle, General Choisy moved his forces to within a mile or two of the British works, effectively sealing off the Gloucester Peninsula.[26] The British were no longer able to forage beyond their lines, and their overland lines of communication to the north were sealed off, making any breakout attempt from Gloucester Point extremely difficult.

*   *   *

On Thursday, October 4th, the day after the Gloucester battle, the army's horse and oxen herds finally arrived at Yorktown, after moving overland from Head of Elk, Maryland, a journey of more than 250 miles. With the arrival of the horses and oxen teams, the movement of the heavy artillery pieces from the landing site on the James River to the Allied lines at Yorktown proceeded at a more rapid pace.

The next day, preparations for the opening of the first parallel were well underway, and the activity did not go unnoticed by the British artillerymen, who kept the allied lines under an incessant fire. The bombardment was particularly heavy in General Wayne's 2nd Division's sector. Captain John Davis of the Pennsylvania Line wrote, "Our works go on day and night some chance Men kill'd with the incessant fire kept up on our works."[27] Another Pennsylvanian, Lieutenant William Feltman, wrote, "This morning a very heavy cannonading and firing with musketry."[28] Later that day Feltman's battalion was ordered to picket duty at Redoubt Number 1. While posting a new group of pickets, a corporal of the Pennsylvania line was mortally wounded when he was struck by a nine-pound cannon ball. On the same day, Captain Duncan's regiment was employed in cutting and making fascines for the trenches. He wrote that, "We had more firing from the enemy last night than any night since the commencement of the siege."[29] It was clear to everyone on both sides of the line that the next phase in the siege operation was about to begin.

After numerous reconnaissance missions and analysis of the terrain by the engineer and artillery officers, the layout of the first parallel was finalized. The line was concave with the right flank anchored near the York River below the town, and the left flank anchored near Goosley Road. The distance between the parallel and the British line was approximately 1,000 yards, except on the extreme right flank opposite British Redoubts 9 and 10, where the distance was somewhat greater.

The excavation of the first parallel was scheduled for the night of 5–6 October, but Washington ordered the operation put on a twenty-four hour hold. Although Washington never revealed the reasons for the delay, it is likely that the British were on high alert and prepared to oppose the opening of the parallel with all means available. It is also probable that the engineers and artillerymen asked for more time to mark the proposed trench line and battery positions. Although there was no actual digging on the night of October 5th, the engineers assisted by the sappers and miners were hard at work marking the projected line of trenches with strips of pinewood. It was dangerous work as British patrols probed the area between the lines throughout the night. Sergeant Joseph Plumb Martin was one of the sappers who accompanied the engineers to assist in laying the pine planks to mark the trench line. He later wrote a vivid description of his experiences that night,

> "We had not proceeded far in the darkness, before the Engineers ordered us to desist and remain where we were, and be sure not to straggle a foot from the spot while they were absent from us. In a few minutes after their departure, there came a man alone to us, having on a surtout, as we conjectured (it being exceedingly dark) and inquired for the Engineers . . . The stranger inquired what troops we were; talked familiarity with us a few minutes, when, being informed which way the officers had gone, he went off in the same direction . . . In a short time the Engineers returned and the aforementioned stranger with them; they discoursed together some time, when, by the officers often calling him "Your Excellency," we discovered that it was Gen. Washington."[30]

Inclement weather continued throughout the daylight hours of Saturday, October 6th. Captain John Davis described it simply as "A rainy day."[31] Despite the inclement weather, work parties continued to construct the necessary siege materials. Each soldier in two Pennsylvania regiments, two Maryland regiments, and a number of militia units were ordered to finish a gabion (a large basket fashioned by tree branches and filled with rocks and dirt) by noon. Once the trenches were dug, the gabions would be carried forward to reinforce the walls to prevent cave-ins.

Troops in the rear areas continued filling sandbags and loading them onto wagons for forward movement. Meanwhile, teams of horses and oxen began dragging the heavy siege cannons toward the front lines. As darkness fell, each soldier was at his assigned station, and officers whispered to their men to, "advance in perfect silence." The sappers and miners moved ahead of the infantry to complete the marking of the trench line.

The American and French troops assigned to open the first parallel trench numbered more than four thousand. In the American sector, six regiments of General Lincoln's troops were assigned the task of opening the parallel, while French General comp de Viomenil's Brigade Soissonois took up the task on the left. The troops were divided into two groups; one consisted of the working party, the men selected to do the actual digging; and the second group was the covering guards, who would form a defensive line 100 yards forward of the proposed trench line.[33] At 8:00 p.m., the covering force marched forward into the murky darkness until they reached their assigned positions. Upon arrival, they took up prone positions on the rain soaked ground peering forward into the darkness. Small reconnaissance patrols crawled forward toward the enemy fortifications to provide early warning of any sorties leaving the British lines to disrupt the opening of the parallel.

As the covering force moved into position, the working parties moved forward in the darkness toward the marked-out trench line. Each man carried an entrenching tool, or a fascine or gabion. Upon arrival, the men were spaced at three to four-foot intervals for the actual digging. When the troops were in position, General Washington rode forward and dismounted near the marked trench line. Grabbing a pick-ax, the commander-in-chief ceremoniously struck the first blow into the rain-soaked ground.

The digging became a race against time. The majority of the work had to be completed before sunrise, when the British sentries would see the massive effort underway, less than a thousand yards from their lines. Once the alarm was sounded, a massive bombardment by the British artillery was certain to occur. The men assigned to the digging worked in silence at a frantic pace. The falling rain muffled the sounds of thousands of pickaxes and spades striking the earth. As the digging continued, wagons loaded with sandbags moved slowly along the parallel, dropping their loads beside the workers. When the diggers were exhausted, relief shifts took their places. While work continued along the trench line, teams of draft horses and oxen dragged the heavy cannon across the sandy soil toward the battery positions along the parallel.

As the Americans worked at a furious pace on their section of the parallel, the French were also hard at work. The Regiment Touraine was constructing a battery position near the cliff overlooking the York River, and a trench line to protect that position. The British were closely monitoring the work on the new French battery, since they suspected that the new battery would support another assault on the Fusiliers Redoubt. Washington and Rochambeau had planned a diversionary action in the French sector, but it was cancelled when British sentinel dogs in the Fusiliers Redoubt became alerted to the digging in the French sector and began to bark. The barking soon spread throughout the British perimeter as more dogs took it up. Soon thereafter, a French Hussar deserter entered the British lines informing them of the work in progress on their right flank near the river. After firing a signal rocket from the Fusiliers Redoubt, the British unleashed an artillery bombardment on the French Touraine soldiers working on the unfinished battery, forcing them to withdraw. Intentional or not, the activity in the French sector drew British attention away from the American sector, allowing the work there to continue uninterrupted.

As dawn approached, the covering force withdrew to the new trench line. Some stayed in the unfinished trenches to assist in completion of the work, but most of the rain-soaked soldiers marched to the rear. Upon arrival, they sat shivering on ground with their muskets cradled in their arms ready to counterattack any British sorties against the still unfinished parallel. By dawn, the Allies had completed sufficient work on the parallel to protect the troops from British artillery fire. It was a remarkable feat that could not have been accomplished without careful planning and the industrious labor of the troops.

As morning sunlight flooded the plain before their works, British sentries were shocked to see a line of new earthworks less than a thousand yards to their front. By moving their lines forward, the Allies had demonstrated that they had the power and strength to methodically demolish the British defenses by moving their heavy artillery ever closer to their fortifications.

The allies anticipated that the British would unleash a barrage of artillery fire to destroy the trenches before they were completed, but the British response was tepid. Only two British cannon opened fired on the new allied works. The guns fired a few salvos at the fortifications, inflicting little damage. Cornwallis was conserving his dwindling supply of ammunition.

Following the European tradition, the allies held a ceremony to mark the opening of the first parallel. Lafayette's Division was tasked to relieve Lincoln's Division in the American sector, and the Regiments Agenois and Saintonge were similarly ordered to relieve the French regiments manning the parallel in the French sector. At noon on the 7th of October, Lafayette's Division marched forward with its colors unfurled and drummers beating the marching cadence. After crossing the mill dam on Wormley Creek, Lafayette's Division entered the new parallel. Once inside, the troops continued marching to the steady beat of the drummers, until each unit reached its assigned position. Regimental flags were then hoisted on the breastworks. General Lincoln's Division then marched out of the parallel reversing the route of Lafayette. The British greeted the newly arrived regiments with a salvo of cannon balls; however, other than kicking up the sandy soil, the balls did minimal damage. Then, in an act of sheer bravado, Lieutenant Colonel Alexander Hamilton, commanding the second battalion of Hazen's Brigade, ordered his troops to mount the parapet in front of their trench and execute the Manual of Arms, a drill described in Baron von Steuben's Drill Regulations. The British stared at the Americans but held their fire during the performance. Not all of the American officers appreciated Hamilton's bravado. Captain James Duncan wrote in his journal that, "Colonel Hamilton gave the orders, and although I esteem him one of the first officers in the American army, must beg leave in this instance to think he wantonly exposed the lives of his men."[34]

Over the next several days, work continued on the artillery positions and the four new infantry redoubts along the first parallel. Barrier ditches were dug around the redoubts, and palisades were constructed and placed over the rear entrances. As a finishing touch, fraises—long wooden poles sharpened at the end—were mounted in the outer walls of the fortifications to prevent attacking infantry from climbing the earthen walls. The parallel trench line was widened and deepened, and the dirt walls were reinforced by additional fascines. When the work on the artillery batteries was complete, the heavy cannon and mortars were hoisted onto the firing platforms. The first firing of the forward batteries was set for Tuesday, the 9th of October.

Eighteenth-century doctrine for siege operations stipulated that no firing should commence until all new battery positions were completed, with all guns mounted and ready to fire. When Washington learned that the Grand French battery would not be prepared to fire before October 10th, he made a decision to ignore the doctrine. All completed batteries began firing on October 9th.

The first allied guns opened fire at 3:00 p.m. Washington gave the honor of firing the first salvo to a French battery on the extreme left of the first parallel. That battery was a full day ahead of the other French batteries. The French targeted the two British ships, the *Formidable* and *Guadaloupe,* that were providing fire support to the Fusiliers Redoubt. Under heavy bombardment from the French battery, the ships weighed anchor and sailed to the Gloucester side of the river, where they were out of range of the French guns. Two hours later, the American Grand Battery on the right opened fire on the left and center of the main British defensive line. Washington lit the fuse of an 18-pounder, and the cannon ball flew across the British lines in a low arc, striking a wooden house in the town where a group of British officers were dining. The shot killed British Commissary-General Perkins, and wounded three other officers. After the first lethal shot, the other cannon and mortars in the battery opened fire, raining death and destruction on the British line. Many of the first rounds fell short or overshot their targets, but the gunners quickly made the necessary adjustments, and the fires grew more accurate and lethal as darkness descended on the plain.

The opening of the allied batteries had a tremendous impact on morale on both sides of the line. On the allied side, the troops saw for the first time the results of all their marching and arduous labors. On the British side, the bombardment belied the words of General Cornwallis, who had assured his troops that the allies lacked the heavy artillery to mount an effective siege. The British troops now knew that it was just a matter of time before their fortifications were battered to pieces by the heavy artillery, leaving them exposed to a massive assault by the Americans and French troops.

The allied artillery continued to bombard the British fortifications throughout the night drawing a spirited response from the British guns. The ground shook and explosions echoed across the plain as the cannon and siege mortars belched fire, launching their missiles into the night sky. Major Ebenezer Denny, observing the bombardments from the Pennsylvania encampment, wrote, "The scene viewed from the camp now was grand . . . a number of shells from the works of both parties passing high in the air, and descending in a curve, each with a long train of fire, exhibited a brilliant spectacle."[35] As the allied shells exploded among the British batteries, a number of guns were dismounted and put out of action. The firing slackened later that night, but occasional rounds continued to disrupt British efforts to repair their damaged fortifications.

While the American and British batteries dueled in the darkness, General Rochambeau's engineers and artillerymen rushed to complete work on their batteries. Freed from their labors in the American sector, teams of draft horses dragged the heavy French siege guns to the front, while hundreds of laborers worked to complete the batteries and manhandle the guns onto their mounts.

Cornwallis was well aware that his options were limited after the allies opened their first parallel. A breakout attempt up the Yorktown peninsula was no longer a viable option. The allied lines were too strong. His best chance for a breakout was on the Gloucester side of the river, where the opposing force was not as strong. To test the strength of the allied forces on the Gloucester Peninsula, Cornwallis ordered eight flatboats loaded with troops to sail upstream from Yorktown and land at a point from which they could flank the forces that were stretched across the Gloucester peninsula, sealing it off. The flatboats shoved off in darkness shortly after midnight on October 10th. French Brigadier General Choisy's forces on the Gloucester Peninsula were on high alert and spotted the boats before they could land. The boats were then taken under fire by the French artillery and scattered. Most of them managed to land within the British lines at Gloucester Point, but at least one boat was captured.[36] It was not the last attempt by Cornwallis to use Gloucester Point as an avenue of escape for his besieged army.

At 9:00 a.m. on October 10th, the allied artillery opened with a thunderous barrage of cannon, mortar, and howitzer fire.. The Grand French battery, in action for the first time, unleashed the fire of more than two-dozen artillery pieces.[37] The British artillery gave a measured response but ceased firing entirely after one hour, and afterward kept up only a sporadic fire for the remainder of the day. The allied batteries, on the other hand, kept up their fire throughout the daylight hours. Most of them concentrated their fire on the British batteries that were located in the Hornwork, near the center of their line. The Fusilier's Redoubt and the detached Redoubts 9 and 10 also received heavy bombardments.

British General Samuel Graham, who was a captain during the siege of Yorktown, described the bombardment in his memoirs:

> An incessant cannonade now commenced on both sides, but our batteries and newly constructed works soon began to feel the effects of the powerful artillery opposed to them, and on the 10th scarcely a gun could be fired from our works, fascines, stockade platforms, and earth, with guns and gun-carriages, being all pounded together in a mass.[38]

Some of the allies' shells overshot their targets and fell on the town, damaging houses and businesses, while others exploded along the wharf and among the British vessels anchored in the river. Civilians who had not fled the town dug shelters in the sand under the cliffs overhanging the river. Hessian Private Johann Conrad Dohla described the plight of the civilians in his diary: "Many were seriously and fatally wounded by the broken pieces of the bombs that were exploding, partly in the air, partly on the ground, which broke arms and legs, or killed them."[39]

During the heavy artillery barrage, the allies relieved their infantry manning the first parallel. Around noon, Lafayette's light infantry division relieved Lincoln's men in the American sector, and the French Agenois and Saintonge regiments took over the trenches in the French sector. When the American and French troops were relieved on the front lines, they had the opportunity to rest and enjoy hot meals in the relative safety of their camps.

There were no safe areas within the British perimeter where the troops could rest, and their rations continued to dwindle. Allied artillery batteries continued to pound the rear areas as well as the fortifications along the main defensive line, making life miserable for all those within the British perimeter.

As the siege continued, Washington remained concerned that Cornwallis's army would either escape or that British reinforcements from New York would arrive. Therefore, the American commander-in-chief insisted on pushing his advantages in troop strength and artillery to the limit in order to force Cornwallis into submission as quickly as possible. With that in mind, Washington ordered his engineers to begin surveying the ground for a second parallel. Additionally, to prevent a British escape across the river, Washington ordered the French artillery nearest the river to destroy the remaining British vessels in the channel off Yorktown. The French moved two 24-pounder cannon from their Grand Battery to a position near the river. During the evening of October 10th, the gunners heated the heavy cannon balls until they were red hot. At 8:00 p.m., the French gunners began sending the glowing projectiles across the night sky toward the British vessels. The prime targets were the frigates *Guadaloupe* and *Charon*, and the transports. The *Guadaloupe* managed to reach safety by moving close to the steep cliffs overhanging the riverbank, but the frigate *Charon* was not as fortunate.

British Navy Lieutenant Bartholomew James, who commanded a shore battery of navy guns that were dismounted from the *Charon*, saw his ship come under bombardment and described the scene in his journal:

> The enemy having opened fresh batteries on this day, and also commenced an additional fire on the Charon with red-hot shot, she was set on fire at half-past six o'clock in three different places, and in a few minutes in flames from the hold to the mastheads... and she broke adrift from her moorings and drove on board a transport to which she also set fire, and they both grounded on the Gloucester side, where they burnt to the waters edge.[40]

American surgeon James Thatcher also observed the firing from a position close to the riverbank and wrote:

The ships were enwrapped in a torrent of fire, which spreading with vivid brightness among the combustible rigging, and running with amazing rapidity to the tops of several masts, while all around was thunder and lightning from our cannon and mortars . . . Some of our shells, overreaching the town, are seen to fall into the river, and bursting throw up columns of water like the spouting of the monsters of the deep.[41]

By dawn of October 11th, all the British vessels that were still afloat had moved to the Gloucester side of the river. Cornwallis's naval support was seriously weakened, and only the *Guadaloupe* and a few small, unarmed transports and open boats remained afloat. The evacuation of Yorktown using boats suddenly became much more difficult and time-consuming.

OPENING THE SECOND PARALLEL

Work on the second parallel was scheduled to begin on the evening of October 11th. Baron von Steuben's Division marched forward early in the day to relieve the troops manning the first parallel. In the French sector, Major General de Chastellux was assigned responsibility for advancing a second parallel. By sunset, the troops were ready to begin the grueling and dangerous work. Part of General Nelson's Virginia militia moved forward to occupy the first parallel, and General von Steuben's men moved forward with entrenching tools, gabions, and fascines. Since the new parallel would be within 400 yards of the British lines, and on line with the detached British Redoubts 9 and 10, creating the new parallel was even more dangerous than opening the first. The sound of the digging was sure to carry to the British lines, and it was anticipated that the British would do everything possible to disrupt the work. American and French artillery batteries were ordered to provide covering fire for the laborers, and keep the British troops pinned down in their fortifications.

At dusk, Lieutenant William Feltman led eighty-two of his fellow Pennsylvanians forward to work on the new parallel. Feltman wrote, "Every second man of the whole detachment carried a fascine and a shovel or spade, and every man a shovel, spade, or grubbing hoe." It wasn't long before Feltman's men came under British cannon fire, and one of his men was wounded. French artillery responded, but their shells fell short, killing two of Feltman's men and seriously wounding another.[42] With enemy and friendly artillery shells bursting all around them, the troops worked at a frantic pace to complete the trench. Soon the trench was three and a half feet deep and seven feet in width, affording some protection from the artillery fire. Feltman's exhausted Pennsylvanians were relieved by the militia before daylight. Similar scenes were playing out all along the new parallel.

Work on the advanced line progressed rapidly throughout the night and the next morning. Fatigue details quickly raised the parapets of the new redoubts and placed palisades in the ditches to deter the British from storming the redoubts. Meanwhile, artillerymen began to move their cannons forward to provide direct fire support to the new parallel. Before dawn, British patrols moved forward, reconnoitering and probing the new line for weaknesses. Occasional firefights erupted in the no-man's land between the lines as the British patrols exchanged musket fire with the Allied covering forces.

When Cornwallis saw the extent of the new parallel shortly after daybreak, he ordered a heavy barrage of artillery, hoping to disrupt the completion of the work. In the short term, the British artillery had the desired effect, and the workers were forced to temporarily cease their efforts and take cover in the trench line. However, the American and French artillery soon began to zero in the British batteries, suppressing their fire. With the allied second parallel within four hundred yards of his defensive line, the British commander was desperate. He expected an all out infantry assault on his defensive line, and knew that he needed additional men to adequately man the fortifications. He therefore ordered Lieutenant Colonel Thomas Dundas to ferry a portion of his brigade from Gloucester Point to the Yorktown defenses. Lieutenant Colonel Tarleton assumed command of the Gloucester Point lines after Dundas's departure.

THE CAPTURE OF REDOUBTS 9 AND 10

On the morning of October 12th, Washington and Rochambeau began planning attacks on the outlying British redoubts, 9 and 10. Capture of these fortifications would allow the Allies to complete the eastern portion of the second parallel all the way to the York River. The Allies began to reconnoiter and study the defenses of the two redoubts. while work continued on the second parallel.

During the night of 12–13 October, work continued on the new Allied redoubts and five new artillery emplacements. Once the five battery positions were completed and the artillery was emplaced, the allies would be able to fire directly into the British fortifications at close range, tearing them apart. However, this could not be accomplished until Redoubts 9 and 10 were captured. Washington knew that he did not have unlimited time to complete the siege. As the month of October wore on, French Admiral de Grasse became increasingly anxious to leave the Chesapeake and return to the West Indies, and neither Washington nor Rochambeau could prevent his departure. Once the French fleet departed the Chesapeake, there was no way to prevent British ships from entering the Bay and landing reinforcements.

At noon on Saturday October 13th, Lafayette's division took over the defense and construction work in the American sector of the second parallel, and the Regiments Agenois and Saintonge took over in the French portion of the line. The volume of British fire increased during the relief operations and continued after nightfall. Allied casualties continued to mount, prompting Washington to write, "The fire of the enemy this night became brisk, and more injurious to us than it had been; several men being killed and many wounded in the Trenches, but the works were not in the smallest degree retarded by it . . ."[43]

Despite the British fire, the allied soldiers continued their work throughout the night of 13–14 October. After daylight the troops were exposed to the fire of Hessian marksmen, as well as artillery. American sharpshooters responded with deadly accurate rifle fire that silenced the Hessian snipers. By afternoon, the allied artillery began to concentrate its fire on the outlying Fusiliers Redoubt and Redoubts 9 and 10. Washington ordered the artillery to smash the abatis and palisades that protected the outer walls of the redoubts. The Fusiliers Redoubt was included in the bombardment to create uncertainty among the British as to which positions were targeted for ground attacks by the allied infantry.

On the afternoon of October 14th, Washington assembled his senior commanders to finalize plans for the assaults on Redoubts 9 and 10. The two detached positions protected Yorktown's southeastern flank, and were critical to the defense of the main British works. If the allies captured them, the weakest section of the British line would be exposed to a direct assault. Redoubt 9, the larger of the two, was located some 350 yards east of the main British line, and 330 yards south of Redoubt 10. Narrow ditches connected both redoubts to the main defensive line. Redoubt 9 was a pentagonal fort with a protective ditch, fraising, and palisade surrounded by a single row of abatis. Redoubt 10 sat at the edge of the bluff that overlooked the York River and was about 200 yards to the right of where the second parallel ended

The French commanders wanted to conduct both attacks, but after much debate and discussion, the allies agreed that the French would launch a major attack on the more formidable Redoubt 9, and the Americans would assault Redoubt 10. Two feint attacks were also planned to distract the British: one against Gloucester Point and the other on the far left of the allied line.

The 71st Regiment, Fraser's Highlanders, augmented by a force of Hessians, defended both Redoubts 9 and 10. A mixed force of Highlanders and Hessians numbering about 120 men defended Redoubt 9 under the command of Lieutenant Colonel Duncan McPherson. Forty-five men under the command of Major James Campbell defended Redoubt 10.

Major General Antoine Charles de Houx, baron de Viomenil, commander of the Brigade Bourbonnois, was assigned responsibility for the assault on Redoubt 9, and his subordinate, Colonel Guillaume de Deux-Ponts, was chosen to lead the assault force of 400 handpicked grenadiers and chasseurs from the Regiment Gatenois and Regiment Royal Deux-Ponts. On the American side, General Lafayette was in overall command of the assault on Redoubt 10. Lafayette selected another Frenchman, Lieutenant Colonel de Gimat, commander of a mixed battalion of Connecticut, Massachusetts, and Rhode Island troops, to lead the assault. It is noteworthy that most of the Rhode Island troops serving in Gimat's battalion were free African-Americans who had volunteered to serve their country.

In addition to Gimat's battalion, two additional Continental battalions were selected for the attack. These were led by Lieutenant Colonel Alexander Hamilton and Lieutenant Colonel John Lauren. In addition to serving as a battalion commander, Hamilton was also the army's Officer of the

Day on October 14th, and he strongly argued that he should have the honor of leading the assault rather than the Frenchman, Gimat. When Lafayette refused to reconsider his appointment of Gimat, Hamilton went over his head and sought General Washington's intervention. Washington overruled Lafayette's decision, and the honors went to his former aide-de-camp, Lieutenant Colonel Hamilton, who had long sought recognition as a battlefield commander.

As night fell, the allied artillery fire slackened, and then the firing stopped completely. A mixture of smoke and fog blanketed the silent landscape. In the American sector, Hamilton gave last minute instructions to his officers and men before introducing the Commander-in-Chief, who would say a few words. Captain Steven Olney, leading a company of Rhode Islanders in the assault force, wrote that, "Washington made a short address or harangue, admonishing us to act the part of firm and brave soldiers..." Washington himself may have been emotionally caught up in the moment, as Olney wrote that, "his Excellency's knees rather shook . . ."[44]

Sergeant Joseph Plumb Martin was one of the Sappers and Miners selected to participate in the night assault on Redoubt 10. It was not until he arrived in the forward trenches that he learned the details of the plan, in which he was to play a critical role. He later described the preparations before the attack: "The Sappers and Miners were furnished with axes, and were to proceed in front and cut a passage for the troops through the abatis."[45] At dark, Martin's detachment moved forward of the trenches and lay down on the ground to await the signal for the attack, which was the firing of three shells from a nearby battery. Everyone's nerves were frayed, including Martin's, and when he turned his head and gazed into the night sky he spotted two brilliant planets, Jupiter and Venus, and almost mistook them for the attack signal. Martin wrote, "I was ready to spring on my feet, thinking they were the signal for starting."[46]

In the French assembly area, similar preparations for the attack were in the final stages. The French commander of the assault force, Guillaume, Comte de Deux-Ponts, said goodbye to his brother, Major General Antoine Charles de Houx, baron de Viomenil. Jean Baptise Antoine de Verger, a sub-lieutenant in the Royal Deux-Ponts regiment, recorded in his journal that the French assault column was lined up on the right flank of an American five-gun battery, with the grenadiers and chasseur companies of the

Gatenois regiment at the head of the column.[47] Deux-Ponts wrote in his account of that night that,

> The chasseurs of the regiment had the head of the column. They were in column by platoons; the first fifty carried fascines; of the other fifty there were only eight who carried ladders; after them came the grenadiers and chasseurs of the regiment of Royal Deuxponts, in column by sections. The whole was proceeded by the two sergeants of the regiment of Gatinois . . . , and by eight carpenters . . .[48]

Antoine Charles de Houx, the overall French commander, decided to accompany the assault force, and when the signal for the attack to begin was given, he marched out into the open ground with his troops. The French troops had not marched far, between 120 to 130 paces, when a Hessian sentry on the redoubt's parapet called out in the darkness, "Werda," a German version of "Who goes there." When the challenge went unanswered, the Hessians opened fire. Ignoring the firing, the French moved forward toward the redoubt. The abatis, which was located about twenty-five paces from the redoubt, was in much better shape than the French anticipated.

The fortifications had been pounded by artillery for several days, but the shells had done little damage. French pioneers wielding their axes chopped openings in the abatis, and the assault troops leapt into the ditch that surrounded the redoubt, where they began breaking through the fraises and climbing the parapet. Despite the heavy fire of the defenders, small groups of men made it to the parapet and began firing down into the defenders. A group of defenders attempted a bayonet charge, but were driven off by the fire. Meanwhile, the pioneers were successful in breaching the palisade, enabling the main body of troops to rush in. Then, according to Deux-Ponts, the defenders, ". . . placed themselves behind a kind of intrenchment of barrels . . ."[49]

The French concentrated their fires on the improvised barricade, and Deux-Ponts was about to order his men to leap down into the redoubt and charge the survivors with bayonets, when the British and Hessians laid down their arms. Then, according to Deux Ponts, his men were able to leap down into the redoubt, "with more tranquility and less risk." However the fight was not yet over. Sub-lieutenant de Verger recalled that a few defenders chose to challenge the attackers. He wrote in his journal, "Several wishing to continue the fight with bayonets paid with their lives."[50] The final assault lasted only about seven minutes.[51]

The French lost 92 enlisted men killed and wounded in the assault. Additionally, one French officer was killed and three others were wounded. After the redoubt was taken, Lieutenant Colonel Deux-Ponts nearly lost his own life as he peered over the parapet to see if the British were mounting a counterattack. A cannon ball ricocheted off the parapet near his head, spraying him with sand and dirt.

The French counted 18 enemy dead inside the redoubt. They also captured three officers and forty enlisted men. Another 120 to 170 British and Hessian soldiers managed to escape, including the redoubt's commander, Lt. Colonel McPherson.

In front of Redoubt 10, the Americans advanced on the same signal as the French. The troops moved forward into the dark and eerie landscape in two columns. Hamilton had ordered his men not to load their weapons. It was to be a silent attack using only bayonets. Gimat's battalion led the right column, followed by Hamilton's battalion. An advance guard of 20 men and a detachment of sappers and miners marched ahead of the right column. Captain Steven Olney wrote that, "The column marched in silence, with guns unloaded and in good order."[52] Olney whispered to several of his men, telling them of his confidence in them, and instructing them to recover the weapons of those who fell in battle. Lieutenant Colonel Lauren's battalion formed the left column. Its mission was to circle around to the rear of the redoubt to prevent the defenders from escaping.

About halfway to the redoubt, the assault column was ordered to halt, and each company was asked to provide a volunteer for the forlorn hope. The column then resumed its march with Sergeant Martin's small detachment of sappers and miners in the lead, followed by the forlorn hope detachment led by Lieutenant John Mansfield of the Fourth Connecticut. Martin wrote that, "Just as we arrived at the abatis, the enemy discovered us and directly opened a sharp fire upon us."[53]

Peering into the darkness, Martin thought he saw a number of his men drop to the ground, presumably hit by the enemy fire. In fact, the ground around the abatis was pock marked with large shell holes, "large enough to bury an ox in," and several men stumbled into the holes. Upon reaching the abatis, the sappers and miners went to work with their axes, clearing paths through the obstacles. Members of Lieutenant Mansfield's forlorn hope and Gimat's advance guard crawled through the gaps and entered the ditch surrounding the redoubt. All the while, the British kept up a steady fire from the parapet.

Lieutenant Mansfield was one of the first Americans to enter the redoubt. One of the Highlanders rushed forward and bayoneted him, seriously wounding the gallant leader of the forlorn hope. Captain Olney entered the ditch where he found about a dozen of his men. He led them through a gap between two palisades, and climbed the earthen parapet. Reaching the top he shouted, "Captain Olney's company, form here!"[54] To his surprise, he soon found himself in the midst of a group of six to eight enemy soldiers with fixed bayonets.

Olney tried to parry the bayonets with his espontoon, but the blade of his weapon broke. A British bayonet slid down the espontoon, scaling Olney's fingers. Another British bayonet pierced Olney's thigh, and a third soldier stabbed him in the abdomen; but Captain Olney was far from finished. He made a thrust with his damaged espontoon, striking one of his assailants in the forehead. At that moment, two of Olney's men, who had loaded their muskets in the ditch, climbed the parapet and fired into the mass of enemy soldiers that surrounded their captain, driving them off. The life-and-death struggle continued as more Americans climbed the parapet, standing on each other's shoulders and backs to leap over the sandbag breastwork atop the parapet. Colonel Hamilton was among them, and as he pulled himself up and over the wall, he found himself in the middle of the furious bayonet fight.

More and more men from Gimat's and Hamilton's battalions entered the redoubt. Captain Kirkpatrick and his sappers were under orders not to enter the works, but they disregarded the order. Sergeant Martin found a spot along the abatis that had been shot away by cannon fire, and after crawling through jumped into the ditch. A man running beside Martin across the ditch was shot in the head with a musket ball and dropped to the ground. Sapper Martin also recalled that the British were hurling hand grenades into the ditch as he ran toward the parapet. Lieutenant Colonel

Gimat never made it into the ditch, as he was shot in the foot when he reached the abatis. The British were soon overwhelmed by sheer numbers as the Continentals swarmed over the parapet. Meanwhile, Lieutenant Colonel Lauren led two companies of Continentals to the rear of the redoubt and took a number of Highlanders prisoner as they attempted to flee. One of those captured was the redoubt's wounded commander, Major Campbell. At least one British soldier made good his escape by sliding down the steep 20-foot riverbank and running down the beach toward the town.

After ten minutes of furious fighting, Redoubt 10 was in American hands. The dead and wounded lay strewn on the ground inside and outside, and 20 British prisoners were under guard at bayonet point within the redoubt. Nine Americans were killed in the lightning attack, and another 25 were wounded. The British had eight soldiers killed or wounded. Army surgeon James Thatcher moved forward to treat the wounded after the fight was over. He wrote that he counted one sergeant and eight men, "dead in the ditch." He also witnessed an incident with the prisoners. A New Hampshire infantry captain threatened the life of the wounded Major Campbell, "to avenge the death of his favorite, Colonel Scammel . . ." who was shot in the back by a British officer earlier in the siege. According to Thatcher, Lt. Colonel Hamilton interposed himself between the two men, putting an end to the affair.[55]

After the fighting, the sky clouded over and it began to rain. Work began immediately to incorporate the captured redoubts into the second parallel. A short time later, a fresh battalion of Continentals rushed forward to Redoubt 10 to forestall any British attempt to retake it. British artillery fired continuously during the allied attacks on the redoubts, targeting positions all along the length of the second parallel. The British assumed that the assaults on Redoubts 9 and 10 signaled the beginning of a general assault on their main defensive line. Their artillery continued firing throughout the night.

General Washington, General Lincoln, and the Chief of Artillery, General Knox, observed the assaults on the two redoubts from the French Grand Battery. Washington summed up his impressions of the American and French assaults, recording in his journal that, "The bravery exhibited by the attacking Troops was emulous and praiseworthy; few cases have exhibited stronger proofs of intrepidity coolness and firmness than were shown upon this occasion."[56]

Shortly after dawn, General Cornwallis left his headquarters in the town to observe the Allied positions that were now within 300 yards of his defensive line. Returning to his headquarters, Cornwallis wrote a brief letter to General Henry Clinton describing his dire situation. After reporting the loss of his two redoubts, he wrote,

> My situation here becomes very critical…Experience has shown that our fresh earthen works do not resist their powerful artillery, so that we shall soon be exposed to an assault in ruined works . . . with weakened numbers. The safety of this place is therefore so precarious, that I cannot recommend that the fleet and army should run great risk in endeavoring to save us.[57]

Lord Cornwallis fully realized his army's dire situation, but he was not yet ready to concede defeat.

DESPERATE MEASURES

Despite the pessimism expressed in his letter to Clinton, Cornwallis remained a dangerous adversary. His artillery continued to pound the second parallel throughout the daylight hours on Monday, the 15th of October. The incoming shells exacted a heavy toll on the allied work parties. Late in the afternoon, the new allied batteries on the second parallel opened fire, even as work continued on the fortifications. Shells rained down on the town and the wharf. There was no longer any safe anchorage for British vessels in the channel. Ebenezer Denny wrote, "A shell from one of the French mortars set fire to a British frigate; she burnt to the water's edge, and blew up—made the earth shake. Shot and shell raked the town in every direction."[58]

As darkness fell the Allied fire slackened, but the British batteries kept up a steady fire. The night sky was filled with shot and shell until 4:00 a.m. on Tuesday morning. when the British artillery suddenly ceased firing. Then, in the pre-dawn darkness, some 350 British troops slipped quietly out of the Hornwork area of the British lines, and moved toward the allied works. In an act of desperation, Cornwallis had ordered Lieutenant

Colonel Robert Abercrombie, commander of the left portion of the defensive line, to conduct a sortie against the new allied batteries. Abercrombie's raiding force included a detachment from the Royal Foot Guards, a company of Grenadiers, and a light infantry company. The raiders targeted two unfinished batteries, one French and one American, that were deemed the most dangerous to the British defenses.

Abercrombie led his men toward a vulnerable point in the second parallel, right between the two batteries and directly on the boundary line between the American and French sectors. The British surprised the French sentries guarding a redoubt, and then entered a communications trench leading to the French battery. The soldiers assigned to guard the battery were asleep, and the British bayoneted them as they slept. The attackers then spiked the battery's four cannon, thrusting their bayonets into the vents, and breaking them off. Meanwhile, the remainder of Abercrombie's force moved toward an American battery defended by soldiers from the 2nd New York and Virginia militia. When the raiders were challenged by American sentries, they identified themselves as French troops, and the sentries let them pass unmolested. When they neared the battery, Abercrombie's men charged with fixed bayonets, scattering the American troops and spiking three 18-pound cannon. The shouting and firing alerted a French guard force that was positioned behind the two batteries. The French charged into the batteries, routing the raiders and driving them back toward their own lines.

The British sortie did not inflict lasting damage to the two allied batteries. The cannon were easily repaired by removing the bent bayonet points from the fuse holes, and they were back in action the next day. Nonetheless, the raid demonstrated that the British were still dangerous foes. Washington ordered his commanders to improve their preparedness for such attacks, particularly during the hours of darkness.

On Tuesday, October 16th, the Allies hurried to complete their work on the new line. The guns and ordnance still in place on the old line were moved forward under the covering fire of the artillery already in place. The firing was relentless, battering the British fortifications at close range. As evening approached, the allies prepared for additional nocturnal British sorties by posting strong detachments of infantry in each of the new batteries. The mid-October weather turned cold and rainy, but the allied gun crews stood by their pieces ready to unleash a thunderous barrage. On General Knox's order, some one hundred cannon and mortars opened fire. The guns belched their projectiles into the blackened sky, and hundreds of shells exploded in Cornwallis's defenses. Fraises, abatis, and palisades were ripped apart, and parapets came tumbling down. Many of the British artillery pieces were dismounted from their firing platforms. Other shells landed in the town, battering the few remaining structures, and setting some of the buildings on fire.

Cornwallis knew that the heavy artillery fire was opening breaches in his lines and decided to undertake one last desperate measure. The British commander ordered the bulk of his army to prepare for an immediate evacuation across the York River to the Gloucester shore. A small detachment was to remain in Yorktown to cover the crossing and negotiate surrender terms for the wounded and sick soldiers who were unable to make the crossing. All baggage and heavy artillery were to be left behind.

Before midnight, the British managed to assemble sixteen serviceable boats along the shoreline to ferry the troops across to Gloucester. Officers calculated that at least three round trips would be needed to ferry all the troops across the river. Once his army was safely across, Cornwallis planned to link up with Lieutenant Colonel Tarleton's force and break through the Allied cordon before marching north toward New York or back to the Carolinas by way of Richmond.

The operation began in absolute secrecy. Around 11 p.m., sixteen boats loaded with soldiers from the British light infantry, the Guards, and the 23rd Regiment shoved off from the Yorktown wharf under the cloudy night sky. As the crews rowed toward the distant shoreline, strong winds began to blow, followed by a severe thunderstorm. High waves tossed the boats about in the channel, and the rain-soaked troops prepared for the worst. Fourteen of the boats managed to reach the Gloucester shore, however the remaining two were blown downstream and landed on the Yorktown shoreline, where the seasick British soldiers were quickly taken prisoner by the Americans.

The storm continued until around 2:00 a.m. Cornwallis realized that the breakout attempt had failed, and ordered the troops who had completed the crossing to return to Yorktown. Allied artillerymen attempted to sink the boats, but most returned safely. Stumbling ashore on unsteady legs, the demoralized troops marched back to their battered fortifications. In Banastre Trarleton's words, "Thus expired the last hope of the British army."[59]

12

CAPITULATION

"In the morning, before relief came, (I) had the pleasure of seeing a drummer mount the enemy's parapet, and beat a parley, and immediately an officer, holding up a white handkerchief, made his appearance outside their works; the drummer accompanied him, beating. Our batteries ceased. An officer from our lines ran and met the other, and tied the handkerchief over his eyes. The drummer (was) sent back, and the British officer (was) conducted to a house in rear of our lines. Firing ceased totally."
—Major Ebenezer Denny,
Pennsylvania Line

As dawn broke on October 17th, the intense bombardment of the British fortifications continued unabated. The day marked the fourth anniversary of the British surrender at Saratoga, and Americans across the land celebrated, but most were unaware that another victory was unfolding at Yorktown; one that would far eclipse Saratoga. The batteries along the second parallel were fully operational that morning. Washington wrote, "The French had opened another Battery of 24s and two 16s and a Mortar Battery of 10 Mortars and two Howitzers."[1] The new American grand battery was also in action early that morning with fires from its 12- and 24-pounders, mortars, and howitzers.[2] British fortifications were pulverized, and almost every structure in the town was demolished to piles of rubble. American Surgeon Thatcher wrote:

197

The whole peninsula trembles under the incessant thunderings of our infernal machines, we have leveled some of their works in ruins and silenced their guns; they have almost ceased firing. We are so near as to have a distinct view of the dreadful havoc and destruction of their works, and even see the men in their lines torn to pieces by the bursting of our shells.[3]

Much of the allies cannon, howitzer, and mortar fire was directed at the British stronghold called the Hornwork and along the British left flank. Hessian Captain Johann Ewald's detachment was in the Hornwork that morning, and he wrote in his journal that, "One saw nothing but bombs and balls raining on our whole side. They battered our works so badly in the flank and rear that all of our batteries were silenced within a few hours. My nerves suffered extremely."[4]

Hessian Private Johann Dohla was also in the Hornwork early the same morning, writing that, "They fired from all positions without letup . . . There was nothing to be seen but bombs and cannonballs raining down on our entire line."[5] Dohla was present when General Cornwallis entered the Hornwork that morning to "observe the enemy and his preparations." Cornwallis had to confirm for himself the damage being done by the allied artillery. He knew that once there were a number of breaches in his fortifications, the allies would launch a final infantry attack with no quarter given. A general assault could be just hours away. Cornwallis was a vain man with a high opinion of his own generalship, but he was not an inhumane individual. He was not prepared to sacrifice the lives of his soldiers for a lost cause.

After watching the devastating effects of the bombardment on his fortifications, and conferring with his officers and engineers, Cornwallis returned to his headquarters and penned a letter to General Washington asking for a 24-hour cessation of hostilities and the appointment of two officers from each side to "settle terms of Surrender of the Posts of York & Gloucester."[6]

Shortly after 10:00 a.m., a British drummer appeared on the parapet of the Hornwork beating for a parley, but the drumbeat was drowned out by the allied cannonade. The drummer was soon spotted by Allied marksmen, who stared in amazement, but held their fire. Then a British officer waving a white handkerchief joined the drummer, and the pair climbed down the parapet and walked toward the allied lines. The artillery fire slackened, then ceased, and the drumbeat calling for a parley could finally be clearly heard as the pair strode across the no-man's land between the lines. As they neared the allied works an American officer walked forward to meet the British. After instructing the drummer to return to the British lines, the American blindfolded the British officer and guided him to Washington's headquarters in a house to the rear.[7] After delivering Cornwallis's letter, the British officer was sent back to his own lines. The allied bombardment resumed as Washington prepared his reply.

After conferring with his staff, Washington wrote his answer to Cornwallis. In his firm and terse response, Washington asked for his opponent's proposed terms for the surrender, adding that there would be no meeting of Commissioners before he received those terms in writing. Also included in Washington's response was a proviso warning his opponent that he would grant only a two-hour suspension of hostilities, while waiting for the proposed British terms for the surrender.[8]

When Washington's letter was signed and ready for delivery, the artillery ceased firing, and the same British officer returned to the American lines under a flag of truce to receive the letter. There is little doubt that Cornwallis was miffed at the short two-hour ceasefire granted by Washington for the preparation of the proposed British terms for the surrender. It was to Cornwallis's advantage to delay the proceedings as long as possible. There was still a possibility, however remote, that British reinforcements would arrive from New York. Nevertheless, he complied with Washington's ultimatum, and stated his surrender terms in a succinct and unambiguous manner. Cornwallis wrote, ". . . the Garrisons at York and Gloucester shall be Prisoners of War with customary honours . . . and that the British shall be sent to Britain, & Germans to Germany, under the engagement not to serve against France, America, or their Allies until released, or regularly exchanged." Cornwallis also specified that all arms and public stores were to be turned over to the allies, with the exception of officers' personal side arms and private property of all solders. Additionally, the British commander wanted Washington's guarantee that the interests of individuals working for the British in a civilian capacity would be protected.[9]

Upon receiving Cornwallis's proposed terms for surrender, Washington suspended hostilities for the night while he prepared his own specific terms for the surrender. While the Commander-in-Chief worked through the night, the American, French, and British soldiers slept peacefully in the chilly October air. Lieutenant Colonel St. George Tucker, a Virginian, wrote in his journal:

> Hostilities have ceased ever since five OClock. It was pleasing to contrast the last night with the preceding—A solemn stillness prevaild—the night was remarkably clear & the sky decorated with ten thousand stars—numerous Meteors gleaming thro' the Atmosphere afforded a pleasing resemblance to the Bombs which had exhibited a noble Firework the night before, but happily divested of all their Horror.[10]

In drafting his terms for the British surrender, Washington was negotiating from a position of strength, and the terms reflected his firmness. First, Washington would not countenance the return of the British and German troops to their native countries. He granted the ground troops and mariners fighting under the British flag prisoner-of-war status; however, they were to remain in American or French custody. Washington was well aware of the poor treatment meted out to American troops who were captured after the fall of New York and Charleston. It was not his intent to imprison the surrendered British troops under such harsh conditions, but he did insist that they would remain captive on American soil.

Secondly, Washington refused to grant the British and their mercenaries the customary military honors during the formal surrender ceremony. During 18th-century European/American wars, it was customary to grant a surrendering army that had fought gallantly and honorably the right to march with their colors unfurled and playing a marching song of the victorious army. Such honors had been denied General Lincoln's force when the American garrison at Charleston surrendered in May 1780, and Washington was determined that Cornwallis's army would suffer the same insult.

To his credit, Washington did grant the British officers the right to retain their side arms, and all officers and soldiers were permitted to keep their personal effects and baggage, with the exception of property confiscated during the campaigns. All other military arms, to include small arms and artillery, and other equipment and stores were to be turned over to the allied forces. Washington did not commit himself on the disposition of civilians who were working for the British, writing that, ". . . until they are more particularly described, nothing definite can be settled."[11] The unspoken issue was that Washington suspected that Cornwallis was attempting to classify American Loyalists and deserters as civilians in service to the British. On the issue of the Loyalist troops, Washington took the position that the disposition of those individuals was completely within the jurisdiction of the United States government. Further, he had announced on several occasions that those soldiers who deserted to the British would be hanged.

To ensure that there would be no unnecessary delay in opening the formal negotiations, Washington insisted that each side appoint two Commissioners to finalize the Articles of Capitulation. He also specified that the Commissioners had to be appointed within two hours of the receipt of his letter or hostilities would be renewed. After Washington's terms for the British surrender were delivered to Cornwallis in the early morning hours of the 19th of October, the British general sent out another flag of truce. The British commander requested further time to digest Washington's proposals. The American Commander-in-Chief agreed.

The temporary truce continued throughout the morning and early afternoon of Thursday, October 18th. Thousands of troops on both sides of the lines stood on the ramparts of their works staring at their opponents as British and French musicians serenaded the troops with martial tunes. Meanwhile, the American and French artillery stood ready to continue the bombardment if the negotiations failed. Taking full advantage of the cease-fire, Cornwallis ordered all serviceable British ships unloaded and scuttled, with the exception of the sloop of war, *Bonetta*. Cornwallis intended to use the *Bonetta*, to carry his dispatches and select passengers to New York. At two o'clock, Cornwallis accepted the surrender terms, and formal negotiations were set to begin.

Washington appointed two officers, one American and one French, to represent the allies as peace commissioners. The American officer he selected was his own aide de camp, Lieutenant Colonel John Laurens of South Carolina. General Rochambeau nominated Viscount de Noailles to represent the French in the negotiations. Cornwallis was responsible for appointing two officers of equal rank to conduct the negotiations for the British. He chose his own aide de camp, Major Alexander Ross, and Lieutenant Colonel Thomas Dundas of the 80th Regiment. The Moore house, located behind the allies' first parallel near the river, was the designated location for the final negotiations.

Laurens and de Noailles arrived at the Moore house before the British Commissioners, who arrived shortly thereafter. The negotiations continued throughout the day and into the night, with Dundas and Ross insisting that full military honors be afforded to the British during the surrender. Lauren's and de Noailles remained adamant that those honors would not be granted. Finally, a compromise was reached under which only the Gloucester garrison would be allowed to surrender with full military honors, since Tarleton's garrison was not under imminent threat of destruction. It was agreed by the Commissioners that Tarleton's legion would be permitted to lead the surrender march with drawn sabers, but all colors would remain furled. The issue of what to do with the American Loyalist troops, primarily Colonel Simcoe's "Queens Rangers," was also discussed at length. Washington's position was that the surrendering Loyalists were under the jurisdiction of the American government, and their disposition was a political and legal matter. He did, however, leave the British a way out of the dilemma. He agreed that the sloop *Bonetta* that was to sail to New York with Cornwallis's dispatches, would not be inspected before departing. Thus Cornwallis was provided a means to evacuate his Loyalist troops if chose to do so.

The Commissioners finally agreed upon Articles of Surrender during the early morning hours of Friday, the 19th of October, and copies were sent to General Washington and Lord Cornwallis. Washington informed Cornwallis that he was to sign the Articles by 11:00 a.m. and that the formal surrender would commence three hours later. Cornwallis signed the surrender document around 11:00, and it was promptly sent to General Washington, who was waiting in Redoubt 10 with his major commanders. After reading the document and examining the signatures, the commander-in-chief affixed his signature after writing, "Done in the trenches before York Town in Virginia, Oct. 19 1781." Then Rochambeau signed for the Army of France, and Admiral de Barras signed for the French Navy in lieu of Admiral de Grasse, who was ill and unable to be present.[12] All that remained to complete the capitulation was the turnover of the British fortifications to the Americans and the formal surrender ceremony.

Hessian Private Dohla was standing his final watch in the Hornwork that morning, and recorded in his diary that, "At twelve o'clock noon all watches and posts were cancelled."[13] Major Ebenezer Denny was one of the Americans who led his men into one of the British forts. At noon, he recorded in his journal:

> All is quiet. Articles of capitulation signed. Detachments of French and Americans take possession of the British forts. Major (James) Hamilton commanded a battalion which took possession of a fort immediately opposite our right and on the bank of the York River. I carried the standard of our regiment on that occasion. On entering the fort, Baron Steuben, who accompanied us, took the standard from me and planted it himself.[14]

Baron von Steuben's action reportedly angered Colonel Richard Butler, commander of the 2nd Pennsylvania, to the point that he was ready to challenge von Steuben to a duel before Washington and Rochambeau cooled him down.[15] By mid-afternoon, Allied troops had occupied all the British fortifications and batteries, including the Hornwork, the strongest fortification of the British line.

Meanwhile, soldiers of the allied army lined up in three ranks along the Hampton Road. The formation stretched for more than a mile, from the allied second parallel to a meadow known thereafter as the Surrender Field. The American troops stood on the east side of the road and the French stood opposite them on the west side. The day was warm for mid-October, and the leaves were beginning to turn to their fall colors. The French soldiers were attired in spotless white uniforms with colored lapels, collars, and buttons on their waistcoats that designated their regiments. Black gaiters pulled over their white broadcloth leggings completed the handsome uniforms. In sharp contrast to the French troops, the Americans were garbed in a mixed assortment. American Continentals wore their soiled, faded blue uniforms, while the militia wore any assortment of hunting shirts and homespun clothing, Despite their shabby attire the Americans stood proudly in their formations eager to get an up-close look at their defeated foes.

Hundreds of civilian spectators from Yorktown and the surrounding countryside were present as well. Some were residents of the Tidewater and surrounding areas, who traveled to Yorktown view the surrender. Others came to reclaim their slaves, who had joined the British hoping to gain their freedom. A number of other civilians were also on hand to witness the surrender. Among them was Sarah Osborn, wife of a New York Continental soldier, who had marched south with Washington's army and busied herself washing, mending, and cooking for the troops. On several occasions she had risked her life carrying provisions to the American front lines. She had come to witness the British surrender firsthand.[16]

On the far right of the American line nearest the British works, General Washington and his generals waited on horseback for the arrival of the British. Across the road, General Rochambeau and his major army and naval commanders, all on horseback, faced the American generals.

Between 2:00 and 3:00 p.m., the long column of British and Hessian troops emerged from the fortifications. The British appeared in clean new uniforms with scarlet red coats and white breeches, while the Hessian regiments wore mostly blue uniforms. At a distance, the allies could make out that the British colors were furled and cased, and the drummers were beating a British march. As the column neared the waiting American and French commanders, it became apparent that the officer leading the British column was not General Cornwallis but the easily recognizable ruddy-faced Irishman, General O'Hara.

As General O'Hara approached the waiting allied generals, Rochambeau's aide-de-camp, Dumas, rode forward to meet him. O'Hara asked Dumas to point out General Rochambeau, and then the Irishman began to move toward him. Realizing that O'Hara intended to surrender to Rochambeau, Dumas intercepted him and led him across the road where Washington was calmly waiting. O'Hara apologized for his error and for Cornwallis's absence, and then attempted to surrender the British army to General Washington. The allied commander, in a display of his well known sang-froid, directed O'Hara to surrender to General Benjamin Lincoln. Washington knew full well that if Cornwallis sent a subordinate to surrender, it was proper to have his own second in command accept it. After accepting the British surrender, General Lincoln directed General O'Hara to lead his troops up the road between the American and French troops toward a large meadow, where the British and Hessian troops were to be disarmed.

It was a humiliating experience for the proud British soldiers, who had to march between the American and French lines for more than a mile to reach the disarmament area. American surgeon Thatcher wrote that their conduct was "disorderly and unsoldierly, their step was irregular and their ranks were frequently broken."[17] Joseph Plumb Martin wrote:

> The British did not make so good an appearance as the German forces; but there was certainly some allowance to be made in their favour; the English felt their honour wounded, the Germans did not greatly care whose hands they were in. The British paid the Americans but little attention as they passed them, but eyed the French with considerable malice depicted in their countenances.[18]

After passing through the allied ranks, the British column turned off the road to the right, and entered the field designated for the disarmament. Mounted French Hussars encircled the field. After the furled colors of each British regiment were surrendered to the Americans, the British soldiers were required to ground their muskets, bayonets, cartridge boxes, swords, and musical instruments, while under the watchful eyes of the Hussars, and the mounted American and French officers. It was a humiliating experience, and a blow to the pride and spirit of the British. Thatcher wrote, "Some of the platoon officers were exceedingly chagrined when giving the word, '*ground arms*,' and I am a witness that they performed this duty in a very unofficerlike manner, and that many of the soldiers manifested a *sullen temper* throwing their arms on the pile with violence, as if determined to render them useless."[19]

A British officer wrote in his memoir that, "A corporal next to me shed tears, and embracing his firelock, threw it down, saying, 'May you never get so good a master.'"[20] Lieutenant William Feltman of the Pennsylvania Line described the whole affair in his journal, writing that, "The British army marched out and grounded their arms in front of our lines. Our whole army drew up for them to march through, the French army on the right and the American army on their left. The British prisoners all appeared to be much in liquor."[21]

Once the last regiment grounded its arms, the disarmed troops marched back toward the town between the same two lines of American and French troops. At least some of the American troops began to taunt and shout threats at their enemies, but the American officers soon silenced their men, and the humiliated, defeated troops marched back to Yorktown without further incident.[22]

Across the York River, a similar ceremony took place when the British Gloucester Point garrison surrendered. French Brigadier General Choisy, the commander of French troops and American militia, accepted the British surrender. At 3:00 pm, Lieutenant Colonel Tarleton, the commander of British forces at Gloucester Point, rode forward followed by his Legionnaires, all with drawn swords. They were followed by Lieutenant Colonel Simcoe's Rangers and a long column of Redcoats and Hessians. The British and Hessians were disarmed in the same manner as the Yorktown garrison. The disarmed troops were then marched back into their fortifications as prisoners of the allied force.

Lieutenant Colonel Tarleton feared for his safety after the surrender, and with good reason. There were many Americans, particularly members of the Virginia militia, who, given the opportunity, would have killed him. With the exception of Benedict Arnold, he was the most notorious and hated British officer in America. Soon after the surrender, Tarleton crossed the river to Yorktown and asked to placed under the protection of General Rochambeau. In keeping with the rules of war, the French general granted the request. Tarleton suffered yet another humiliation when he was accosted on the street in Yorktown after the surrender. A Virginian recognized the horse that Tarleton was riding as one that was stolen during one of Tarleton's forays into the Virginia countryside. The Virginian ordered the lieutenant colonel to dismount, and took the horse to return it to its rightful owner.

With the surrender of the Gloucester garrison, the Yorktown campaign was officially over. Nine weeks after marching from their encampments along the Hudson, the American and French troops accomplished what many thought impossible. After a three-week siege, the Allied army compelled the surrender of Lord Cornwallis's army. It was a stunning turn of events.

*   *   *

On the day after the surrender, Cornwallis wrote a lengthy letter to General Clinton. He informed his commander-in-chief that he had surrendered his army to the allied army, writing that, "I have the mortification to inform your Excellency that I have been forced to give up the posts of York and Gloucester, and to surrender the troops under my command, by capitulation on the 19th inst as prisoners of war to the combined forces of America and France."[23] He then continued to give his own detailed account of the siege, beginning with the statement that he "never saw this post in a very favourable light . . ."[24] That was a remarkable statement, since it was his own decision to occupy and fortify Yorktown for use as a naval base. Continuing, Cornwallis attempted to defend each decision he had made during the siege. By implication, Cornwallis also attempted to shift the blame for the defeat to General Clinton. He took great care to remind his commander-in-chief that he'd promised that, "every possible means would be tried by the navy and army to relieve us."[25] Cornwallis's letter left little doubt that he would never accept responsibility for the British defeat at Yorktown. His letter was the opening salvo in a feud between the two generals that would last throughout their lifetimes.

*   *   *

As soon as the guns went silent, both sides began to report the casualties suffered during the siege. Although some researchers have questioned the accuracy of the casualty reports, the numbers are generally consistent with the various events that occurred during the siege.

Washington's journal extract for the siege listed a total of two officers and 21 enlisted men killed, and six officers and 57 enlisted men wounded, for a total of 86 casualties. The same journal reports the French losses from the beginning of the siege through the attacks on the redoubts as significantly higher than the American losses, probably as a result of their attack on Redoubt 9.[26] Overall, the French lost two officers and 50 enlisted men killed, and nine officers and 137 enlisted men wounded, for a total of 198. The figures reported by Washington do not include the allied casualties sustained during the period 15–19 October, nor do they include the number of wounded who later died as a result of their wounds.

British losses were considerably higher than those suffered by the allies.

Their reports indicate that a total of 156 officers and rank and file were killed and another 326 were wounded, for a total of 482. In addition to the killed and wounded, the British reported that 70 men were missing at the end of the siege. It is probable that most of the men reported as missing deserted to the allies during the siege.

Washington also reported to Congress on the number of prisoners taken after the British surrender. The numbers of British, Hessians, and Loyalists taken prisoner on the 19th of October were 7,247 soldiers and 840 seamen.[27] It is presumed by many historians that many of the Loyalist troops avoided becoming prisoners of war by boarding the sloop *Bonettta* and sailing to British-occupied New York. According to the terms of the surrender, the *Bonetta* was permitted to sail without any inspection of cargo or passengers.

Most of the British officers who surrendered at Yorktown avoided months of captivity in American prison camps by signing parole affidavits that allowed them to return to New York, and eventually to Great Britain. However, some officers were required to march with their troops to the prison camps in Virginia, Maryland, and Pennsylvania to ensure that good order and discipline were maintained in the ranks. Those officers were chosen by lottery after the surrender. After arrival at the camps, the officers were permitted to find lodgings in private quarters nearby. General Cornwallis was also paroled and he sailed north to New York a few days after the surrender. He later sailed home to England, where he was received more as a hero than a disgraced general who was largely responsible for losing the Crown's southern colonies.

There is no accurate count of the numbers of civilians and other noncombatants who perished during the siege. Most of the residents of Yorktown fled before it began, but many of those who remained saw their homes blown to pieces by the allied artillery, and without doubt many were killed or seriously wounded during the bombardments. Others died from smallpox and other diseases that spread through the town during the siege. Many of the African-Americans who followed the British to Yorktown hoping to gain their freedom also perished. Some were forced to leave the British lines after they fell ill with smallpox or other diseases. Most of those died in the woods or along the roads of the peninsula. Others were hunted down by their owners and returned to bondage.

* * *

General Clinton set sail from New York with the long-awaited reinforcements for Yorktown on October 19th, the same day as the surrender. The British fleet commanded by Admiral Thomas Graves arrived off the Virginia Capes on the morning of October 24th, three days after most of the British prisoners departed Yorktown for prison camps in the north. Word of the surrender had not reached the British fleet, and Admiral Graves issued orders to his captains to prepare to break through Admiral de Grasse's blockading fleet. However, before the fleet could enter the Chesapeake, a British naval officer reached Grave's flagship with important news. The naval officer, who had departed Yorktown the day before the surrender, informed Admiral Graves and General Clinton that he had heard no firing from the defenses of Yorktown or Gloucester Point for several days. General Clinton decided to wait for additional confirmation of Cornwallis's surrender. By the 29th of October, General Clinton and Admiral Graves were convinced that Cornwallis had surrendered, and on that day the British fleet set sail back for New York.[28]

13

AFTERMATH

"Sir, I have the Honor to inform Congress, that a Reduction of the British Army under the command of Lord Cornwallis, is most happily effected—The unremitting Ardor which actuated every Officer & Soldier in the Combined Army on this Occasion, has principally led to this Important Event, at an earlier period that my most sanguine Hopes had induced me to expect . . ."
—GO: Washington
Head Quarters near York[town] 19th Octo. 1781

After signing the Articles of Surrender, Washington selected one of his trusted aides, Lieutenant Colonel Tench Tilghman of Maryland, to carry dispatches announcing the surrender to the Congress. After a perilous 300-mile journey, Tilghman arrived in Philadelphia shortly after midnight on the 24th of October. He rode directly to the residence of Thomas McKean, President of Congress. Tilghman was nearly arrested by a city watchman as he knocked vigorously on the President's door. After McKean read the dispatches, news of the victory spread rapidly throughout the city. Night watchmen announced the news as they made their rounds shouting, "Cornwallis is taken." Before long, church bells across the city, along with the bell at Independence Hall, began to peal. At dawn, cannons were fired in celebration of the victory, and Congress convened, an hour earlier than scheduled, to hear the news. The citizens of Philadelphia left their homes and gathered on street corners and in the city's taverns to celebrate the great victory. After delivering the news, Lieutenant Colonel Tilghman came down with a fever, and had to find lodgings to recuperate from his arduous journey. He had arrived penniless in Philadelphia, having spent all of his funds purchasing fresh horses and hiring a boat to sail the Chesapeake. Members of Congress contributed money to pay room and board for the fever-ridden colonel. Congress later voted to provide Tilghman a horse, saddle, bridle, and dress sword for his service.[1]

News of the victory spread quickly across the thirteen states, and celebrations were held in towns and cities from New England to Georgia. The celebrations continued for days, and church bells rang throughout the land. Local militia units paraded through towns, and salutes were fired on village greens. Taverns were crowded with celebrants, and local political leaders read long orations heralding the victory. After more than six long years, war weary Americans wondered if peace was at last at hand.

In British-occupied New York City the mood was subdued among the Tory population and troops. While there was no official word of Cornwallis's surrender, the British troops on Staten Island reported hearing the celebratory ringing of church bells and the firing of muskets and cannon in the rebel-held towns in nearby New Jersey.[2] By the end of October, there was no longer any doubt that Yorktown had fallen to the allies, and the city's large population of Loyalists wondered if the end of the war was at hand. Many had fled to New York when they were driven from their homes in rebel-occupied territory. An American victory meant that most Loyalists would live out their lives in permanent exile and never see their homes again.

VERSAILLES, FRANCE

General Rochambeau appointed the Duc de Lauzun to carry the news of the Allied victory to France. After a hazardous twenty-three day voyage, during which the British Navy pursued his ship, Lauzun disembarked at Brest and then traveled by coach to Versailles. Lauzun personally delivered the news to King Louis XVI in the Queen's chambers. The 27-year-old king was overjoyed at the news. France had finally avenged the loss of Canada to the British during the Seven Years War. Britain would soon lose all thirteen of its colonies along the Atlantic seaboard. To celebrate the great victory, the King ordered a *Te Deum* to be sung in the Metropolitan Church in Paris, and the residents of the city were ordered by the city council to illuminate the fronts of their houses.[3]

French Foreign Minister de Vergennes was no less pleased than his King. Vergennes was the key figure in forging the Franco-American alliance. He also ensured that financial aid as well as supplies, arms, and troops flowed to America, keeping the American Revolution alive during some of its darkest years. Vergennes' gamble had finally paid off for France, and Great Britain's dominance on the international stage was now seriously challenged. Minister Vergennes continued to play an important role in French politics until his death in 1787.

While the victory at Yorktown did much to restore French national pride, the gifts of money and military support had nearly bankrupted the national treasury. This along with the extravagances of the court of Louis XVI and France's ruling class had seriously damaged the national economy, sowing the seeds of discontent. Before the decade was over, France would have its own revolution, leading to the collapse of the monarchy, and the execution of most of France's nobility and aristocrats, including King Louis XVI.

LONDON, ENGLAND

News of Cornwallis's surrender at Yorktown reached London one day after Lauzun delivered the news to the French king. At noon on Sunday, November 25th, a messenger arrived at Lord George Germain's house in London. Lord Germain, Cabinet Secretary of the American Department, read the alarming letter from General Clinton that announced the news of Cornwallis's surrender. Germain and three other cabinet members then rode to the home of First Secretary (Prime Minister) Lord North, where they delivered the bad news. According to those present, North exclaimed wildly, "Oh God! It is all over!" Asked later how North took the news, an eyewitness replied, "As he would have taken a ball in his breast."[4] After consultation with the British government's Cabinet Secretaries, North sent a dispatch to King George III, who was spending the weekend with his family at the White House in Kew Gardens. Later that evening, Germain received his King's reply. In his own words, the King wrote, ". . . I trust that neither Lord George Germain nor any Member of the Cabinet will suppose that it makes the smallest alteration in those principles of my conduct, which have directed me in past time, and which will always continue to animate me under every event, in the prosecution of the present contest."[5] The King appeared ready to fight on in America, no matter the cost.

Two days later, the King officially opened the new session of Parliament. During his welcoming speech, he announced his intention to continue the fight to retain his thirteen American colonies, setting the stage for two more years of war. King George's remarks set off a firestorm among the Whigs in Parliament. Charles James Fox, a prominent Whig statesman who opposed the war, delivered a fiery speech denouncing the policies of George III and his Cabinet. The heated debate continued in Parliament for four months, ending with Lord North's resignation on March 20th, 1782, after a motion of "no confidence." Lord North's admonition that, "It is all over!" proved accurate. King George III finally had to accept the defeat of his government's policies, and sank into a deep depression that lasted for years. American, French, and British peace commissioners met for the first time in Paris in April of 1782, one month after the fall of the North government.

* * *

On October 20th, one day after the British surrender, Washington once again sought Admiral de Grasse's agreement to keep the French fleet in American waters to assist in driving the British from Charleston and Savannah. Five days later, he received the Admiral's reply. De Grasse informed Washington that he had prior instructions from the French government to return his fleet to the West Indies, along with the troops that he had landed at Yorktown. Therefore, he was unable to commit his fleet to additional operations off the Atlantic coast. On November 4th, most of the ships of Admiral de Grasse's fleet departed the Chesapeake and sailed for the West Indies, leaving the British navy in control of the waters off the American coast. Washington knew that without the support of the French fleet, he had little chance of liberating Charleston and Savannah in the coming months. He therefore began to reconsider the deployment of the allied troops at Yorktown.

After consulting with his generals, the commander-in-chief decided to split his forces between the southern and northern theaters. He was well aware that Nathaniel Greene's southern army badly needed reinforcements. Although General Greene had driven the British from the interiors of the

Carolinas and Georgia, it was still possible that the British would attempt to reinforce their garrisons at Charleston and Savannah. He therefore ordered Major General Arthur St. Clair to march south with General Anthony Wayne's Pennsylvanians and General Mordecai Gist's Maryland and Delaware troops to reinforce Greene's southern army. The remaining Continental troops would march north to winter camps in New York. By mutual agreement, General Rochambeau's troops were to remain in southern Virginia to deter the British from launching another incursion.

The French siege artillery, supported by the Regiment Soissonois and a force of hussars and grenadiers, remained at Yorktown, while the remainder of Rochambeau's regiments, including the headquarters, established their camps in and around Williamsburg. As a precautionary measure, Lauzun's Legion was deployed to Hampton. Admiral de Grasse did agree to leave four ships to guard the entrances of both the York and James Rivers. The French forces remained in Virginia until August 1782, when Rochambeau's entire force was redeployed to Rhode Island.

After General St Clair marched south toward the Carolinas on November 4th, General Washington departed Yorktown and moved his headquarters from Yorktown to Williamsburg. After a days' rest, he rode north, spending a week at Mount Vernon before continuing his journey north to rejoin the Continental army.

* * *

The British surrender at Yorktown in October 1781 did not end the American Revolutionary War. The British still had 26,000 troops deployed in North America. The cities of New York, Charleston, and Savannah remained in British hands. In addition, the British still had a number of outposts around the Great Lakes and around Lake Champlain. Altogether, some 9,000 British troops were stationed in Canada. The British also maintained a garrison at St Augustine in Florida. At sea, the British navy continued to patrol along the Atlantic coast, blockading American ports and interdicting commerce. Fighting would continue sporadically during the winter and spring of 1782, primarily in the southern theater and along the frontiers. However, due to the lack of political and public support for the war on the home front, there would be no further major British campaigns in America.

In July of 1782 the British evacuated Savannah, and in December of the same year their forces evacuated Charleston, ending once and for all their hopes of retaining their southern colonies. On November 30th, 1782, provisional articles of peace between the United States and Great Britain were signed, and in April 1783, Congress ratified the provisional articles of peace, officially ending hostilities. Then on September 3rd, 1783, the Treaty of Paris was signed, ending the war and officially recognizing the United States as an independent sovereign nation. Two months later the British army evacuated New York City, their last remaining garrison on American soil. However, it was the dramatic events that occurred during the year 1781 that set the stage for final victory and for America's independence.

EPILOGUE

To Major General Nathaniel Greene

Newburgh Feby 6th 1783

. . . If Historiographers should be hardy enough to fill the page of History with the advantages that have been gained with unequal numbers (on the part of America) in the course of this contest, & attempt to relate the distressing circumstances under which they have been obtained, it is more than probable that Posterity will bestow on their labors the epithet & marks of fiction for it will not be believed that such a force as Great Britain has employed for eight years in this Country could be baffled in their plan of Subjugating it by numbers infinitely less—composed of Men oftentimes half starved—always in Rags—without pay—and experiencing, at times, every Species of distress which human nature is capable of undergoing.

—Go. Washington

THE BRITISH
"I never saw such fighting, since God made me."
—*General Cornwallis*

LORD CHARLES CORNWALLIS

After returning to New York on parole, General Cornwallis was exchanged for Henry Laurens on the 31st of December 1781. After retuning to England, Cornwallis began to repair his damaged reputation by shifting the blame to Sir Henry Clinton for the humiliating British defeat at Yorktown. He found a sympathetic listener in King George III, who appointed him as Governor General and Commander-in-Chief in India in 1786. In that capacity, he achieved success in several military campaigns, and was recognized for his military and civil administration reforms. After his success in the Third Anglo-Mysore War, he was awarded the title Marquess Cornwallis. In 1794, he retuned to England to assume duties as Master-General of the Ordnance, and in 1798 he was appointed Lord Lieutenant of Ireland and Commander-in-Chief Ireland. He was reappointed as Governor-General of India in 1805, but died that October, shortly after his arrival. He was sixty-seven years old. To the end of his life, he continued to point the blame for his loss at Yorktown toward General Clinton. Unfairly or not, British public opinion generally agreed with Lord Cornwallis, and his reputation as one of Britain's great generals remains intact.

GENERAL SIR HENRY CLINTON

Sir Guy Carleton replaced General Clinton as Commander-in-Chief in 1782, after which Clinton returned to England. In 1783, he published a *Narrative of the Campaign of 1781 in North America*, in which he attempted to blame Cornwallis for the failure of the British southern strategy. He then resumed his seat in Parliament in 1784, and won reelection in 1790. Three years later he was promoted to the rank of full General in the army. In July of 1794, he was appointed Governor of Gibraltar, but he became ill and died before he could assume the position. He was 65 years old. Although he worked for more than a decade to clear his name, Henry Clinton's legacy is inextricably linked to the events of 1781, culminating with the disastrous British defeat at Yorktown. It happened on his watch as Commander-in-Chief North America.

GENERAL CHARLES O'HARA

General O'Hara, who fought courageously at Guilford Courthouse, and despite his disabling wounds returned to the field in time to preside over the British surrender at Yorktown, returned to England on parole after the surrender. In 1784, he fled England to the Continent because of gambling debts. After Lord Cornwallis helped him pay off his debts, he returned to England. In 1793, he was promoted to Lieutenant General, and a year later he was captured in Toulon France. He spent two years in prison in Paris, and after his exchange he was named Governor of Gibraltar. In 1798, he was promoted to full general. General O'Hara died in 1802, as a result of wounds he received at Guilford Courthouse. He was 62 years old. General O'Hara remained loyal to General Cornwallis throughout his life-time.

REAR ADMIRAL THOMAS GRAVES

A year after the Battle of the Capes, Admiral Graves' fleet was caught in a violent storm off the coast of Newfoundland. The fleet lost four major warships and 3,500 sailors perished. Admiral Graves subsequently returned to England and served as Admiral Richard Howe's second in command during the French Revolutionary Wars. He was later promoted to full admiral, and was elevated to the Irish peerage as Baron Graves. He died in 1802 at the age of seventy-six.

BRIGADIER GENERAL BENEDICT ARNOLD

Benedict Arnold departed New York with his family on December 8th, 1781. After reaching England, he tried to convince the North government and King George III to carry on the fight with he Americans. He then attempted unsuccessfully to return to America after General Carleton was appointed to replace General Clinton. Further attempts to secure positions with the government, or with the British East India Company, were also unsuccessful. Rejected by British society, Arnold moved with his family to New Brunswick, Canada, where he engaged in land speculation and made a series of bad business deals. Arnold and his family returned to London in 1791. He later outfitted a ship and operated as a privateer against the French in the West Indies. His career as a privateer was cut short when the French captured him. Arnold managed to escape by bribing his guards, but his privateering venture was at an end. Benedict Arnold returned to England penniless and in declining health. The American turncoat, who had ravaged southern Virginia and New London, Connecticut during the year 1781, died in June of 1801 at the age of sixty.

LIEUTENANT COLONEL BANASTRE TARLETON

The infamous Lieutenant Colonel Tarleton returned to England on parole after the American victory at Yorktown. He ran unsuccessfully for Parliament in 1784, but afterwards won a seat in 1790, representing Liverpool. In 1794 he was promoted to Major General in the British Army, and assumed the position of Commissioner of the Cork District in Ireland. He continued to earn promotions, and in 1812 he achieved the rank of full general. Tarleton hoped to command British forces in the Peninsular campaign, but the appointment went instead to Wellington. In 1815, Tarleton was made a Baronet. General Banastre Tarleton married the daughter of a duke in 1798, and he lived until the year 1833, dying at the age of seventy-eight. Americans most remember Tarleton for his role as Cornwallis's ruthless cavalry commander, while his own countrymen remember him as a general officer and Member of Parliament.

LIEUTENANT COLONEL JOHN GRAVES SIMCOE

The leader of the Loyalist Queen's Rangers, who was in poor health during the siege of Yorktown, was granted a parole, and sailed home to England in December of 1781. He was elected to Parliament in 1790, and in 1791 he was appointed lieutenant governor of Upper Canada, a post he held until 1798. He later served as commander of British forces in Haiti with the rank of major general. After returning to England, he was promoted to lieutenant general, and was appointed Commander-in-Chief of India. He became ill during the voyage to India, and was forced to return to England, where he died in October 1806 at the age of fifty-four.

LORD GEORGE GERMAIN

The British Secretary of State for the American colonies, Lord Germain, received much of the blame for the loss of the American colonies. With little understanding of the American people and the geography of the colonies, he attempted to micro-manage the prosecution of the war from London. His tenacity in refusing to concede the loss of any of the colonies led to his forced resignation from both his cabinet post and his seat in Parliament in 1782. He was subsequently elevated to peerage by King George III, with the title Viscount Sackville. However, he never took his seat in the House of Lords due to his failing health. Germain died in 1785 at the age of sixty-nine.

LORD FREDERICK NORTH

After his government received a vote of no confidence in Parliament in March 1782, Lord North's 12-year term as Prime Minister of Great Britain was at an end. The career politician returned to power as Home Secretary in April 1783, but he was forced out of that office eight months later. North retained his seat in the House of Commons until 1790. Soon thereafter, he entered the House of Lords upon the death of his father, the Earl of Guilford. He died in London in 1792. He was sixty years old.

THE FRENCH

Humanity has won its battle. Liberty now has a country.
—Marquis de Lafayette

GENERAL JEAN-BAPTISE-DONATIEN DE VIMEUR, COMTE DE ROCHAMBEAU

General Rochambeau returned to France in 1783, where he was decorated by King Louis XVI and appointed governor of Picardy, a province in the north of France. During the French Revolution, he was arrested and narrowly escaped execution during the Reign of Terror. He was later made a marshal of France, and in 1804 he was awarded the Legion of Honor by Napoleon Bonaparte. Rochambeau died in 1807 at the age of eighty-one.

ADMIRAL FRANCOIS JOSEPH PAUL COMTE DE GRASSE

After his fleet returned to the Caribbean, Admiral de Grasse was defeated by Admiral Hood in the battle of St. Kitts, and later at the Battle of the Saintes. De Grasse was taken prisoner when his badly damaged flagship, *Ville de Paris*, was captured. When de Grasse returned to France, he stood court-martial for his defeats, but he was acquitted on all charges. He died in 1788 at the age of sixty-five.

ARMAND-LOUIS DE GONTAUT-BIRON, DUC DE LAUZUN

The commander of Lauzun's Legion returned to France soon after Cornwallis's surrender, carrying the news of victory to King Louis XVI. During the French Revolution, he aligned himself with the revolutionaries, and was promoted to lieutenant general. The Revolutionary Tribunal later accused him of political crimes, and on 31 December 1793, Lauzun met his end on the guillotine at the age of forty-six.

GILBERT DU MOTIER, MARQUIS DE LAFAYETTE

Lafayette returned to France in December 1781, where his countrymen greeted him as a hero. He gave valuable assistance to the Americans during peace negotiatons that led to the 1783 Treaty of Paris. As commander-in-chief of the National Guard during the French Revolution, he tried to maintain order, but ran afoul of the radical factions. Lafayette fled the country, but he was apprehended by the Austrians and spent over five years in prison. After Napoleon Bonaparte arranged his release in 1797, Lafayette returned to France. He later served in the Chamber of Deputies, and in 1824 he accepted an invitation from President James Monroe to visit the United States. During his return visit, he toured the country, visiting many of his former comrades-in-arms. Lafayette died in Paris in 1834 at the age of seventy-seven.

CHARLES GRAVIER, COMTE DE VERGENNES

After 1781, the French Foreign Minister continued to support the American cause. During the peace negotiations that led to the Treaty of Paris in 1783, Vergennes tried to balance the conflicting interests of France, the United States, and Spain. He was concerned that France had carried most of the financial burden of the war, but had gained very little at the peace table. Nonetheless, Vergennes remained in the government until his death in 1787, two years before the outbreak of the French Revolution. He was seventy years old.

THE AMERICANS

"The times that tried men's souls are over—and the greatest and completest revolution the world ever knew, gloriously and happily accomplished."
—*Thomas Paine*

GENERAL GEORGE WASHINGTON

No other American could have kept the Patriot cause alive during the tumultuous events of 1781. George Washington stayed with the army until the last British troops departed New York in November of 1783. Prior to the departure of the British, Washington was faced with the possibility of another mutiny; this one led by his own officers. In what historians have labeled the "Newburgh Conspiracy," officers of the Continental Army were prepared to take action against Congress to secure the pay that they had been promised but never received. At a meeting held on March 15th, 1783, Washington gave an impassioned speech counseling his officers to exercise patience and recognize the supremacy of Congress. The majority of those present affirmed their loyalty to the nation, and the crisis was averted. On December 4th, 1783, Washington bid farewell to his officers at Fraunces Tavern in New York City, and then traveled to Annapolis Maryland, where he formally tendered his resignation as Commander-in-Chief of the army to Congress. George Washington then returned to Mount Vernon to resume his private life.

In May of 1787, Washington returned to public life to serve as presiding officer during the Constitutional Convention in Philadelphia. After the Constitution was ratified by the states, Washington was elected the first President of the United States. After serving two four-year terms, he again returned to his home at Mount Vernon, and once again resumed his private life. George Washington died at Mount Vernon on December 14th, 1799 at age sixty-seven.

MAJOR GENERAL NATHANIEL GREENE

Next to General Washington, Nathaniel Greene was the officer most responsible for the remarkable American strategic victories achieved during the year 1781. Afterwards, Greene kept the pressure on British and Loyalist forces until they evacuated Charleston in December 1782. After the war, Greene was plagued by debts that he had incurred during his war-time service. He was forced to sell his home in Warwick, Rhode Island, and moved with his family to Georgia. The grateful people of South Carolina and Georgia awarded Greene grants of land and money, including an estate north of Savannah. However, he was not able to make his plantation a financial success. In 1786, Nathaniel Greene, the former Quaker and self-taught general, died of a heat stroke. He was forty-four years old.

MAJOR GENERAL BENJAMIN LINCOLN

The American general who surrendered Charleston to the British, and later accepted the surrender of the British at Yorktown, served as Secretary of War from 1781 to 1783. In 1787, he played a key role in crushing Shay's Rebellion, an uprising by New England farmers and businessmen who were opposed to a strong central government. The rebellion threatened to plunge the new nation into civil war. Benjamin Lincoln remained active in public life until his retirement in 1809. He died in 1810 at the age of seventy-seven.

MAJOR GENERAL "MAD" ANTHONY WAYNE

After Yorktown, Wayne marched his Pennsylvania Continentals south to join Greene's army, where he remained until the British evacuated Charleston. He was promoted to major general in 1783. After the war, Wayne returned to Pennsylvania and served a term in the Pennsylvania legislature. He then moved to Georgia, and settled on land awarded to him by the state of Georgia. In 1792, President Washington appointed Wayne as commander of the Legion of the United States to bring peace to the nation's troubled northwest frontier. After taking command, General Wayne led the American forces against Indian tribes in Ohio, where he won a decisive battle against the tribes at Fallen Timbers. He died in Erie Pennsylvania in 1796 at the age of fifty-one.

MAJOR GENERAL FRIEDRICH WILHELM VON STEUBEN

General von Steuben remained on active duty until 1783, when he was discharged with honors. A year later, he was awarded American citizenship by the Pennsylvania legislature. Beset with financial problems, Congress finally granted von Steuben a lifetime pension, and he eventually settled on a small estate near Utica, New York. General Von Steuben remained a lifelong bachelor, and was a beloved hero of the American people. He died in 1794 at the age of sixty-four.

MAJOR GENERAL HENRY KNOX

Henry Knox, Washington's Chief of Artillery, was promoted to Major General in March of 1782. He continued to serve throughout the remainder of the war and during the demobilization of the Army after the ratification of the Treaty of Paris. Knox remained on active duty and was present at Washington's farewell address to his officers at Francuses Tavern in New York City. Knox resigned his army commission in 1784, and returned to his family's home in Massachusetts. In March of 1785, he was appointed as the nation's second Secretary of War under the Articles of Confederation, and later as the first Secretary of War under the newly ratified United States Constitution. He served in Washington's Cabinet as Secretary of War until 1795. After his retirement, Knox moved with his family to his estate, Montpelier, at Thomaston, Maine where he was involved in finding many new businesses in the area. Henry Knox died unexpectedly in 1806 at the age of fifty-six.

BRIGADIER GENERAL DANIEL MORGAN

The Virginian who defeated Tarleton at the Cowpens in January 1781 retuned to his home after the British surrender at Yorktown. He then began to invest in land, eventually acquiring more than a quarter of a million acres. In 1794, Daniel Morgan was recalled to active service to help suppress the Whiskey Rebellion. He later served a term in the U.S. House of Representatives from 1797 to 1799. He died in 1802 on his sixty-sixth birthday.

BRIGADIER GENERAL THOMAS SUMTER

After the war ended, the "The Carolina Gamecock" served two separate terms in the U.S. House of Representatives, and later in the U.S. Senate. He retired from his Senate seat in 1810, and died in 1832 at the age of ninety-eight. He earned the distinction of being the last surviving general of the American Revolution.

BRIGADIER GENERAL FRANCIS MARION

The renowned leader of South Carolina's militia and partisan forces, known as "The Swamp Fox," carried on a relentless campaign against the British and Loyalist forces in South Carolina and Georgia until the end of the war. Afterward he served several terms in the South Carolina State Senate. Marion married late in his life, and died childless in 1795. He was sixty-three years old.

BRIGADIER GENERAL THOMAS NELSON JR.

The Governor of Virginia, militia commander, and signer of the Declaration of Independence was in failing health by the end of the siege of Yorktown. As a result of his illness, Nelson was forced to resign from office as governor of Virginia. Poor health was not his only problem. His home in Yorktown was destroyed during the siege, and he was two million dollars in debt having spent his fortune supporting the Revolution. The Virginia legislature also ordered an investigation of Nelson's actions during his term as governor. His political adversaries accused him of exceeding his authority while in office, but he was subsequently cleared of all wrongdoing. Thomas Nelson later retired to a small estate in Hanover County, though bankrupt and in broken health. He died in 1789 at the age of fifty-one.

COLONEL WILLIAM WASHINGTON

After his capture at Eutaw Springs, Greene's daring cavalry leader spent the remainder of the war as a prisoner, under house arrest in the Charleston area. After the war he married Jane Elliot, and settled in South Carolina. He served in the South Carolina Legislature from 1787 to 1804. He was also commissioned at the rank of Brigadier General in the United States Army in 1798, and served until 1800. During that period, he was responsible for the defenses of South Carolina and Georgia. William Washington died in 1810 at the age of fifty-eight.

COLONEL RICHARD BUTLER

The Pennsylvania Colonel who kept a detailed journal at the siege of Yorktown was put in charge of Indian affairs in the Northwest Territory after the war. He negotiated the treaties of Fort Stanwix and Fort McIntosh, before returning to Pennsylvania where he accepted a judgeship in Allegheny County, and later served in the state legislature. When the Native Americans in Ohio resisted American troops, Butler was appointed as a major general, and was second-in-command of a 1791 expedition led by General Arthur St . Clair. He was killed in a battle with the Miami Indians at the Battle of the Wabash in Ohio on November 4, 1791.

LIEUTENANT COLONEL "LIGHT HORSE HARRY" LEE

Henry Lee left the army shortly after the British surrender at Yorktown, due to illness. From 1786 to 1788, he served as a delegate to the Continental Congress, and was Governor of Virginia from 1791 to 1794. He was later commissioned as a major general in the United States Army, and served from 1798 to 1800. Afterward, he served in the U.S. House of Representatives. Despite his success in public life, Lee was unable to manage his financial affairs, and he soon found himself deep in debt. As a result, he was sentenced to debtors prison in 1808. After his release, Lee was seriously injured in a Baltimore riot, and in 1813 he sailed to the Caribbean to recover. He died in Georgia in 1818, while attempting to travel home to Virginia. Henry Lee, the father of future Confederate General Robert E. Lee, was sixty-two years old.

LIEUTENANT COLONEL ALEXANDER HAMILTON
Following the war Hamilton served in the Continental Congress from 1782 to 1783, after which he founded a successful law practice. He later authored the majority of the Federalist Papers, and in 1789 was appointed as the nation's first Secretary of the Treasury. He resigned from the cabinet in 1795 and returned to his law practice in New York. He remained politically active, advocating a strong central government and the establishment of a national bank. After the 1804 gubernatorial election in New York, Hamilton was killed in a duel with Aaron Burr, who had lost the election. Hamilton had backed Burr's opponent, Morgan Lewis, during the campaign. Hamilton was forty-nine years old at the time of his death.

LIEUTENANT COLONEL JOHN LAURENS
The young South Carolinian, who was one of Washington's most trusted aides, traveled south to join General Greene's army after the British surrender at Yorktown. Laurens was killed on August 27, 1782 during a skirmish with a large British foraging party near the Combahee River. Laurens was killed two months before his 28th birthday.

LIEUTENANT COLONEL DAVID HUMPHREYS
General Washington's trusted aide and confidant, David Humphreys, remained on Washington's staff until 1784, when he was appointed to a commission that was negotiating treaties of commerce with European nations. In 1791 he was appointed minister to Portugal. He was later

appointed minister to Spain, and served the Connecticut House of Representatives. During the War of 1812, Humphreys was commissioned a
brigadier general in the Connecticut militia. The highly respected soldier,
citizen, and businessman died in 1818 at the age of sixty-six.

LIEUTENANT COLONEL TENCH TIIGHMAN
The trusted aide and confidant of General Washington, who carried the
news of Lord Cornwallis's surrender to Congress, stayed with the Commander-in-Chief until he submitted his resignation to Congress at Annapolis in December 1783. The Marylander then returned to the mercantile
business in Baltimore, forming a company in partnership with Robert
Morris. Tench Tighlman died on April 18, 1786 at the age of forty-one.

ROBERT MORRIS
Robert Morris, who is aptly called the financier of the American Revolution, continued his efforts to put the country's financial house in order
after 1781. In 1787 he became a delegate to the Constitutional Convention, and later served as a United States Senator. As a Senator representing
Pennsylvania, Morris generally supported the Federalist agenda and Hamilton's economic policies. Despite his financial acumen, Morris' personal
finances collapsed in 1798, due to his overuse of credit and margin to
finance his endeavors in land speculation. He was imprisoned for debt in
Philadelphia from 1798 to 1801. After his release he spent the remainder
of his life in retirement, and died in 1806 at the age of seventy-two.

DR. JAMES THATCHER
The Army surgeon, who kept one of the most detailed journals of the
American Revolutionary War, remained with the Continental Army until
1783. After leaving the army he began a medical practice in Plymouth,
Massachusetts. In addition to his widely acclaimed journal, Thatcher
authored a number of books on medicine and other topics. Doctor
Thatcher died in 1844 at the age of ninety.

MAJOR EBENEZER DENNY
After leaving the army in 1795, the army major, who wrote one of the
most intriguing accounts of the siege of Yorktown, returned to civilian life

in his native state of Pennsylvania. In 1797, Denny was elected as Allegheny County Commissioner, and in July of 1816 he became the first mayor of the city of Pittsburgh. He retired from public service in 1817 and died in 1822 at the age of sixty-one.

CAPTAIN JAMES DUNCAN

The twenty-five-year-old captain in the Pennsylvania Line, who kept an excellent journal of his service, continued to serve in Colonel Hazen's regiment until the end of the war. He then returned to Pennsylvania, and was appointed as Adams County's first prothonotary, a court position he held for twenty-one years. In 1823, he moved to Mercer County, Pennsylvania, where he resided until his death in 1844 at the age of eighty-eight.

SAPPER AND MINER SERGEANT JOSEPH PLUMB MARTIN

After his discharge from the Continental Army in 1783, Martin taught school in New York for a year. He then moved to Maine and became one of the founders of the town of Prospect near Stockton Springs. He was a farmer, and over the years he held positions as selectman, Justice of the Peace, and town clerk. In his spare time, Martin wrote numerous stories and poems, including his well known "Narrative of a Revolutionary Soldier." In 1818, Martin received a war pension of $96 dollars a year for the rest of his life. Joseph Plum Martin died in 1850 at the age of eighty-nine.

SERGEANT PETER FRANCISCO

After recovering from the serious wounds that he suffered at the Battle of Guilford Courthouse, the "Virginia Giant" returned to duty and served under General Lafayette at Yorktown. After the war, Francisco spent four years pursuing a basic education. He was married three times and raised six children According to his third wife, Peter Francisco served during the War of 1812 with the 5th Regiment of U.S. Infantry. He died in 1831 at the age of seventy-one. A monument honoring the heroic Virginian stands on the Guilford Courthouse Battlefield, and another is located in New Bedford, Massachusetts.

SARAH OSBORN

After the British surrender at Yorktown, Sarah Osborn returned to West

Point with her husband. After he was discharged in 1783, Sarah and her husband moved to nearby New Windsor. Her husband later deserted her, and she returned to her home in Orange County, New York. She later married John Benjamin, who was also a veteran of the Revolution. The couple later moved to Wayne County Pennsylvania. Sarah filed a pension deposition in 1837, at the age of eighty-one, under the pension act for Revolutionary War veterans and their widows. Her application was approved, and she received a double pension for both her husbands. Her deposition is on file at the National Archives. Sarah Osborn died in 1854 at the age of ninety-eight.

NOTES

Chapter One: The Darkest New Year
1. Russell Roberts, Mitchell Lane, *Holidays and Celebrations in Colonial America* (Hockessin: DE, 2006), p. 19.
2. *Heath's Memoirs of the American War*, reprinted from original addition of 1798, (New York, 1904), p. 282.
3. Ibid.p.282. See also Frank Landon Humphreys, *Life and times of David Humphreys* (New York & London, 1917), pp. 194–195.
4. Piers, Mackesy, *The War in America 1775–1783* (Lincoln NE & London, 1964) pp. 367–368.
5. Ibid. p. 370.
6. Jeremy Black, *George III, America's Last King* (New Haven & London, 2006) pp. 227–241.
7. David McCullough, *John Adams* (New York, London, Sidney, Singapore, 2001) p. 241.
8. John Ferling, *Almost a Miracle* (New York, 2007) pp. 472–473.

Chapter Two: Disorder, Fear, and Mutiny
1. Robert K. Wright, Jr. *The Continental Army* (Washington, DC, 1983) pp. 153–161.
2. Carl Van Doren, *Mutiny in January* (New York, 1943) pp. 34–35.
3. Ibid.
4. General Wayne to Colonel Francis Johnston, Dec.16, 1780, in Charles Stille's, *Major General Anthony Wayne and The Pennsylvania Line* (Philadelphia, 1893) pp. 240–241.
5. Pennsylvania in the War of the Revolution, Battalions and Line 1775–1883. Volume II (Harrisburg, 1780) p. 631.

6. Enos Reeves Letterbook Extracts, January 2–17, 1781 in The American Revolution, Writings from the War of Independence (New York, 2001) pp. 630–637.
7. Van Doren, Mutiny in January, p. 42.
8. Ibid.
9. Reeves, p. 630.
10. Ibid.
11. General Wayne to General Washington, January, 1, 1781, in Charles Stille's, Major General Anthony Wayne and the Pennsylvania Line (Philadelphia, 1893) p. 242.
12. Reeves, p. 631.
13. Ibid.
14. ibid. p. 632.
15. General Wayne to General Washington in Stille's, p. 242.
16. General Washington to Brigadier General Anthony Wayne, January 3d, 1781, from The writings of George Washington from the original manuscript sources, Electronic Text Center, University of Virginia Library.
17. Ibid.
18 Van Doren, p. 66.
19. Oliver De Lancey: Journal, January 3–21, 1781 in The American Revolution, Writings from the War of Independence, p. 639.
20. Van Doren, p. 73.
21. Ibid. p. 74.
22. Ibid. p. 75
23. Ibid. p. 128
24 George Washington to Meshech Weare, et al, January 5, 1781, Circular Letter on Pennsylvania Line Mutiny. George Washington Papers at the Library of Congress, 1741–1799.
25. Heath's Memoirs, p. 286.
26. James Thatcher, A Military Journal During the American Revolutionary War, From 1775 to 1783. pp 245–247.

Chapter Three: Hills of the South Country
1. Charles Cornwallis to Henry Clinton, 29 August 1780, in Correspondence of Charles, first Marquis Cornwallis, Vol. I, Charles Ross, Esq., (London, 1859). p. 58.
2. Lawrence E. Babits, A Devil of a Whipping The Battle of the Cowpens (Chapel Hill, 1998) p. 3.
3. Ibid. p. 49.
4. Terry Golway, Washington's General (New York, 2006) p. 241.

Chapter Four: Hell in Virginia
1. Michael Kranish, Flight from Monticello-Thomas Jefferson at War (New York, 2010) p. 164.

2. Ibid. p. 173
3. Ibid. p. 175
4. Ibid. p. 195
5. Thomas Jefferson to George Washington, 10 January 1781, in The Project Gutenberg, EBook of Memoir, Correspondence, and Miscellanies, From the Papers of Thomas Jefferson, by Thomas Jefferson.

Chapter Five: Sunrise at the Cowpens
1. Pension application of John Whelchel W6498, Transcribed by Will Graves, in Southern Campaign Revolutionary War Pension Statements and Rosters at http://southerncampaign.org/pen/Index.htm
2. Tarleton to Cornwallis, January 4, 1781, in History of the Campaigns of 1780 and 1781 in the Southern Provinces of North America by Lieutenant Colonel Tarleton. p. 251.
3. Don Higginbotham, *Daniel Morgan Revolutionary Rifleman* (Chapel Hill, 1961) p. 130 and Edwin C. Bearss, *Battle of the Cowpens* (Washington D.C., 1967) p. 11.
4. William Johnson, *Sketches of the Life and Correspondence of Nathaniel Greene, Major General of the Armies of the United States in the War of the Revolution, Vol. I* (Charleston, 1822) p. 376.
5. Ibid.
6. George Scheer and Hugh Rankin, *Rebels and Redcoats* (New York, 1957) p. 428.
7. Tarleton, p. 220.
8. Ibid. p. 222.
9. Pension application of John Jolly W9276.
10. Lawrence Babits, *A Devil of a Whipping, the Battle of Cowpens* (Chapel Hill, 1998) p. 92.
11. James Collins, *Autobiography of a Revolutionary War Soldier* (1859, Reprint New York, 1979) p. 52.
12. Tarleton, p. 224
13. Pension application of Henry Wells S11712.
14, Babbits, p. 143
15. Bearss, p. 44
16, Pension application of John Whelchel W6498.

Chapter Six: The Race to the Dan
1. Charles Cornwallis letter to Henry Clinton, 18 January 1781.
2. Correspondence of Cornwallis, Vol 1, p. 517
3. Ibid. p. 518
4. Nathaniel Greene letter to George Washington, 9 February 1781.
5. Ibid.
6. Nathaniel Greene letter to George Washington, 28 February 1781.

7. Nathaniel Greene letter to George Washington, 10 March 1781.

8. Gilbert du Motier Lafayette to George Washington, 7 March 1781.

9, Gilbert du Motier Lafayette to George Washington, 15 March 1781.

10. Ibid.

11. Ellis Oberholtzer, *Robert Morris Patriot and Financier* (New York, 1903) p. 74.

Chapter Seven: We Fight, Get Beat, and Fight Again

1. Golway, p. 255

2. Ibid.

3. Henry Lee, *The Campaign of 1781 in the Carolinas* (Philadelphia, 1824) p. 169.

4. Lawrence Babits & Joshua Howard, *Long, Obstinate, and Bloody* (Chapel Hill, 2009) p. 108.

5. Pension application of Nathan Slade W6071.

6. Pension application of Benedict Wadkins W11709.

7. Sir John Ross, *Memoirs and Correspondence of Admiral Lord de Saumarez, Vol. II* (London, 1838) pp. 337–338.

8. Ibid.

9. Major Rowland Broughton-Mainwaring, *Historical Record of the Royal Welch Fusiliers*, (London, 1889) p. 101.

10. Pension application of John Warren S3457.

11. Pension application of Westwood Armistead W8100.

12. Babits & Howard, p. 129.

13. Ibid. p. 140.

14. Charles Ross, *Correspondence of Charles, First Marquis Cornwallis Vol. I* (London, 1859) p. 86–87.

15. Pension application of Peter Francisco W11021.

16. Lee, p. 175.

17. Tarleton, p. 282.

18. John Buchanan, *The Road to Guilford Courthouse* (New York, 1997) p. 379.

19. Babbits & Howard, p. 175.

20. Ross, p. 87.

Chapter Eight: Everything Has Changed

1. George Washington to Benjamin Tallmadge, 30 April 1781.

2. George Washington to John Laurens, 9 April 1781.

3. Charles Cornwallis to George Germain, 18 April 1781.

4. Charles Cornwallis to Henry Clinton, 23 April 1781.

5. Charles Cornwallis to George Germain, 23 April 1781.

6. George Washington to Chevalier de la Luzerne, 23 May 1781.

7. John Ferling, *Almost a Miracle-The American Victory in the War of Independence* (New York, 2007) p. 505.

8. David Lee Russell, *The American Revolution in the Southern Colonies* (Jefferson, NC, 2000) p. 243.

9. Charles Caldwell, *Memoirs of the Life and Campaigns of the Hon. Nathaniel Greene* (Philadelphia, 1819) p. 440.

10. Charles Cornwallis to Henry Clinton, 26 May 1781.

11. *Military Journal of Major Ebenezer Denny* (Philadelphia, 1859) 1–15 May 1781.

Chapter Nine: The Lion Sleeps at Yorktown

1. John Rhodehamel, *The American Revolution, Writings from the War of Independence* (New York, 2001) p. 695

2. Ibid. p.697.

3. Michael Kranish, *Flight from Monticello-Thomas Jefferson at War* (New York, 2010) p. 366.

4. Tarleton, p. 369.

5. Claude Blanchard, *Journal of Claude Blanchard* (New York, 1969) p. 115.

6. George Washington to Count de Rochambeau, 13 June 1781.

7. George Washington to Admiral Alexandre de Grasse, 17 August 1781.

8. Ellis Oberholtzer, *Robert Morris, Patriot and Financier* (New York, 1903) p. 83.

9. John Fiske, *The American Revolution, Vol. II.* (Cambridge, MA, 1891) p. 277.

10. Henry Clinton to Charles Cornwallis, 11 June 1781, and Ferling, p. 513.

11. Charles Cornwallis to Henry Clinton, 27 July 1781.

12. Charles Cornwallis to Henry Clinton, 12 July 1781.

13. Charles Cornwallis to Henry Clinton, 23 August 1781.

14, George Washington to Gilber du Motier Lafayette, 15 August 1781.

15. Gilbert du Motier Lafayette to George Washington, 21-22 August 1781.

16. Thatcher, p. 261.

17. Ferling, p. 525.

18. Thatcher, p. 263.

19. Ibid.

20. Oberholtzer, p. 84.

21. Ibid. p. 88.

22. Robert Selig, *March to Victory, Washington Rochambeau and the Yorktown Campaign of 1781* (Washington D.C., 2005) p. 40.

23. Ibid.

24. Jerome Greene, *The Guns of Independence—The Siege of Yorktown* (New York, 2005, 2009) p. 33.

25. Ibid.

Chapter Ten: We Have Pursued Them to the Eutaws

1. Lee, p. 300.

2. Scheer and Rankin, p. 460.

3. Ibid.
4. Nathaniel Greene to George Washington, 6 August 1781.
5. Lee, p. 100.
6. Christine Swager, *The Valiant Died* (Westminster, MD, 2006) p.69.
7. Ibid. p. 73.
8. Alexander Stewart to Charles Cornwallis, 9 September 1781.
9. John Rhodehamel, *The American Revolution, Writings from the War of Independence* (New York, 2001); Otho Williams, *Narrative of the Battle of Eutaw Springs*, pp. 707–720.
10. Ibid.
11. Ibid.
12. Nathaniel Greene to the President of Congress, 11 September 1781.
13. Ibid.
14. Steven Haller, *William Washington: Cavalryman of the Revolution* (Westminster, MD, 2001).
15. Pension application of William Griffis R4323.
16. Lee, p. 473.
17. Pension application of Hezekiah Carr W3509.

Chapter Eleven: The Siege of Yorktown

1. *Military Journal of Major Ebenezer Denny* (Philadelphia, 1859) September 15 1781. p. 39.
2. William Feltman, *The Journal of William Feltman of the First Pennsylvania Regiment, 1781–82.* (Philadelphia, 1853) p.12.
3. *Diary of Captain James Duncan in the Yorktown Campaign* in Journals and Diaries of the War of Revolution with Lists of Officers and Soldiers, 1755–1783 (Harrisburg, 1893) p. 744–752.
4. Joseph Plum Martin, *A Narrative of a Revolutionary War* (New York, 2001).
5. Greene, p. 79.
6. Ibid. p. 92.
7. Martin, p. 197.
8. Greene, p. 92.
9. Feltman, p. 3.
10. John Davis, *The Yorktown Campaign. Journal of Captain John Davis of the Pennsylvania Line.* Pennsylvania Magazine of History and Biography V (Philadelphia, 1881) pp. 290–305.
11. Martin, p. 198.
12. Greene, p. 100.
13. Denny, p. 40.
14. *Washington's Journal,* Extracts of the Siege. Sept. 28–Oct. 20, 1781.
15. Ibid.

16. Thatcher, 272.
17. Ibid.
18. Tarleton, p. 387.
19. Ibid.
20. Ibid.
21.Thatcher, p. 221.
22. Ibid.
23. Ibid.
24. Tarleton, p. 387.
25. *Lauzun's Memoirs*, Magazine of American History, VI, p. 53.
26. Greene, p. 148.
27. Davis, p. 304.
28. Feltman, p. 17.
29. Duncan, p. 749.
30. Martin, pp. 198–199.
31. Davis, p. 304.
32. Thatcher, p. 272.
33. Greene, p. 159.
34. Duncan, p. 749.
35. Denny, p. 41.
36. Greene, p. 207.
37. Ibid, p. 196.
38. *Memoir of General Graham* (Edinburgh, 1862) p. 60.
39. Johann Conrad Dohla, *A Hessian Diary of the American Revolution* (Norman, OK, 1990) p. 167.
40. James Bartholomew, *Journal of Rear Admiral Bartholomew James* (London, 1896) p. 121.
41. Thatcher, p. 274.
42. Feltman, p. 19.
43. Washington's Journal, p. 168.
44. Mrs. Williams, *Biography of Revolutionary Heroes Containing the Life of Brigadier Gen. Barton and also Captain Stephen Olney* (New York, 1839) p. 276.
45. Martin, p. 202.
46. Ibid.
47, Howard Rice and Anne Brown, *American Campaigns of Rochambeau's Army, 1780–1783: The Journals of Clermont-Crevecoeur, Verger and Berthier* (Princeton, 1972) pp. 141–143.
48. Samuel Abbot Green, *My Campaigns in America, A Journal dept by Count William de Deux-Ponts 1780–81* (Boston, 1868) p. 144.
49. Ibid. p. 146.
50. Rice & Brown, pp 141–143.

51. Ibid.
52. Williams, p 276.
53. Martin, p. 202
54. Williams, p. 277.
55. Thatcher, p. 275–276.
56. Washington's Journal, p. 168.
57. Charles Cornwallis to Henry Clinton, 15 October 1781.
58. Denny, p. 43.
59. Tarleton, p. 400.

Chapter Twelve: Capitulation
1. Washington's Journal, p. 169.
2. Ibid.
3. Thatcher, p. 277.
4. Johann Ewald, *Diary of the American War: A Hessian Journal* (New Haven, CT, 1979).
5. Dohla, p. 172.
6. Charles Cornwallis to George Washington, 17 October 1781.
7. Denny, p. 144.
8. George Washington to Charles Cornwallis, 17 October 1781.
9. Charles Cornwallis to George Washington, 17 October 1781, ½ past 4 p.m.
10. St George Tucker: Journal, September 28–October 20, 1781, in *The American Revolution, Writings from the War of Independence*. p. 738.
11. George Washington to General Cornwallis, 18 October 1781.
12. Greene, p. 289.
13. Dohla, p. 173.
14. Denny, p. 44.
15. Richard Butler, *Journal of the Siege of Yorktown*, in Historical Magazine (New York, 1864) 102–112.
16. Pension application of Sarah Osborn.
17. Thatcher, p. 280.
18. Martin, p. 207.
19. Thatcher, p. 280.
20. Graham, p. 64.
21. Feltman, p. 22.
22. William Hallahan, *The Day the Revolution Ended 19 October 1781* (Hoboken, NJ, 2004), pp. 202–203.
23. Charles Cornwallis to Henry Clinton, 20 October 1781.
24. Ibid.
25. Ibid.
26. Washington's Journal, 14 October 1781.

27. Greene, p. 465.
28. Ibid. pp. 316–317.

Chapter Thirteen: Aftermath
1. *Memoir of Lieut. Col. Tench Tilghman* (Albany, 1876), & Hallahan, p. 218.
2. Hallahan, p. 233.
3. Ibid. p. 253.
4. *Memoirs of Sir Nathan Wraxall*, in Commanger & Morris, p. 1243.
5. Hallahan, p. 249.

BIBLIOGRAPHY

Books

Babits, Lawrence E. *A Devil of a Whipping, The Battle of the Cowpens.* Chapel Hill, NC: The University of North Carolina Press, 1998.

Babits, Lawrence E. and Joshua B. Howard. *Long, Obstinate, and Bloody: The Battle of*
Guilford Courthouse. Chapel Hill, NC: The University of North Carolina Press, 2009.

Bearss, Edwin C. *Battle of Cowpens.* Johnson City, TN: The Overmountain Press, 1996.

Black, Jeremy. *George III, America's Last King.* New Haven, CT: Yale University Press, 2006.

Bobrick, Benson. *Angel in the Whirlwind: The Triumph of the American Revolution.* New York: Simon & Schuster, 1997.

Brands, H. W. *The First American: The Life and Times of Benjamin Franklin.* New York: Doubleday, 2000.

Broughton-Mainwaring, Rowland. *Historical Record of the Royal Welch Fusiliers.* London: Hatchards, Piccadilly, 1889.

Buchanan, John. *The Road to Guilford Courthouse: The American Revolution in the Carolinas.* New York: John Wiley & Sons, Inc., 1997.

Carbone, Gerald M. *Washington: Lessons in Leadership.* Washington DC: Palgrave Macmillan, 2010.

Chadwick, Bruce. *The First American Army: The Untold Story of George Washington and the Men behind America's First Fight for Freedom.* Naperville, IL: Source Books, Inc., 2005.

Churchill, Winston. *The Great Republic: a History of America*. New York: Random House, 1999.

Commager, Henry Steele, and Richard B. Morris, eds. *The Spirit of Seventy-Six: The Story of the American Revolution as told by Participants*. New York: Da Capo Press, 1995.

Davis, Burke. *The Campaign that Won America: The Story of Yorktown*. Philadelphia: Eastern Acorn Press, 1970.

Dykeman, Wilma. *The Battle of Kings Mountain 1780, With Fire and Sword*. Washington DC: U.S. Government Printing Office, 1978.

Ellis, Joseph J. *His Excellency George Washington*. New York: Alford A. Knopf, 2004.

Ferling, John. *Almost a Miracle: The American Victory in the War of Independence*. New York: Oxford University Press, 2007.

Fiske, John. *The American Revolution, Vol II*. Boston & New York: Houghton, Mifflin and Company, 1891.

Fleming, Thomas J. *Beat the Last Drum: The Siege of Yorktown, 1781*. New York: St. Martins Press, 1963.

Golway, Terry. *Washington's General: Nathaniel Greene and the Triumph of the American Revolution*. New York: Henry Holt and Company, 2006.

Greene, Jerome A. *The Guns of Independence: The Siege of Yorktown, 1781*. New York: Savas Beatie, 2005, 2009.

Hairr, John. *Guilford Courthouse: Nathaniel Greene's Victory in Defeat, March 15, 1781*. Cambridge, MA: Da Capo Press, 2002.

Hallahan, William H. *The Day the Revolution Ended, 19 October 1781*. Hoboken, NJ: John Wiley and Sons, Inc., 2004.

Higginbotham, Don. *Daniel Morgan, Revolutionary Rifleman*. Chapel Hill, NC: University of North Carolina Press, 1961.

Johnston, Henry P. *The Yorktown Campaign and the Surrender of Cornwallis 1781*. New York: Harper & Brothers, 1881.

Johnson, William. *Sketches of the Life and Correspondence of Nathaniel Greene, Major General of the Armies of the United States in the War of Revolution, Vol I*. Charleston, SC: Printed for the Author, by A.E. Miller, 1822.

Kennett, Lee. *The French Forces in America, 1780–1783*. Westport, CT: Greenwood Press, 1977.

Ketchum, Richard M. *Victory at Yorktown: The Campaign that Won the*

Revolution. New York: Henry Holt, 2004.

Kranish, Michael. *Flight from Monticello: Thomas Jefferson at War*. Oxford, New York: Oxford University Press, 2010.

Lengel, Edward G., ed. *The Glorious Struggle: George Washington's Revolutionary War Letters*. New York: HarperCollins Publishers, 2007.

Linn, John Blair and William H. Egle, *Pennsylvania in the War of the Revolution, 1775–1783, Volume II*. Harrisburg: Lane S. Hart, State Printer, 1880.

Mackesy, Piers. *The War for America, 1775–1778*. Cambridge, MA: Harvard University Press, 1964.

Matloff, Maurice ed. *American Military History*. Washington, DC: U.S. Government Printing Office, 1969,

McCullough, David. *John Adams*. New York: Simon & Schuster, 2001.

Middlekauff, Robert. *The Glorious Cause: The American Revolution, 1763–1789*. Oxford & New York, 1982, 2005.

Mitchell, Broadus. *Alexander Hamilton, The Revolutionary Years*. New York: Thomas Y. Crowell Company, 1970.

Moncure, John. *The Cowpens Staff Ride and Battlefield Tour*. Leavenworth, KS: U.S. Army Command and General Staff College, 1996.

Moore, H.N. *Life and Services of Gen. Anthony Wayne*. Philadelphia: Published by John B. Perry, 1845.

Morrissey, Brendan. *Yorktown 1781*. Oxford, UK: Osprey, 1999.

Nelson, Paul David. *Anthony Wayne: Soldier of the Early Republic*. Bloomington, IN: Indiana University Press, 1985.

Oberholtzer, Ellis Paxson. *Robert Morris, Patriot and Financier*. New York: The Macmillan Company, 1903.

Phillips, Donald T. *On the Wings of Speed: George Washington and the Battle of Yorktown*. New York: iUniverse Star, 2006.

Rhodehamel, John H. ed. *The American Revolution: Writings from the War of Independence*. New York: Literary Classics of the United States Inc., 2001.

Ross, Charles, Ed. *Correspondence of Charles, First Marquis Cornwallis, Vol. I*. London: John Murray, 1859.

Royster, Charles. *A Revolutionary People at War: The Continental Army and American Character, 1775–1783*. Chapel Hill, NC: University of North Carolina Press, 1996.

Scheer, George F. and Hugh F. Rankin. *Rebels and Redcoats, the American Revolution through the Eyes of those who Fought and Lived It.* New York: Da Capo Press, 1957.

Simms, W. Gilmore. *The Life of Francis Marion.* Philadelphia: G.G. Evans, Publisher, 1860.

Southern, Ed, ed. *Voices of the American Revolution in the Carolinas.* Winston Salem, NC: John F. Blair Publisher, 2009.

Stedman, C. *History of the Origin, and Termination of the American War, Vol. II.* London: Printed by the Author, 1794.

Stille, Charles J. *Major General Anthony Wayne and the Pennsylvania Line in the Continental Army.* Philadelphia: J.B. Lippincott Company, 1893.

Swager, Christine R. *The Valiant Died: The Battle of Eutaw Springs, September 8, 1781.* Westminster, MD: Heritage Books, Inc., 2007.

Van Doren, Carl. *Mutiny in January.* New York: The Viking Press, 1943.

Wallace, Willard M. *Traitorous Hero: The Life & Fortunes of Benedict Arnold.* New York: Harper & Brothers, 1954.

Weigley, Russel F. *The American Way of War: A History of the United States Military Strategy and Policy.* Bloomington, IN: Indiana University Press, 1973.

Williams, Mrs. *Biography of Revolutionary War Heroes, containing the Life of Brigadier Gen. William Barton and also of Captain Stephen Olney.* Providence RI: Published by the author, 1839.

Wright, Robert K. *The Continental Army.* Washington DC: U.S. Government Printing Office, 1983.

Diaries, Journals, and Memoirs

Blanchard, Claude. *The Journal of Claude Blanchard, Commissary of the French Auxiliary Army sent to the United States during the American Revolution, 1780–1783.* Translated from a French manuscript by William Duane. Edited by Thomas Balch. Albany: J. Munsell, 1876.

Clinton, Henry. *Narrative of the Campaign in 1781 in North America.* Philadelphia: Printed by John Campbell, 1865.

Davis, John. *Journal of Captain John Davis of the Pennsylvania Line.* Printed in The Pennsylvania Magazine of History and Biography, Volume 5. Philadelphia: The Historical Society of Pennsylvania, 1881.

Denny, Ebenezer. *Military Journal of Major Ebenezer Denny, an officer in the Revolutionary and Indian Wars*. Philadelphia: J.B. Lippincott & Co. for the Historical Society of Pennsylvania, 1859.

Deux-Ponts, William de. *My Campaigns in American, a Journal kept by Count William de Ponts, 1780–81*. Translated from a French Manuscript with an introduction by Samuel Abbot Green. Boston: J.K. Wiggin and Wm. Parsons Lunt, 1868.

Dohla, Johann Conrad. *A Hessian Diary of the American Revolution*. Translated, editied, and with an introduction by Bruce E. Burgoyne. Norman OK: University of Oklahoma Press, 1990.

Duncan, James. *Diary of Captain James Duncan, of Colonel Moses Hazen's Regiment in the Yorktown Campaign, 1781*. In Journals and Diaries of the War of Revolution with lists of officers and soldiers, 1775–1783. Edited by William Henry Egle. Harrisburg PA: E.D. Myers State Printer, 1893.

Feltman, William. *The Journal of Lieut. William Feltman, of the First Pennsylvania Regiment, 1781–82*. Philadelphia: Published for the Historical Society of Pennsylvania by Henry Carey Baird, 1853.

Graham, Samuel. *Memoir of General Graham, with Notices of the Campaigns in which he was engaged from 1779 to 1801*. Edited by his son, Colonel James J. Graham. Edinburgh: Privately Printed by R&R Clark, 1862.

Greene, Nathaniel. *Memoirs of the Life and Campaigns of Hon. Nathaniel Greene*. Edited by Charles Caldwell. Philadelphia: Published by Robert Desilver, 1819.

Heath, William. *Heath's Memoirs of the American War*. Reprinted from the original edition of 1798. With introduction and notes by Rufus Rockwell Wilson. New York: A. Wessels Company, 1904.

Humphreys, David. *Life and Times of David Humphreys, Soldier-Statesman-Poet*. By David Humphreys in two volumes. New York & London: G.P. Putnam's Sons, 1917.

James, Bartholomew. *Journal of Rear-Admiral Bartholomew James, 1752–1828*. Edited by John Knox Laughton. London: Printed for the Navy Records Society, 1896.

Lafayette, Gilbert M. *Memoirs of Gilbert M. Lafayette*. By Gen. H.L.V. Duooudray Holstein, 2d edition. Geneva: Printed and published by John Gretes & Co., 1885.

Lee, Henry. *Memoirs of the War in the Southern Department of the United*

States. In two volumes. Philadelphia & New York: Published by Bradford and Innskeep, 1813.

Martin, Joseph Plumb. *A Narrative of a Revolutionary War Soldier*. With an introduction by Thomas Fleming. New York: Signet Classic, 2001.

Saumarez, Lord de. *Memoirs and Correspondence of Admiral Lord De Saumarez from Original Papers in Possession of the Family*. By John Ross, in two volumes. London: Richard Bentley, 1838.

Simcoe, J.G. *Simcoe's Military Journal, a History of the Operations of a Partisan Corps, the Queen's Rangers during the American Revolution*. New York: Bartlett & Welford, 1844.

Tarleton, Banastre. *A History of the Campaigns of 1780 and 1781, in the Southern Provinces of North America by Lieutenant Colonel Tarleton, Commandant of the Late British Legion*. Dublin: Printed for Colles, Exshaw, White, Whitestone, Burton, Byrne, Moore, Jones, and Dorin, 1787.

Thatcher, James. *A Military Journal* during the American Revolutionary War, from 1775 to 1783—Describing Interesting Events and Transactions of the Period: With Numerous Historical Facts and Anecdotes, From the Original Manuscript. Kellock Robertson Press, 2009.

Tilghman, Tench. *Memoir of Lieut. Col. Tench Tilghman, Secretary and Aid to Washington*. Albany NY: J. Munsell, 1876.

Verger, Jean Baptise Antoine. *American Campaigns of Rochambeau's Army, 1780–1783: The Journals of Clermont-Crevecoeur, Verger and Berthier*. By Howard C. Rice & Anne S. Brown, Princeton: Princeton University Press, 1972.

Washington, George, *Washington's Journal Extracts on the Siege. Sept. 28–Oct. 20, 1781*. In The Yorktown Campaign and the Surrender of Cornwallis 1781, by Henry P. Johnston. New York: Harper & Brothers, 1781.

Correspondence

The correspondence cited in the text and chapter notes can be found in a number of sources including: The Library of Congress American Memory Collection, George Washington Papers at the Library of Congress, 1741–1799, Journals of the Continental Congress, Volumes 19–21, the writings of George Washington from the original manuscript sources (Electronic

Text Center, University of Virginia Library). An excellent online archives of letters from primary American, French and British Revolutionary War military and civilian leaders, can be found on the Family Tales website, http://www.familytales.org/

Pension Applications/Statements
Revolutionary War Pension Records are held at the National Archives, Washington D.C. Over 10,000 transcribed pension applications and 70 rosters from the Southern Campaign of the Revolutionary War can be accessed online at the website http://southerncampaign.org/pen/index.htm

INDEX

Abercrombie, Lt. Col. Robert, 193
Adams, John, 8, 73, 122–123
Adkins, Josiah, 127
Alexander, Gen. William, 131
American Military Units
　American Grand Battery, 180
　Connecticut Continentals, 162
　Continental Corps of Sappers and Min-
　　ers, 163, 165, 188
　Delaware Continentals, 29, 52, 82, 86–
　　87, 114, 150
　Lee's Legion, 77, 82–83, 90, 105, 112–
　　114, 147, 150
　Maryland Continentals, 29, 52, 67, 77,
　　86, 102, 114, 150, 156; 1st Regi-
　　ment, 87–90, 104; 2nd Regiment,
　　87–88, 90, 104
　New Jersey Brigade, 25–26
　New York Continentals, 2nd Infantry,
　　194
　North Carolina Continentals, 113, 152
　North Carolina militia, 29
　Pennsylvania Continentals, 2nd In-
　　fantry, 16–17, 203; 4th Infantry,
　　16–17; 5th Infantry, 15; 9th In-
　　fantry, 15–17; 10th Infantry, 14–15;
　　11th Infantry, 14
　Pennsylvania Line, 100, 116, 118,
　　161–162, 167, 175, 205, 224
　Virginia Continentals, 11, 82–83, 86,
　　102, 104, 114, 156; 2nd Regiment,
　　104
　Virginia militia, 52
Annapolis, Maryland, 142
Antoine de Verger, Jean Baptiste, 188
Arbuthnot, Adm. Marriot, 92
Archer's Hope, 142
Armistead, Westwood, 81
Arnold, Gen. Benedict, 95, 107–108,
　116, 206; advances on Richmond, 42;
　aggressive leader, 38; approaches
　Hood's Point, 41; attacks New Lon-
　don, Connecticut, 139; colonists ha-
　tred of, 141; defection to British, x, 4,
　8, 37; departs Richmond, 45; dis-
　appointed he didn't capture Jefferson,
　45; failed New London raid, 141; in-
　vasion of Virginia, 26; leaves the coun-
　try, 141, 219; Newport News, arrives
　at, 39–40; plan to capture West Point,
　5; Portsmouth, 40, 91, 93, 99;
　Portsmouth, ordered to occupy, 38–
　39; postwar, 219; returns to New York,
　117; Richmond, capture and sacking
　of, 43, 45; wants to lead attack on
　Philadelphia, 132
Articles of Capitulation, 201
Articles of Confederation, 72
Articles of Surrender, 202, 211
Audibert, Philip, 141

Augusta, Georgia, 112–113, 115

Barras, Adm. Comte de, 109, 138–139, 202
Battle of the Capes, 138–139, 219
Beatty, Capt. William, 104
Bettin, Capt. Adam, 17–18
"Board of Sergeants", 14, 20–24
Bonaparte, Napoleon, 221–222
HMS *Bonetta*, 201–202, 208
Bouzar, Sgt. William, 22
Brandywine, battle of, 11, 16, 34
Brierly's Ferry, South Carolina, 31
British Military Units
    1st Dragoon Guards, 48
    1st Guard Battalion, 79, 82, 84
    2nd Battalion Guards, 80
    3rd Regiment of Foot, 147, 153
    7th Fusiliers, 48, 55–57, 59
    16th Light Dragoons, 48
    17th Dragoons, 48, 116
    19th Regiment of Foot, 147, 153
    23rd Regiment of Welsh Fusiliers, 80, 89, 91, 195, 171, 174
    30th Regiment of Foot, 147, 153
    33rd Regiment of Foot, 80, 82, 84–85, 87–88
    63rd Regiment of Foot, 103
    71st Infantry (Highlanders), 55–59, 79, 85, 89–90, 187
    80th Regiment of Foot, 38, 133, 202
    British Legion, 48
    Edinburgh Volunteers, 38
    Grenadier Guards, 21, 80, 84, 87–88, 91, 195
    King's American Regiment, 103
    New York Volunteers, 103
    Queen's Rangers, 38, 42, 125, 202, 206, 220
    Simcoe's Rangers, 43
    South Carolina Royalists, 103
    Tarleton's Legion, 48–50, 55–56, 61, 63, 128, 167, 170
    Volunteers of Ireland, 103
British Secret Service, 21

Brooklyn, battle of, 11
Browne, Lt. Col., 113, 150
Brunswick, New Jersey, 3
Buford, Col. Abraham, 48
Burr, Aaron, 226–227
Butler, Gen. John, 77, 81, 84, 126
Butler, Col. Richard, 16–17, 19, 203, 226
Byrd Plantation, 42, 44–45, 116
Byrd, Mary, 42

Camden, 1780 battle of, ix, 6, 8, 29–31, 34, 36, 49
Camden, South Carolina, 94, 101, 105–107, 110–111, 148–150
"Camp of Repose", 33
Campbell, Maj. James, 187, 191–192
Campbell, Lt. Col. Richard, 104, 114
Campbell, Col. William, 77, 80, 82–83, 121, 152, 156
Carleton, Sir Guy, 218–219
Charleston, South Carolina, ix, 31–32, 36, 64, 91, 95, 101–102, 105, 112, 115, 146–147, 153, 155, 200, 214–216, 224
Charleston, South Carolina, siege of, 6, 8, 27, 29, 48
HMS *Charlestown*, 37
Charlotte, North Carolina, 32
Charlottesville, Virginia, 107, 119–120
Charon, 183
Chastellux, Gen. Francois-Jean, Chevalier de, 184
Cheraw, South Carolina, 29, 31, 33, 35, 64–65
Cherokee and Creek Indians, 47
Choisy, Gen. Claude-Gabriel, Duc de, 174–175, 181, 206
Clarke, Col. Elijah, 113
Claude-Anne, Gen. Marquis de Saint-Simon Montbleur, 164
Clinton, General Sir Henry, ix, 4, 21, 23–24, 27, 37, 116, 128, 171, 219;
    Arnold allowed to leave the country, 141; Benedict Arnold, 38; blamed by Cornwallis for Yorktown, 217–218;

capture of Charleston, South Carolina, 29; Cornwallis praises Tarleton, 63; Cornwallis' surrender letter, 208; Cornwallis's letter for offense, 105–106; Cornwallis's pessimism, 193; defending New York, 109; hopes to rally the Loyalists, 38; New London, Connecticut, 139; orders Cornwallis to send troops to New York, 122, 126, 132; plan to capture, 5; postwar, 218; reinforces Arnold, 93; reports surrender to Lord Germain, 213; Rochambeau departs Rhode Island, 131; sailed from New York to support Cornwallis, 209; thinks Washington will attack New York, 135; Yorktown, 192

Coates, Col. John, 147

Coffin, Maj. John, 151

Collins, James, 57

Columbia, South Carolina, 111

Committee of Congress, 24

Continental Army, viii–x, 12, 19, 22, 33–34, 41, 107

Continental Congress; 34, 72, 122–123, 137, 211–212, 223; bounties, 12; Pennsylvania Line mutiny, 14, 19, 21–22; shortage of everything, 13; Washington's supply issues, viii

Cornwallis, Gen. Charles, Earl, ix, 26, 35, 38, 47–48, 61, 72, 101–102, 107, 121, 127–128, 132, 141, 144, 162, 218–220; abandons the Carolina's, 105–106; allows men no rest, 67; approves Tarleton's plan, 48; army is now isolated, 139; Articles of Capitulation, 201; Charlotte, arrival at, 30; Clinton orders 3,000 troops, 122, 132; Clinton, orders from, 27; Clinton, surrender letter to, 207; close to capturing Otho Williams, 27, 68–69; Cowpens disaster, 63–64; crackdown on rebel leaders, 29; crossing the James, 116; decides to return to North Carolina, 69; exchanged for Laurens, 217; gives up pursuit of Lafayette, 119; Gloucester breakout attempt, 181; Greene has a numerical advantage, 75; Greene plans to lure into Virginia, 65; Greene, plans to move against, 32–33; Greene, pushing hard to capture, 67, 70; Guilford Courthouse, battle of, 79–80, 83, 85–86, 88–90, 93; has to deal with Morgan, 32; Hillsboro, 30; hoarding ammunition, 179; invasion of North Carolina, 30; joins with Phillips, 108; Lafayette, 117; launches a winter campaign, 32; marches to Wilmington, 94; Morgan, last chance to destroy, 66; Morgan, pushing hard to catch, 65, 67; needs Loyalist support, 29; opposition growing daily, 143; out-generaled by Greene, 94; paroled and sent to New York, 208; Petersburg, arrival at, 109; Portsmouth, departure from, 133, 134; postwar, 217; requests 24-hour cessation of hostilities, 198–200; Richmond evacuation, 121–122, 125; Richmond, arrival at, 110; Tarleton, praise of, 63; Virginia campaign, 115–116; Virginia, arrival at, 71, 108–109; Williamsburg, 125; Wilmington, departure from, 105–106; Winnsboro, departure from, 31, 49; "winter of discontent", 27; Yorktown made a base, 133; Yorktown, arrival at, 133; Yorktown, assessment of, 217; Yorktown, blames Clinton for, 217; Yorktown, British defenses, 134, 142; Yorktown, siege of, 167, 170–171, 173, 179–185, 192–195, 198; Yorktown, surrender at, 201–202, 204, 206, 211–213

Cowpens, battle of, 47, 50–52, 55–61, 63, 65, 76, 155, 224

Dan River, 68–69

Darley, Thomas, 60

Davidson, Gen. William, 66

Davis, Capt. John, 167, 175–176

De La Luzerne, Chevalier Anne-César, 110, 137

Declaration of Independence, 42, 44, 164, 225
DeKalb, Gen. Baron Johan, 29
DeLancey, Jr., Maj. Oliver, 21, 135
Denny, Ensign Ebenezer, 118, 161–162, 168, 181, 193, 197, 203, 228
Detouches, Adm. Rene, Chevalier, 71–72, 91–93, 99
Deux-Ponts, Col. Guillaume de, 187–188, 190
Dobbs Ferry, 5
Dohla, Pvt. Johann C., 161, 182, 198, 203
Dorchester, South Carolina, 115
Du Portail, Gen. Luis, 130, 168, 172
Duc de Lauzun, Gen. Armand-Louis, 164, 170, 174, 212–213, 215, 221
Dumas, Count, 204
Duncan, Capt. James, 162, 175, 179, 228
Dundas, Lt. Col. Thomas, 38, 174, 185, 202
"duration of the war", 12
Dutch Republic, 6
Duval, Lt. Isaac, 156

Eaton, Gen. Thomas, 77, 81–82, 84
Elbert, Col. Samuel, 172
Eutaw Springs, battle of, 149–153, 155–157
Evans, Pvt. Absalom, 15
Ewald, Johann von, 39–40, 43, 45, 198
Eyre, Lt. Col. Edmund, 140
Fallen Timbers, battle of, 224
Feltman, Lt. William, 162, 175, 184–185, 205
Ferguson, Maj. Patrick, 30–31, 51, 95
fireships, 143

Fishbourne, Maj. Benjamin, 19
Ford, Lt. Col. Benjamin, 104
HMS *Formidable*, 180
Fort Granby, South Carolina, 110–111
Fort Motte, South Carolina, 110–111, 148
Fort Ticonderoga, battle of, 16

Fort Washington, 34
Fort Watson, South Carolina, 102, 110–111
Fort Williams, 47
Fox, Charles James, 214
Francisco, Sgt. Peter, 89, 229
Franklin, Benjamin, 8, 73–74, 123
Fraser, Maj. Thomas, 148
French military units
    Brigade Bourbonnois, 164, 187
    Brigade D'Agenois, 164
    Brigade Soissonois, 164, 177
    French Legion, 164
    Grand French Battery, 182–183
    Lauzun's Legionnaires, 174
    Regiment Agenois, 179, 182, 186
    Regiment Gatenois, 187–189
    Regiment Royal Deux-Ponts, 187–189
    Regiment Saintonge, 179, 182, 186
    Regiment Soissonois, 215
    Regiment Touraine, 164, 178
Fusiliers Redoubt, Yorktown, 166, 170–171, 178, 180, 182, 186

Gates, General Horatio, ix, 29, 31, 33–34
George III, King, 6, 30, 213–214, 218–219
Germain, Lord George, 91, 105–106, 116, 125, 213, 220
German military units
    Fusilier Regiment, 81, 85, 90
    Hessians, 4, 21, 38–40, 42–43, 45, 82, 125, 187, 198, 203, 206
    Jaegers, 43, 48, 80, 82, 84–85, 87
    Regiment von Bose, 79–80, 82, 84
Germantown, battle of, 11, 16, 34
Giles, Maj. Edward, 63
Gimat, Lt. Col. Jean-Joseph Sourbader de, 187–188, 190–191
Gist, Gen. Mordecai, 215
Gloucester Point, battle of, 172–175, 181–182
Gloucester Point, Virginia, 117, 133, 142, 144, 170, 180, 184–185, 187, 195, 202, 206

Graham, Gen. Samuel, 182

Grasse, Adm. Francois Joseph Paul, Comte de, Admiral de, 8, 100, 110, 129, 135, 139, 142, 144, 186, 209; arrives off Chesapeake Bay, 137–138; British surrender at Yorktown, 202; ordered to sail to North America, 74, 109; postwar, 221; Washington seeks help, 214; Yorktown, 170; postwar, 219

Graves, Adm. Thomas, 138, 209, 219

Gravier, Charles, comte de Vergennes, 7

Green Springs, battle of, 162

Greene, General Nathaniel, ix, 32, 35, 38, 64, 66, 72, 95, 100, 106–107, 115, 121, 128, 145, 147, 148, 214, 224, 227; appointed to command, 31, 34–35; army intact after Guilford Courthouse, 93; Camden, 102; continues his campaign in South Carolina, 110; Cornwallis plans to move against, 32–33; Cornwallis tries to lure into a battle, 70; Cowpens victory, news of, 63, 65; detaches Morgan, 35–36; Eutaw Springs, battle of, 149–151, 153, 155–157; fight a war of attrition, 35; follows Cornwallis, 94; Fort Watson, 102; Guilford Courthouse, battle of, 76–77, 80, 83, 86–87, 90; has a superior force, 75; Hobkirks Hill, 103–104; looking for troops and supplies, 146; Morgan's emaciated condition, 68; Morgan's request to be relieved of command, 68; Ninety-Six, 113; orders from Washington, 34; out-generaled the British, 94, 95, 115; plans attacks on British outposts, 111; plans for a campaign against Cornwallis, 33; plans to lure Cornwallis into Virginia, 65; postwar, 223; pre-war, 34; question about willingness to fight, 68; race "the race for the Dan", 69; steals a march on Cornwallis, 67; strategic success at Hobkirks Hill, 105; to reunite his army, 61; Washington's assessment of,

217; Washington's most trusted general, 33; Wayne sent to reinforce, 215

Griffis, William, 155–156

HMS *Guadaloupe*, 171, 180, 183–184

Guilford Courthouse, battle of, 67–68, 70, 76–77, 79–91, 93, 155, 218–219, 229

Gunby, Col. John, 87–88, 104

Hamilton, Lt. Col. Alexander, 179, 187–188, 190–192, 203, 226–227

Hampton Roads, Virginia, 39, 92, 99, 128, 133, 138

Hampton, Col. Wade, 152

Harrison, Benjamin, 42

Hartford Conference of 1780, 73–74

Hawes, Lt. Col. Samuel, 104

Hayne, Col. Isaac, 148

Hazen, Gen. Moses, 163, 179

Head of Elk, Maryland, 130, 137, 141, 162, 175

Heath, Gen. William, 4, 25, 131

Henderson, Lt. Col. William, 145, 150–152, 156

Highlands Department, 4

Hillsboro, North Carolina, 30

Hillsborough, engagement at, 70

Hobkirks Hill, engagement at, 102–105

Hood's Point, 41–43

Houx, Gen. Antoine Charles de, Baron de Viomenil, 187, 164, 188–189

Houx, Gen. Joseph Hyacinthe du, Compe de Viomenil, 164, 177

Howard, Lt. Col. John, 57–59, 88, 156

Howe, Adm. Richard, 219

Howe, Gen. Robert, 25–26

Huger, Gen. Issac, 65, 67–68, 77, 86, 102

Humphreys, Lt. Col. David, 3–5, 227

James, Lt. Bartholomew, 183

Jamestown, Virginia, 127, 161, 163

Jay, John, 123

Jefferson, Thomas, 45, 107, 117, 123; calls on von Steuben, 41; Charlottesville, 119; flees Charlottesville,

119–121; flees Richmond, 43–44; Governor of Virginia, 40; orders call up of militia, 40; relieved he had escaped Arnold, 45
Jouett, John, 120

Kings Mountain, battle of, 7, 30–31, 47, 51, 95, 155
Kirkwood, Capt. Robert, 77, 103, 150
Knox, Gen. Henry, 24, 172, 192, 194
Knyphausen, Gen. Wilhelm von, 4–5
Kosciuszko, Thaddeus, 33, 112

Lafayette, Gen. Marquis de, 25–26, 71–72, 99–100, 108, 115, 127–128, 132, 162–164, 186, 229; abandons Richmond, 117–118; Cornwallis out to destroy, 117; defends Richmond, 108; French reinforcements, 138; joins Wayne, 121; Malvern Hill, 134; Portsmouth, 91–92; postwar, 221–222; replaces von Steuben, 71; Richmond, 116; shadows Cornwallis, 125; struggles with supplies for Greene, 107; Yorktown, siege of, 179, 182, 187–188
Laurens, Lt. Col. John, 72, 74, 100, 187, 190–191, 201–202, 227
Laurens, Henry, 123, 217
Lawson, Gen. Robert, 77, 84–85
Ledyard, Col. William, 139
Lee, Gen. Charles, 48
Lee, Col. Henry "Light Horse Harry", 69–70, 75, 105, 111, 145, 152, 156–157; Augusta, 112–113; Camden, 102; chasing the British back to Charleston, 156; Eutaw Springs, 150–151; Guilford Courthouse, battle of, 77, 79, 81, 83; Ninety-Six, 113; postwar, 226; "Pyles' Massacre", 70
Leslie, Gen. Alexander, 32, 38, 49, 64, 79–81, 87, 116
Liamont, Col. Henry Francois, 164
Lincoln, Gen. Benjamin, ix, 164, 177, 179, 182, 192, 200, 204, 223

Linton, William, 81
Louis XVI, King, 7–8, 212–213, 221
Loyalists, ix, 7, 29–31, 35, 43–44, 49, 51, 55, 60, 70, 93–95, 102, 110, 111–112, 115, 133, 148, 201–202, 208, 212, 220
Luzerne, Chevalier de la, 122

Majoribanks, Maj. John, 152–153, 155
Mansfield, Lt. John, 191
Marie D'Aboville, Col. Francois, 172
Marion, Gen. Francis, ix, 31–32, 105, 113, 147–148, 157; chasing the British back to Charleston, 156; Eutaw Springs, 149–151; Fort Motte, 111; ordered to attack British supply lines, 101–102; postwar, 225
Martin, Sgt. Joseph Plumb, 163, 165, 167, 176, 188, 190–191, 228
Mason, John, 23
McClellan, Capt. Joseph, 14
McDowell, Col. Samuel, 86
McKean, Thomas, 211
McLeod, Lt. John, 89
McPherson, Lt. Col. Duncan, 187, 190
Mercer, Lt. Col. John, 174
Moffet, Col. George, 86
Moncks Corner, South Carolina, 105, 115
Monmouth Court House, battle of, 11, 16, 35, 89, 163
Montgomery, Maj. William, 140
Morgan, Gen. Daniel, 32, 35, 64, 95, 157; arrives at Guilford Courthouse, 67; attacks Cornwallis' supply lines, 36; Cornwallis would have to deal with, 32; Cowpens as defensible ground, 50–52; Cowpens battle plan, 53; Cowpens, battle of, 56–59, 61, 76; Greene's decision to avoid an engagement, 68; joins Lafayette, 121; meets up with Huger, 67; news of the Cowpens victory, 63; perilous situation after Cowpens, 64; postwar, 224; requests to be relieved of command, 68;

steals a march on Cornwallis, 64–66; Tarleton chases, 47, 49–51; Tarleton ordered to deal with, 36; Whiskey Rebellion, 224; worn out from campaigning, 68

Morris, Robert, 73, 130–131, 137, 141–142, 227

Morristown mutiny, 163

Mount Kimble, 13–14, 19–21

Mount Vernon, 144, 223, 215

Moylan, Col. Stephen, 165

Muhlenberg, Gen. Peter, 107, 117, 167

Nelson, Jr., Gen. Thomas, 40, 117, 164–167, 184, 225

New London, Connecticut, battle of, 139–141

New Windsor, New York, 3, 19, 25, 71, 92, 99

New York City, vii, x, 5, 200, 212, 215

"Newburgh Conspiracy", 222–223

Newport News, Virginia, 39

Newport, Rhode Island, viii, 8, 71, 91–92, 100, 138

Ninety-Six, 29, 31–32, 47, 64

Ninety-Six, siege of, 101, 110–111, 113–115, 145, 155–156

Noailles, Viscount de, 201–202

North, Frederick, 2nd Earl of Guilford, 6–7, 95, 105, 213–214, 219–221

Ogden, James, 23

Ogilive, Capt., 57, 59

O'Hara, Gen. Charles, 85, 89, 133; British surrender at Yorktown, 204; Guilford Courthouse, battle of, 80, 88, 91, 218–219; postwar, 218

Old Point Comfort, 37

Olney, Capt. Steven, 188, 190–191

Orangeburg, South Carolina, 110–111

Osborn, Sarah, 163, 204, 229

Osborn, Sgt. Aaron, 163,

Paine, Thomas, 222

Pennsylvania Line mutiny, 5, 11–14, 16–19, 22–26

Petersburg, Virginia, 107–108, 115

Philadelphia, Pennsylvania, 17–18, 20, 125, 136–137

Phillips, Gen. William, 93, 106–109, 115

Pickens, Gen. Andrew, ix, 51–52, 57, 59, 101, 112–113, 150, 157

Pickering, Col. Thomas, 131

Portsmouth, Virginia, 38, 40, 46, 71, 91–93, 99, 107–108, 116–117, 126–128, 132, 134

Princeton, battle of, 11, 34

"Pyles' Massacre", 70

Rawdon, Lord Francis, 95, 101, 105–106, 111, 147; Camden, 102, 105; Hobkirks Hill, 103–105; Ninety-Six, 112–114

Redoubt #9, Yorktown, 168, 170, 176, 184–187, 192

Redoubt #10, Yorktown, 168, 170, 176, 184–188 190, 192

Reed, Joseph, 22–24

Reeves, Lt. Enos, 14–15

Reign of Terror, 221

Rhode Island, battle of, 35

Richmond, Virginia, 39–42, 107–108, 117–118, 121; Cornwallis vacates, 122, 125; falls to Arnold, 43–44; sacked by Arnold, 44–45

Robinson, Jr., Lt. Col. Beverley, 38

Rochambeau, Gen. Compe de, viii, 71–72, 100–101, 132, 137, 141, 162, 204, 215; agrees to help Washington, 92; arrives at Williamsburg, 143–144; arrives in Baltimore, 142; Articles of Capitulation, 201; British surrender at Yorktown, 202–204; capture of British redoubts, 185–186; departs Rhode Island, 131; Head of Elk, 141; joins with Washington at White Plains, 128–131; lands at Newport, 8; last troops arrive at Williamsburg, 163; meeting with de Grasse, 144; meeting with Washington about summer cam-

paign, 109–110; meets with Washington, 8; postwar, 221; reconnaissance of New York, 135; reports surrender to King Louis XVI, 212; requesting assistance from France, 73–74; Tarleton's protector, 206; Yorktown, siege of, 164, 166, 168, 172, 178, 181
Roche, Patrick, 152
Ross, Maj. Alexander, 202

Salisbury, North Carolina, 65
Sandy Hook, New Jersey, 38
Saratoga, Battle of, ix, 6, 29, 107
Saratoga, British surrender at, 197
Saumarez, Capt. Thomas, 81
Savage, John, 56
Savannah, Georgia, 101, 112, 115, 157, 214–216
Scammell, Lt. Col. Alexander, 170, 192
Seven Years War, 8, 212
Shippen, Peggy, 37, 42
Simcoe, Lt. Col. John, 38, 42–43, 45, 125; British surrender at Yorktown, 202; Charlottesville, 119–121; Gloucester Point, 174; Portsmouth, 127; postwar, 220; Richmond, 116; Spencer's Ordinary, 126; surrender of, 206
Singleton, Capt. Anthony, 82, 86, 88
Slade, Nathan, 81
Southern Army, ix
Southern Department, ix, 33, 35
Spain, 6
Speedwell Iron Works, 77, 90
Spencer's Ordinary, 126
St. Augustine, Florida, 215
Stanton, Virginia, 120
Steuben, Gen. Friedrich von, 36, 43–44, 69, 107–108, 119–120, 179; British surrender at Yorktown, 203; "de facto" commander of the militia, 41; drilling troops at Williamsburg, 163; Jefferson calls for help, 41; Lafayette replaces, 71–72; postwar, 224; Yorktown, siege of, 164, 184

Stevens, Gen. Edward, Guilford Courthouse, battle of 77, 84–85
Stewart, Lt. Col. Alexander, 147–151, 153, 155–156
Stewart, Ensign Dugald, 80
Stewart, Col. Walter, 16–17, 19
Stono, battle of the, 47
Stony Point, battle of, 11, 16, 89
Stuart, Lt. Col. James, 88–89, 91
Sumter, Gen. Thomas, ix, 31–32, 101, 105, 113, 147, 150, 225

Tallmadge, Benjamin, 99
Tarleton, Lt. Col. Banastre, 32, 115, 167, 224; British surrender at Yorktown, 202; Charleston, 1780 siege of, 48; Charlottesville, 120; chasing Morgan, 47–51, 53; Cornwallis praises, 63; Cowpens, battle of, 55–56, 58–61, 63–64; follows Lafayette, 118; Gloucester Point, 173–174, 185, 195; Guilford Courthouse, battle of, 79, 83; Hillsborough, engagement at, 70; massacre at the Waxhaws, 49; moves on Charlottesville, 119; moves on Cowpens, 55; Petersburg, 108; postwar, 219; requests protection, 206; requests reinforcements, 48; Richmond, 116; sent to deal with Morgan, 36; surrender of, 206; Yorktown, siege of, 166, 171, 173
HMS *Terrible*, 138
Thatcher, James, 125, 136, 161, 173, 183, 192, 197, 205, 228
Thompson, Capt. John, 47
Tilghman, Lt. Col. Tench, 211–212, 227
Tilly, Capt. Arnaud de, 92
Tolbert, Capt. Samuel, 15
Touches, Adm. De, 92
Treaty of Alliance, 8
Treaty of Paris, 216
Trenton, battle of, 11, 22, 34
Trois-Rivieres, battle of, 16
Troublesome Iron Works, 82
Trumbull, Jonathan, 109

Tucker, Lt. Col. St. George, 200

Valley Forge, vii, 16, 162–163
Vergennes, Charles Gravier, comte de, viii, 7–8, 73–74, 122, 213, 222
Ville de Paris, 144
Virginia Assembly, 121
Virginia House of Delegates, 42

Walpole, Robert, 6
Warren, John, 81
Washington, Gen. George, 101, 132, 137, 224, 227; angered about French navy, 99; appeal to Congress, viii; Arnold's defection, x, 4; Articles of Capitulation, 201; asks for proposed terms, 199; British plan to capture him, 4–5, 44; British plan to capture West Point, 5; capture of British redoubts, 185–186; casualties, 208; Cornwallis requests 24-hr cessation of hostilities, 199; de Grasse, meeting with, 144, 214; deceives the British, 135; elected President, 223; failure of French naval effort, 92; French fleet, 71; Gloucester Point, 175; Greene, 34–35; Greene was a wise choice, 95; Greene, assessment of, 217; Greene, his decision to appoint, 68; Head of Elk, 141; Humphreys' mission, 3; January 1, 1781, 3; January 1, 1781, 4; January 1, 1781, 5; Joseph Reed, 22; needs French support, 100; New "Newburgh Conspiracy", 222–223; New Jersey Brigade mutiny, 25; obsession with New York, 100; Pennsylvania Line mutiny, 5, 19; postwar, 222; proposal for the French fleet, 110; reconnaissance of New York, 135; requesting assistance from France, 73–74; Rochambeau and the summer campaign, 109–110; Rochambeau at White Plains, 129–131; Rochambeau, meeting with, 8; six weeks to destroy Cornwallis, 144; spreading mutiny, 24;

struggle to save his army, x; supply issues, vii–viii, 13–14; terms for British surrender, 200–201; toughest challenge of the war, 26; Wayne, high opinion of, 17; Wayne's Pennsylvania Line letter, 18; Wayne's second Pennsylvania Line mutiny letter, 19; Williamsburg, arrival at, 143–144, 161; Williamsburg, last troops arrive, 163; Yorktown, British surrender at, 202–204, 211; Yorktown, siege of, 166, 168, 170, 172–173, 176–178, 180, 183, 188, 192, 194
Washington, Martha, 4–5
Washington, Col. William, 47, 50–52, 145, 157; captured, 155–156, 225; Charlotte, 32; Cowpens, battle of, 57, 59–60, 63; Eutaw Springs, battle of, 153, 225; Guilford Courthouse, battle of, 77, 85–86, 88–90; Hobkirks Hill, battle of, 103–104; moves on Ninety-Six, 32; postwar, 225
Watkins, Benedict, 81
Waxhaws, battle of, 48–49, 70, 102
Wayne, General Anthony, 18, 116, 118, 127, 162; British spies, 23; end of the mutiny, 24; joins Lafayette, 121; ordered to Virginia, 100; Pennsylvania Line mutiny, 13–16, 20; Pennsylvania Line mutiny letter to Washington, 18; Pennsylvania Line negotiations, 20–23; postwar, 224; quote, 1; respected by his men, 17; second Pennsylvania Line mutiny letter, 19; sent to reinforce Greene, 215; Spencer's Ordinary, 126; Washington's opinion of, 17; Yorktown, siege of, 175
Webster, Lt. Col. James, 80–82, 87–88, 91
Weedon, Gen. George, 170
Wells, Henry, 60
West Point, New York, x, 4, 25
Whelchel, John, 47, 61
Whiskey Rebellion, 224
White Plains, New York, 128, 134

White, Lt. Francis, 15
Williams, Benjamin, 82
Williams, John, 23
Williams, Col. Otho, 77; arrives at Guilford Courthouse, 67; Eutaw Springs, battle of, 150, 152, 156; Greene's decision to avoid an engagement, 68; Guilford Court house, battle of, 86, 90–91; Hobkirks Hill, 102
Williamsburg, Virginia, 122, 126, 142–144, 161–165, 170, 215

Wilmington, North Carolina, 91, 94–95, 101, 115
Winnsboro, South Carolina, 27, 31–32, 49, 67, 105

Yorktown, siege of, 163–198, 208, 212, 218–219, 223–225, 229
Yorktown, British surrender at, 201–204, 206, 213, 215,
Yorktown, Virginia, 71, 117, 133, 139, 141–143, 164, 166, 167-168, 170, 173, 181, 195, 197, 204

ABOUT THE AUTHOR

Born and raised in Pittsburgh, PA, Robert L. Tonsetic graduated in 1964 from the University of Pittsburgh with a BA in English Literature, and then joined the U.S. Army as an infantry second lieutenant. After completing Special Forces training in 1966 he served in Thailand with the 46th Special Forces Company. He was subsequently assigned to the 199th Light Infantry Brigade in Vietnam, serving as a rifle company commander during the Tet and May Offensives of 1968. In 1970, he returned to Vietnam as a senior advisor to South Vietnamese Ranger and Airborne battalions. His decorations for wartime service include the Distinguished Service Cross, the Silver Star, and the Bronze Star for Valor. He retired from the Army at the rank of Colonel in 1991.

He subsequently completed his Doctorate at the University of Central Florida and taught at the graduate level for five years as a member of the adjunct faculty. His previous books include *Warriors: An Infantryman's Memoir of Vietnam* (2004); *Days of Valor: An Inside Account of the Bloodiest Six Months of the Vietnam War* (2007); and *Forsaken Warriors: The Story of an American Advisor with the South Vietnamese Rangers and Airborne, 1970– 71* (2009). He currently resides with his wife, Polly, on Maryland's eastern shore.